The Knights T

By

C. G. Addison Esq.

Coming Soon
How I Stole 5.6 Million from Walmart
The Gods Return Loki's Trial
Zombie Squirrels

Loki's Publishing

Seattle, WA

The Knights Templars

C. G. Addison

Contents

The Knights Templars

Introduction

"Go forth to battle and employ your substance and your persons for the advancement of God's religion. Verily, God loveth those who fight for his religion in battle array."—Koran, *chapter 56, entitled* Battle Array.

"O Prophet, stir up the faithful to war! If twenty of you persevere with constancy they shall overcome two hundred, and if there be one hundred of you they shall overcome one thousand of those who believe not."—*Chapter 8, entitled* The Spoils.

"Verily, if God pleased, he could take vengeance on the unbelievers without your assistance, but he commandeth you to fight his battles that he may prove the one of you by the other; and as to those who fight in defense of God's true religion, God will not suffer their works to perish."—Koran, *chapter 47, entitled* War.

To be propagated by the sword was a vital principle of Mahommedanism. War against infidels for the establishment and extension of the faith was commanded by the Prophet, and the solemn injunction became hallowed and perpetuated by success.

A century after the death of Mahomet, the Moslems had extended their religion and their arms from India to the Atlantic Ocean; they had subdued and converted, by the power of the sword, Persia and Egypt, and all the north of Africa, from the mouth of the Nile to the extreme western boundary of that vast continent; they overran Spain, invaded France, and turning their footsteps towards Italy they entered the kingdoms of Naples and Genoa, threatened Rome, and subjected the island of Sicily to the laws and the religion of their Prophet. But at the very period when they were about to plant the Koran in the very heart of Europe, and were advancing with rapid strides to universal dominion, intestine dissensions broke out amongst them which undermined their power, and Europe was released from the dread and danger of Saracen dominion.

In the tenth century of the Christian era, however, the ferocious and barbarous Turcomans appeared as the patrons of Mahommedanism, and the propagators of the Koran. These were wild pastoral tribes of shepherds and hunters, who descended from the frozen plains to the north of the Caspian, conquered Persia, embraced the religion and the law of Mahomet, and became united under the standard of the Prophet into one great and powerful nation. They overran the greater part of the Asiatic continent, destroyed the churches of the Christians and the temples of the Pagans, and appeared (A. D. 1084) in warlike array on the Asiatic shore of the

Hellespont in front of Constantinople. The terrified emperor Alexius sent urgent letters to the Pope and the Christian princes of Europe, exhorting them to assist him and their common Christianity in the perilous crisis. The preachings of Peter the hermit, and the exhortations of the Pope, forthwith aroused Christendom; Europe was armed and precipitated upon Asia; the Turkish power was broken; the Christian provinces of the Greek empire of Constantinople were recovered from the grasp of the infidels; and the Latin kingdom of Jerusalem was reared upon the ruins of the Turkish empire of sultan Soliman. The monastic and military order of the Temple was then called into existence for the purpose of checking the power of the infidels, and fighting the battles of Christendom in the plains of Asia. "Suggested by fanaticism," as Gibbon observes, but guided by an intelligent and far reaching policy, it became the firmest bulwark of Christianity in the East, and mainly contributed to preserve Europe from Turkish desolation, and probably from Turkish conquest.

Many grave and improbable charges have been brought against the Templars by monks and priests who wrote in Europe concerning events in the Holy Land, and who regarded the vast privileges of the order with indignation and aversion. Matthew Paris tells us that they were leagued with the infidels, and fought pitched battles with the rival order of Saint John; but as contemporary historians of Palestine, who describe the exploits of the Templars, and were eye-witnesses of their career, make no mention of such occurrences, and as no allusion is made to them in the letters of the Pope addressed to the Grand Master of the order of Saint John shortly after the date of these pretended battles, I have omitted all mention of them, feeling convinced, after a careful examination of the best authorities, that they never did take place.

At this distant day, when the times and scenes in which the Templars acted are changed, and the deep religious fervor and warm fresh feelings of bygone ages have given way to a cold and calculating philosophy, we may doubt the sincerity of the military friars, exclaim against their credulity, and deride their zeal; but when we call to mind the hardships and fatigues, the dangers, sufferings, and death, to which they voluntarily devoted themselves in a far distant land, the sacrifice of personal comforts, of the ties of kindred, and of all the endearments of domestic life, which they made without any prospect of worldly gain or temporal advantage, for objects which they believed to be just, and noble, and righteous, we must ever rank the generous impulses by which they were actuated among the sublime emotions which can influence the human character in those periods when men feel rather than calculate, before knowledge has chilled the sensibility, or selfish indifference hardened the heart.

Chapter I.

"Yet 'midst her towering fanes in ruin laid, The pilgrim saint his murmuring vespers paid; 'Twas his to mount the tufted rocks, and rove The chequer'd twilight of the olive grove; 'Twas his to bend beneath the sacred gloom, And wear with many a kiss Messiah's tomb."

The natural desire of visiting those holy spots which have been sanctified by the presence, and rendered memorable by the sufferings, of the Son of God, drew, during the early ages of Christianity, crowds of devout worshippers and pilgrims to Jerusalem. Among the most illustrious and enthusiastic of the many wanderers to the Holy City was the empress Helena, the mother of Constantine, who, with the warm feelings of a recent conversion, visited in person every place and every object in Palestine associated with the memory of him who died for mankind on the blessed cross. With a holy zeal and a lively enthusiasm, she attempted to fix by unquestionable tradition the scene of each memorable event in the gospel narrative; and Christendom is indebted to her for the real or pretended discovery (about two hundred and ninety-eight years after the death of Christ) of the Holy Sepulcher. Over this sacred monument the empress and her son Constantine caused to be erected the magnificent church of the Resurrection, or, as it is now called, the church of the Holy Sepulcher; and they adorned all those places in the Holy Land which remind us most forcibly of the earthly existence and death of Jesus Christ, with magnificent churches and religious houses.

The example of this pious princess, and the pretended discoveries made by her of holy relics, caused a great increase in the pilgrimages to Jerusalem. The conquest of Palestine by the Arabians, (A. D. 637,) stimulated rather than suppressed them; it added to the merit by increasing the danger and difficulty of the undertaking, whilst the enthusiasm which prompted the long and perilous journey was increased by the natural feelings of sorrow and indignation at the loss of the holy places, and the possession of them by the conquering infidels. Year after year, and century after century, hundreds and thousands of both sexes, of all ranks and every age, the monarch and the peasant, the noble and the beggar, flocked to the shrines and the altars of Palestine. They visited, with pious affection, Bethlehem, where the Savior first saw the light; they bathed in the waters of the river Jordan, wherein he was baptized, and wept and prayed upon Mount Calvary, where he was crucified.

The Knights Templars

On the conquest of Jerusalem by the Arabians, the security of the Christian population had been provided for in a solemn guarantee given under the hand and seal of the caliph Omar, to Sophronius the patriarch. One fourth of the entire city, with the church of the Resurrection, the Holy Sepulcher, and the great Latin convent, had been left in the hands of the Christians and the pilgrims were permitted, on payment of a trifling tribute, freely to visit the various objects of their regard. When the scepter was transferred from the family of the Abassides to the Fatimites, and the caliphs of Egypt obtained possession of Palestine, the same mild and tolerant government was continued. In the eleventh century, the zeal of pilgrimage had reached its height, and the caravans of pilgrims had become so numerous as to be styled *the armies of the Lord.* The old and the young, women and children, flocked in crowds to Jerusalem, and in the year 1064 the Holy Sepulcher was visited by an enthusiastic band of seven thousand pilgrims. The year following, however, Jerusalem was conquered by the wild Turcomans, three thousand of the citizens were massacred, and the command over the holy city and territory was confided to the emir Ortok, the chief of a savage pastoral tribe.

Under the iron yoke of these fierce northern strangers, the Christians were fearfully oppressed; they were driven from their churches; divine worship was ridiculed and interrupted; and the patriarch of the Holy City was dragged by the hair of his head over the sacred pavement of the church of the Resurrection, and cast into a dungeon, to extort a ransom from the sympathy of his flock. The pilgrims who, through innumerable perils, had reached the gates of the Holy City, were plundered, imprisoned, and frequently massacred; a piece of gold, was exacted as the price of admission to the holy Sepulcher, and many, unable to pay the tax, were driven by the swords of the Turcomans from the very threshold of the object of all their hopes, the bourne of their long pilgrimage, and were compelled to retrace their weary steps in sorrow and anguish to their distant homes. The intelligence of these cruelties aroused the religious chivalry of Christendom; "a nerve was touched of exquisite feeling, and the sensation vibrated to the heart of Europe." Then arose the wild enthusiasm of the crusades, and men of all ranks, and even monks and priests, animated by the exhortations of the pope and the preachings of Peter the Hermit, flew to arms, and enthusiastically undertook "the pious and glorious enterprize" of rescuing the holy Sepulcher of Christ from the foul abominations of the heathen.

When intelligence of the capture of Jerusalem by the Crusaders (A. D. 1099) had been conveyed to Europe, the zeal of pilgrimage blazed forth with increased fierceness: it had gathered intensity from the interval of its suppression by the wild Turcomans, and promiscuous crowds of both sexes, old men and children, virgins and matrons, thinking the road then open and the journey practicable, successively pressed forwards towards the Holy City. The infidels had indeed been driven out of Jerusalem, but not out of Palestine. The lofty mountains bordering the sea coast were infested by warlike bands of fugitive Mussulmen, who maintained themselves in various impregnable castles and strongholds, from whence they issued forth upon the high-roads, cut off the communication between Jerusalem and the sea-ports, and revenged themselves for the loss of their habitations and property by the indiscriminate pillage of all travelers. The Bedouin horsemen, moreover, making rapid incursions from beyond the Jordan, frequently kept up a desultory and irregular warfare in the plains; and the pilgrims, consequently, whether they approached the Holy City by land or by sea, were alike exposed to almost daily hostility, to plunder, and to death.

To alleviate the dangers and distresses to which they were exposed, to guard the honor of the saintly virgins and matrons, and to protect the gray hairs of the venerable palmer, nine noble knights, who had greatly distinguished themselves at the siege and capture of Jerusalem, formed a holy brotherhood in arms, and entered into a solemn compact to aid one another in clearing the highways, and in protecting the pilgrims through the passes and defiles of the mountains to the Holy City. Warmed with the religious and military fervor of the day, and animated by the sacredness of the cause to which they had devoted their swords, they called themselves the *Poor Fellow-soldiers of Jesus Christ*. They renounced the world and its pleasures, and in the holy church of the Resurrection, in the presence of the patriarch of Jerusalem, they embraced vows of perpetual chastity, obedience, and poverty, after the manner of monks. Uniting in themselves the two most popular qualities of the age, devotion and valor, and exercising them in the most popular of all enterprises, they speedily acquired a famous reputation.

At first, we are told, they had no church, and no particular place of abode, but in the year of our Lord 1118, (nineteen years after the conquest of Jerusalem by the Crusaders,) they had rendered such good and acceptable service to the Christians, that Baldwin the Second, king of Jerusalem, granted them a place of habitation within the sacred inclosure of the Temple on Mount Moriah, amid those holy and magnificent structures, partly erected by the Christian Emperor Justinian, and partly built by the Caliph Omar, which were then exhibited by the monks and priests of Jerusalem, whose restless zeal led them to practise on the credulity of the pilgrims, and to multiply relics and all objects likely to be sacred in their eyes, as the Temple of Solomon, whence the Poor Fellow-soldiers of Jesus Christ came thenceforth to be known by the name of "the Knighthood of the Temple of Solomon."

By the Mussulmen, the site of the great Jewish temple on Mount Moriah has always been regarded with peculiar veneration. Mahomet, in the first year of the publication of the Koran, directed his followers, when at prayer, to turn their faces towards it, and pilgrimages have constantly been made to the holy spot by devout Moslems. On the conquest of Jerusalem by the Arabians, it was the first care of the Caliph Omar to rebuild "the Temple of the Lord." Assisted by the principal chieftains of his army, the Commander of the Faithful undertook the pious office of clearing the ground with his own hands, and of tracing out the foundations of the magnificent mosque which now crowns with its dark and swelling dome the elevated summit of Mount Moriah.

This great house of prayer, the most holy Mussulman Temple in the world after that of Mecca, is erected over the spot where "Solomon began to build the house of the Lord at Jerusalem on Mount Moriah, where the Lord appeared unto David his father, in the place that David had prepared in the threshing-floor of Ornan the Jebusite." It remains to this day in a state of perfect preservation, and is one of the finest specimens of Saracenic architecture in existence. It is entered by four spacious doorways, each door facing one of the cardinal points; the *Bab el D'Jannat*, or gate of the garden, on the north; the *Bab el Kebla*, or gate of prayer, on the south; the *Bab ib'n el Daoud*, or the gate of the son of David, on the east; and the *Bab el Garbi*, on the west. By the Arabian geographers it is called *Beit Allah*, the house of God, also *Beit Almokaddas*, or *Beit Almacdes*, the holy house. From it Jerusalem derives its Arabic name, *el Kods*, the holy, *el Schereef*, the noble, and *el Mobarek*, the blessed.

The crescent had been torn down by the crusaders from the summit of this great Mussulman Temple, and replaced by an immense golden cross, and the edifice was consecrated to the services of the Christian religion, but retained its simple appellation of "The Temple of the Lord." William, Archbishop of Tyre and Chancellor of the Kingdom of Jerusalem, gives an interesting account of the building as it existed in his time during the Latin dominion. He speaks of the splendid mosaic work on the walls; of the Arabic characters setting forth the name of the founder, and the cost of the undertaking; and of the famous rock under the centre of the dome, which is to this day shown by the Moslems as the spot whereon the destroying angel stood, "with his drawn sword in his hand stretched out over Jerusalem."[*] This rock, he informs us, was left exposed and uncovered for the space of fifteen years after the conquest of the holy city by the crusaders, but was, after that period, cased with a handsome altar of white marble, upon which the priests daily said mass.

To the south of this holy Mussulman temple, on the extreme edge of the summit of Mount Moriah, and resting against the modern walls of the town of Jerusalem, stands the venerable Christian church of the Virgin, erected by the Emperor Justinian, whose stupendous foundations, remaining to this day, fully justify the astonishing description given of the building by Procopius. That writer informs us that in order to get a level surface for the erection of the edifice, it was necessary, on the east and south sides of the hill, to raise up a wall of masonry from the valley below, and to construct a vast foundation, partly composed of solid stone and partly of arches and pillars. The stones were of such magnitude, that each

---

[*] *Will. Tyr.* lib. i. cap. 2, lib. viii. cap. 3. *Jac. de Vitr. Hist. Hierosol.* cap. lxii. p. 1080. *D'Herbelot Bib. Orient.* p. 270, 687, ed. 1697.

block required to be transported in a truck drawn by forty of the emperor's strongest oxen; and to admit of the passage of these trucks it was necessary to widen the roads leading to Jerusalem. The forests of Lebanon yielded their choicest cedars for the timbers of the roof, and a quarry of variegated marble, in the adjoining mountains, furnished the edifice with superb marble columns.[*] The interior of this interesting structure, which still remains at Jerusalem, after a lapse of more than thirteen centuries, in an excellent state of preservation, is adorned with six rows of columns, from whence spring arches supporting the cedar beams and timbers of the roof, and at the end of the building is a round tower, surmounted by a dome. The vast stones, the walls of masonry, and the subterranean colonnade raised to support the south-east angle of the platform whereon the church is erected, are truly wonderful, and may still be seen by penetrating through a small door, and descending several flights of steps at the south-east corner of the enclosure. Adjoining the sacred edifice, the emperor erected hospitals, or houses of refuge, for travelers, sick people, and mendicants of all nations, the foundations whereof, composed of handsome Roman masonry, are still visible on either side of the southern end of the building.

On the conquest of Jerusalem by the Moslems, this venerable church was converted into a mosque, and was called *D'Jamé al Acsa*; it was enclosed, together with the great Mussulman Temple of the Lord erected by the Caliph Omar, within a large area by a high stone wall, which runs around the edge of the summit of Mount Moriah, and guards from the profane tread of the unbeliever the whole of that sacred ground whereon once stood the gorgeous temple of the wisest of kings. When the Holy City was taken by the crusaders, the *D'Jamé al Acsa*, with the various buildings constructed around it, became the property of the kings of Jerusalem: and is denominated by William of Tyre "the palace," or "royal house to the south of the Temple of the Lord, vulgarly called the Temple of Solomon." It was this edifice or temple on Mount Moriah which was appropriated to the poor fellow-soldiers of Jesus Christ, as they had no *church* and no particular place of abode, and from it they derived their name of Knights Templars.[†] The canons of the Temple of the Lord conceded to them the large court extending between that building and the Temple of Solomon; the king, the patriarch, and the prelates of Jerusalem, and the barons of the Latin kingdom, assigned them various gifts and revenues for their maintenance and support, and the order being now settled in a regular place of abode, the knights soon began to entertain more extended views, and to seek a larger theatre for the exercise of their holy profession.

Their first aim and object had been, as before mentioned, simply to protect the poor pilgrims, on their journey backwards and forwards, from the sea-coast to Jerusalem; but as the hostile tribes of Mussulmen, which everywhere surrounded the Latin kingdom, were gradually recovering from

---

[*] *Procopius* de ædificiis Justiniani, lib. 5.
[†] *Will. Tyr.* lib. xii. cap. 7, lib. viii. cap. 3. *Hist. Orient. Jac. de Vitr. apud Thesaur. Nov. Anecd. Martene*, tom. iii. col. 277. *Phocæ descript. Terr. Sanct.* cap. 14, col. 1653.

the terror into which they had been plunged by the successful and exterminating warfare of the first crusaders, and were assuming an aggressive and threatening attitude, it was determined that the holy warriors of the Temple should, in addition to the protection of pilgrims, make the defense of the Christian kingdom of Jerusalem, of the eastern church, and of all the holy places, a part of their particular profession. The two most distinguished members of the fraternity were Hugh de Payens and Geoffrey de St. Aldemar, or St. Omer, two valiant soldiers of the cross, who had fought with great credit and renown at the siege of Jerusalem. Hugh de Payens was chosen by the knights to be the superior of the new religious and military society, by the title of "The Master of the Temple;" and he has, consequently, generally been called the founder of the order.

Baldwin, king of Jerusalem, foreseeing that great advantages would accrue to the Latin kingdom by the increase of the power and numbers of these holy warriors, despatched two Knights Templars to St. Bernard, the holy Abbot of Clairvaux, with a letter, telling him that the Templars whom the Lord had deigned to raise up, and whom in a wonderful manner he preserved for the defense of Palestine, desired to obtain from the Holy See the confirmation of their institution, and a rule for their particular guidance, and beseeching him "to obtain from the Pope the approbation of their order, and to induce his holiness to send succor and subsidies against the enemies of the faith."* Shortly afterwards Hugh de Payens himself proceeded to Rome, accompanied by Geoffrey de St. Aldemar, and four other brothers of the order, who were received with great honor and distinction by Pope Honorius. A great ecclesiastical council was assembled at Troyes, (A. D. 1128,) which Hugh de Payens and his brethren were invited to attend, and the rules to which the Templars had subjected themselves being there described, the holy Abbot of Clairvaux undertook the task of revising and correcting them, and of forming a code of statutes fit and proper for the governance of the great religious and military fraternity of the Temple.

Regula Pauperum Commilitonum Christi et Templi Salomonis.

"The rule of the poor fellow soldiers of Jesus Christ and of the Temple of Solomon," arranged by St. Bernard, and sanctioned by the Holy Fathers of the Council of Troyes, for the government and regulation of the monastic and military society of the Temple, is principally of a religious character, and of an austere and gloomy cast. It is divided into seventy-two heads or chapters, and is preceded by a short prologue, addressed "to all who disdain to follow after their own wills, and desire with purity of mind to fight for the most high and true king," exhorting them to put on the armor of obedience, and to associate themselves together with piety and

---

* *Chrysost. Henriq. de Priv. Cist.* p. 477.

humility for the defense of the holy catholic church; and to employ a pure diligence, and a steady perseverance in the exercise of their sacred profession, so that they might share in the happy destiny reserved for the holy warriors who had given up their lives for Christ.

The rule enjoins severe devotional exercises, self-mortification, fasting, and prayer, and a constant attendance at matins, vespers, and on all the services of the church, that "being refreshed and satisfied with heavenly food, instructed and stablished with heavenly precepts, after the consummation of the divine mysteries," none might be afraid of the *fight*, but be prepared for the *crown*. The following extracts from this rule may be read with interest.

"VIII. In one common hall, or refectory, we will that you take meat together, where, if your wants cannot be made known by signs, ye are softly and privately to ask for what you want. If at any time the thing you require is not to be found, you must seek it with all gentleness, and with submission and reverence to the board, in remembrance of the words of the apostle, *Eat thy bread in silence*, and in emulation of the psalmist, who says, *I have set a watch upon my mouth*; that is, I have communed with myself that I may not offend, that is, with my tongue; that is, I have guarded my mouth, that I may not speak evil.

"XI. Two and two ought in general to eat together, that one may have an eye upon another....

"XVII. After the brothers have once departed from the hall to bed, it must not be permitted any one to speak in public, except it be upon urgent necessity. But whatever is spoken must be said in an under tone by the knight to his esquire. Perchance, however, in the interval between prayers and sleep, it may behove you, from urgent necessity, no opportunity having occurred during the day, to speak on some military matter, or concerning the state of your house, with some portion of the brethren, or with the Master, or with him to whom the government of the house has been confided: this, then, we order to be done in conformity with that which hath been written: *In many words thou shalt not avoid sin;* and in another place, *Life and death are in the hands of the tongue.* In that discourse, therefore, we utterly prohibit scurrility and idle words moving unto laughter, and on going to bed, if any one among you hath uttered a foolish saying, we enjoin him, in all humility, and with purity of devotion, to repeat the Lord's Prayer.

"XX. ... To all the professed knights, both in winter and summer, we give, if they can be procured, white garments, that those who have cast behind them a dark life may know that they are to commend themselves to their Creator by a pure and white life. For what is whiteness but perfect chastity, and chastity is the security of the soul and the health of the body. And unless every knight shall continue chaste, he shall not come to perpetual rest, nor see God, as the apostle Paul witnesseth: *Follow after peace with all men, and chastity, without which no man shall see God....*

"XXI. ... Let all the esquires and retainers be clothed in *black* garments: but if such cannot be found, let them have what can be procured in the province where they live, so that they be of one color, and such as is of a meaner character, viz. brown.

"XXII. It is granted to none to wear white habits, or to have white mantles, excepting the above-named knights of Christ.

"XXXVII. We will not that gold or silver, which is the mark of private wealth, should ever be seen on your bridles, breastplates, or spurs, nor should it be permitted to any brother to buy such. If, indeed, such like furniture shall have been charitably bestowed upon you, the gold and silver must be so colored, that its splendor and beauty may not impart to the wearer an appearance of arrogance beyond his fellows.

"XLI. It is in no wise lawful for any of the brothers to receive letters from his parents, or from any man, or to send letters, without the license of the Master, or of the procurator. After the brother shall have had leave, they must be read in the presence of the Master, if it so pleaseth him. If, indeed, anything whatever shall have been directed to him from his parents, let him not presume to receive it until information has been first given to the Master. But in this regulation the Master and the procurators of the houses are not included.

"XLII. We forbid, and we resolutely condemn, all tales related by any brother, of the follies and irregularities of which he hath been guilty in the world, or in military matters, either with his brother or with any other man. It shall not be permitted him to speak with his brother of the irregularities of other men, nor of the delights of the flesh with miserable women; and if by chance he should hear another discoursing of such things, he shall make him silent, or with the swift foot of obedience he shall depart from him as soon as he is able, and shall lend not the ear of the heart to the vender of idle tales.

"XLIII. If any gift shall be made to a brother, let it be taken to the Master or the treasurer. If, indeed, his friend or his parent will consent to make the gift only on condition that he useth it himself, he must not receive it until permission hath been obtained from the Master. And whosoever shall have received a present, let it not grieve him if it be given to another. Yea, let him know assuredly, that if he be angry at it, he striveth against God.

"XLVI. We are all of opinion that none of you should dare to follow the sport of catching one bird with another: for it is not agreeable unto religion for you to be addicted unto worldly delights, but rather willingly to hear the precepts of the Lord, constantly to kneel down to prayer, and daily to confess your sins before God with sighs and tears. Let no brother, for the above especial reason, presume to go forth with a man following such diversions with a hawk, or with any other bird.

"XLVII. Forasmuch as it becometh all religion to behave decently and humbly without laughter, and to speak sparingly but sensibly, and not in a loud tone, we specially command and direct every professed brother that he venture not to shoot in the woods either with a long-bow or a cross-bow; and for the same reason, that he venture not to accompany another who shall do the like, except it be for the purpose of protecting him from the perfidious infidel; neither shall he dare to halloo, or to talk to a dog, nor shall he spur his horse with a desire of securing the game.

"LI. Under Divine Providence, as we do believe, this new kind of religion was introduced by you in the holy places, that is to say, the union of *warfare* with *religion*, so that religion, being armed, maketh her way by the sword, and smiteth the enemy without sin. Therefore we do rightly adjudge, since ye are called Knights of the Temple, that for your renowned merit, and especial gift of godliness, ye ought to have lands and men, and possess husbandmen and justly govern them, and the customary services ought to be specially rendered unto you.

"LV. We permit you to have married brothers in this manner, if such should seek to participate in the benefit of your fraternity; let both the man and his wife grant, from and after their death, their respective portions of property, and whatever more they acquire in after life, to the unity of the common chapter; and, in the interim, let them exercise an honest life, and labor to do good to the brethren: but they are not permitted to appear in the white habit and white mantle. If the husband dies first, he must leave his portion of the patrimony to the brethren, and the wife shall have her maintenance out of the residue, and let her depart therewith; for we consider it most improper that such women should remain in one and the same house with the brethren who have promised chastity unto God.

"LVI. It is moreover exceedingly dangerous to join sisters with you in your holy profession, for the ancient enemy hath drawn many away from the right path to paradise through the society of women: therefore, dear brothers, that the flower of righteousness may always flourish amongst you, let this custom from henceforth be utterly done away with.

"LXIV. The brothers who are journeying through different provinces should observe the rule, so far as they are able, in their meat and drink, and let them attend to it in other matters, and live irreproachably, that they may get a good name out of doors. Let them not tarnish their religious purpose either by word or deed; let them afford to all with whom they may be associated, an example of wisdom, and a perseverance in all good works. Let him with whom they lodge be a man of the best repute, and, if it be possible, let not the house of the host on that night be without a light, lest the dark enemy (from whom God preserve us) should find some opportunity.

"LXVIII. Care must be taken that no brother, powerful or weak, strong or feeble, desirous of exalting himself, becoming proud by degrees, or defending his own fault, remain unchastened. If he showeth a disposition to amend, let a stricter system of correction be added: but if by godly admonition and earnest reasoning he will not be amended, but will go on more and more lifting himself up with pride, then let him be cast out of the holy flock in obedience to the apostle, *Take away evil from among you.* It is necessary that from the society of the Faithful Brothers the dying sheep be removed. But let the Master, who *ought to hold the staff and the rod in his hand,* that is to say, the staff that he may support the infirmities of the weak, and the rod that he may with the zeal of rectitude strike down the vices of delinquents; let him study, with the counsel of the patriarch and with spiritual circumspection, to act so that, as blessed Maximus saith, The sinner be not encouraged by easy lenity, nor hardened in his iniquity by immoderate severity. Lastly. We hold it dangerous to all religion to gaze too much on the countenance of women; and therefore no brother shall presume to kiss neither widow, nor virgin, nor mother, nor sister, nor aunt, nor any other woman. Let the knighthood of Christ shun *feminine kisses*, through which men have very often been drawn into danger, so that each, with a pure conscience and secure life, may be able to walk everlastingly in the sight of God."

After the confirmation by a Papal bull of the rules and statutes of the order, Hugh de Payens proceeded to France, and from thence he came to England, and the following account is given of his arrival, in the Saxon chronicle. "This same year, (A. D. 1128,) Hugh of the Temple came from Jerusalem to the king in Normandy, and the king received him with much honor, and gave him much treasure in gold and silver, and afterwards he sent him into England, and there he was well received by all good men, and all gave him treasure, and in Scotland also, and they sent in all a great sum in gold and silver by him to Jerusalem, and there went with him and after him so great a number as never before since the days of Pope Urban."[*] Grants of lands, as well as of money, were at the same time made to Hugh de Payens and his brethren, some of which were shortly afterwards confirmed by King Stephen on his accession to the throne, (A. D. 1135.) Among these is a grant of the manor of Bistelesham made to the Templars by Count Robert de Ferrara, and a grant of the church of Langeforde in Bedfordshire made by Simon de Wahull, and Sibylla his wife, and Walter their son.

Hugh de Payens, before his departure, placed a Knight Templar at the head of the order in this country, who was called the Prior of the Temple, and was the procurator and vicegerent of the Master. It was his duty to manage the estates granted to the fraternity, and to transmit the revenues to Jerusalem. He was also delegated with the power of admitting members into the order, subject to the control and direction of the Master, and was to provide means of transport for such newly-admitted brethren to the far east, to enable them to fulfill the duties of their profession. As the houses of the Temple increased in number in England, sub-priors came to be appointed, and the superior of the order in this country was then called the Grand Prior, and afterwards Master of the Temple.

An astonishing enthusiasm was excited throughout Christendom in behalf of the Templars; princes and nobles, sovereigns and their subjects,

---

[*] See also Hoveden apud X script. page 479. Hen. Hunting. ib. page 384.

vied with each other in heaping gifts and benefits upon them, and scarce a will of importance was made without an article in it in their favor. Many illustrious persons on their deathbeds took the vows, that they might be buried in the habit of the order; and sovereign princes, quitting the government of their kingdoms, enrolled themselves amongst the holy fraternity, and bequeathed even their dominions to the Master and the brethren of the Temple. St. Bernard, at the request of Hugh de Payens, took up his powerful pen in their behalf. In a famous discourse "In praise of the New Chivalry," the holy abbot sets forth, in eloquent and enthusiastic terms, the spiritual advantages and blessings enjoyed by the military friars of the Temple over all other warriors. He draws a curious picture of the relative situations and circumstances of the *secular* soldiery and the soldiery of Christ, and shows how different in the sight of God are the bloodshed and slaughter perpetrated by the one, from that committed by the other. Addressing himself to the secular soldiers he says "Ye cover your horses with silken trappings, and I know not how much fine cloth hangs pendent from your coats of mail. Ye paint your spears, shields, and saddles; your bridles and spurs are adorned on all sides with gold, and silver, and gems, and with all this pomp, with a shameful fury and a reckless insensibility, ye rush on to death. Are these military ensigns, or are they not rather the garnishments of women? Can it happen that the sharp-pointed sword of the enemy will respect gold, will it spare gems, will it be unable to penetrate the silken garment? Lastly, as ye yourselves have often experienced, three things are indispensably necessary to the success of the soldier; he must be bold, active, and circumspect; quick in running, prompt in striking; ye, however, to the disgust of the eye, nourish your hair after the manner of women, ye gather around your footsteps long and flowing vestures, ye bury up your delicate and tender hands in ample and wide-spreading sleeves. Among you, indeed, nought provoketh war or awakeneth strife, but either an irrational impulse of anger, or an insane lust of glory, or the covetous desire of possessing another man's lands and possessions. In such causes it is neither safe to slay nor to be slain.

"And now we will briefly display the mode of life of the Knights of Christ, such as it is in the field and in the convent, by which means it will be made plainly manifest to what extent the soldiery of God and the soldiery of the *world* differ from one another.... The soldiers of Christ live together in common in an agreeable but frugal manner, without wives, and without children; and that nothing may be wanting to evangelical perfection, they dwell together without separate property of any kind, in one house, under one rule, careful to preserve the unity of the spirit in the bond of peace. You may say, that to the whole multitude there is but one heart and one soul, as each one in no respect followeth after his own will or desire, but is diligent to do the will of the Master. They are never idle nor rambling abroad, but when they are not in the field, that they may not eat their bread in idleness, they are fitting and repairing their armor and their clothing, or employing themselves in such occupations as the will of the

Master requireth, or their common necessities render expedient. Among them there is no distinction of persons; respect is paid to the best and most virtuous, not the most noble. They participate in each other's honor, they bear one another's burthens, that they may fulfill the law of Christ. An insolent expression, a useless undertaking, immoderate laughter, the least murmur or whispering, if found out, passeth not without severe rebuke. They detest cards and dice, they shun the sports of the field, and take no delight in that ludicrous catching of birds, (hawking,) which men are wont to indulge in. Jesters, and soothsayers, and storytellers, scurrilous songs, shows and games, they contemptuously despise and abominate as vanities and mad follies. They cut their hair, knowing that, according to the apostle, it is not seemly in a man to have long hair. They are never combed, seldom washed, but appear rather with rough neglected hair, foul with dust, and with skins browned by the sun and their coats of mail. Moreover, on the approach of battle they fortify themselves with faith within, and with steel without, and not with gold, so that armed and not adorned, they may strike terror into the enemy, rather than awaken his lust of plunder. They strive earnestly to possess strong and swift horses, but not garnished with ornaments or decked with trappings, thinking of battle and of victory, and not of pomp and show, and studying to inspire fear rather than admiration....

"There is a Temple at Jerusalem in which they dwell together, unequal, it is true, as a building, to that ancient and most famous one of Solomon, but not inferior in glory. For truly, the entire magnificence of that consisted in corrupt things, in gold and silver, in carved stone, and in a variety of woods; but the whole beauty of this resteth in the adornment of an agreeable conversation, in the godly devotion of its inmates, and their beautifully-ordered mode of life. That was admired for its various external beauties, this is venerated for its different virtues and sacred actions, as becomes the sanctity of the house of God, who delighteth not so much in polished marbles as in well-ordered behavior, and regardeth pure minds more than gilded walls. The face likewise of this Temple is adorned with arms, not with gems, and the wall, instead of the ancient golden chapiters, is covered around with pendent shields. Instead of the ancient candelabra, censers, and lavers, the house is on all sides furnished with bridles, saddles, and lances, all which plainly demonstrate that the soldiers burn with the same zeal for the house of God, as that which formerly animated their great leader, when, vehemently enraged, he entered into the Temple, and with that most sacred hand, armed not with steel, but with a scourge which he had made of small thongs, drove out the merchants, poured out the changers' money, and overthrew the tables of them that sold doves; most indignantly condemning the pollution of the house of prayer, by the making of it a place of merchandize."

St. Bernard then congratulates Jerusalem on the advent of the soldiers of Christ, "Be joyful, O Jerusalem," says he, in the words of the prophet Isaiah, "and know that the time of thy visitation hath arrived. Arise now, shake thyself from the dust, &c., &c. Hail, O holy city, hallowed by the tabernacle of the Most High! Hail, city of the great King, wherein so many wonderful and welcome miracles have been perpetually displayed. Hail, mistress of the nations, princess of provinces, possession of patriarchs, mother of the prophets and apostles, initiatress of the faith, glory of the Christian people, whom God hath on that account always from the beginning permitted to be visited with affliction, that thou mightest thus be the occasion of virtue as well as of salvation to brave men. Hail, land of promise, which, formerly flowing only with milk and honey for thy possessors, now stretchest forth the food of life, and the means of salvation to the entire world. Most excellent and happy land, I say, which, receiving the celestial grain from the recess of the paternal heart, in that most fruitful bosom of thine, has produced such rich harvests of martyrs from the heavenly seed, and whose fertile soil has no less manifoldly engendered fruit a thirtieth, sixtieth, and a hundredfold in the remaining race of all the faithful throughout the entire world. Whence most agreeably satiated, and most abundantly crammed with the great store of thy pleasantness, those who have seen thee diffuse around them in every place the remembrance of thy abundant sweetness, and tell of the magnificence of thy glory to the very end of the earth to those who have not seen thee, and relate the wonderful things that are done in thee.

"Glorious things are spoken concerning thee, city of God!"

Chapter II.

"We heard the *tecbir*, so the Arabs call Their shout of onset, when with loud appeal They challenge *heaven*, as if commanding conquest."

Hugh de Payens, having now laid in Europe the foundations of the great monastic and military institution of the Temple, which was destined shortly to spread its ramifications to the remotest quarters of Christendom, returned to Palestine at the head of a valiant band of newly-elected Templars, drawn principally from England and France. On their arrival at Jerusalem they were received with great distinction by the king, the clergy, and the barons of the Latin kingdom. Hugh de Payens died, however, shortly after his return, and was succeeded (A. D. 1136) by the Lord Robert, surnamed the Burgundian, (son-in-law of Anselm, Archbishop of Canterbury,) who, after the death of his wife, had taken the vows and the habit of the Templars.* At this period the fierce religious and military enthusiasm of the Mussulmen had been again aroused by the warlike Zinghis, and his son Noureddin, two of the most famous chieftains of the age. The one was named *Emod-ed-deen*, "Pillar of religion;" and the other *Nour-ed-deen*, "Light of Religion," vulgarly, Noureddin. The Templars were worsted by overpowering numbers. The latin kingdom of Jerusalem was shaken to its foundations, and the oriental clergy in trepidation and alarm sent urgent letters to the Pope for assistance.

The Lord Robert, Master of the Temple, had at this period (A. D. 1146) been succeeded by Everard des Barres, Prior of France, who convened a general chapter of the order at Paris, which was attended by Pope Eugenius the Third, Louis the Seventh, king of France, and many prelates, princes, and nobles, from all parts of Christendom. The second crusade was there arranged, and the Templars, with the sanction of the Pope, assumed the blood-red cross, the symbol of martyrdom, as the distinguishing badge of the order, which was appointed to be worn on their habits and mantles on the left side of the breast over the heart, whence they came afterwards to be known by the name of the *Red Friars* and the *Red Cross Knights*. At this famous assembly various donations were made to the Templars, to enable them to provide more effectually for the defense of the Holy Land. Bernard Baliol, through love of God and for the good of his soul, granted them his estate of Wedelee, in Hertfordshire, which afterwards formed part of the preceptory of Temple Dynnesley. This grant

---

* *Will. Tyr.* lib. xiii. cap. 26; *Anselmus*, lib. iii. epistolarum, epist. 43, 63, 66, 67.

is expressed to be made at the chapter held at Easter, in Paris, in the presence of the Pope, the king of France, several archbishops, and one hundred and thirty Knights Templars clad in white mantles.[*]

Brother Everard des Barres, the newly-elected Master of the Temple, having collected together all the brethren from the western provinces, joined the second crusade to Palestine. During the march through Asia Minor, the rear of the Christian army was protected by the Templars, who greatly signalized themselves on every occasion. Odo of Deuil, or Diagolum, the chaplain of King Louis, and his constant attendant upon this expedition, informs us that the king loved to see the frugality and simplicity of the Templars, and to imitate it; he praised their union and disinterestedness, admired above all things the attention they paid to their accoutrements, and their care in husbanding and preserving their equipage and munitions of war, and proposed them as a model to the rest of the army.[†]

Conrad, emperor of Germany, had preceded King Louis at the head of a powerful army, which was cut to pieces by the infidels in the north of Asia; he fled to Constantinople, embarked on board some merchant vessels, and arrived with only a few attendants at Jerusalem, where he was received and entertained by the Templars, and was lodged in the Temple in the Holy City. Shortly afterwards King Louis arrived, accompanied by the new Master of the Temple, Everard des Barres; and the Templars now unfolded for the first time the red-cross banner in the field of battle. This was a white standard made of woollen stuff, having in the centre of it the blood-red cross granted by Pope Eugenius. The two monarchs, Louis and Conrad, took the field, supported by the Templars, and laid siege to the magnificent city of Damascus, "the Queen of Syria," which was defended by the great Noureddin, "Light of religion," and his brother *Saif-eddin*, "Sword of the faith."

The services rendered by the Templars are thus gratefully recorded in the following letter sent by Louis, the French king, to his minister and vicegerent, the famous Suger, abbot of St. Denis: "I cannot imagine how we could have subsisted for even the smallest space of time in these parts, had it not been for their (the Templars') support and assistance, which have never failed me from the first day I set foot in these lands up to the time of my despatching this letter—a succor ably afforded and generously persevered in. I therefore earnestly beseech you, that as these brothers of the Temple have hitherto been blessed with the love of God, so now they may be gladdened and sustained by our love and favor. I have to inform you that they have lent me a considerable sum of money, which must be repaid to them quickly, that their house may not suffer, and that I may keep my word...."[‡]

---

[*] *Reg. Cart. S. Joh. Jerus. in Bib. Cotton. Nero E. b.* No. xx. fo. 118.
[†] *Odo de Diogilo de Ludov.* vii. *profectione in Orientem*, p. 67.
[‡] *Duchesne hist. franc. scrip.* tom. iv. p. 512; epist. 58, 59.

The Knights Templars

Among the English nobility who enlisted in the second crusade were the two renowned warriors, Roger de Mowbray and William de Warrenne. Roger de Mowbray was one of the most powerful and warlike of the barons of England, and was one of the victorious leaders at the famous battle of the standard: he marched with King Louis to Palestine; fought under the banners of the Temple against the infidels, and, smitten with admiration of the piety and valor of the holy warriors of the order, he gave them, on his return to England, many valuable estates and possessions. Among these were the manors of Kileby and Witheley, divers lands in the isle of Axholme, the town of Balshall in the county of Warwick, and various places in Yorkshire: and so munificent were his donations, that the Templars conceded to him and to his heirs various special privileges. About the same period, Stephen, King of England, granted and confirmed "to God and the blessed Virgin Mary, and to the brethren of the Knighthood of the Temple of Solomon at Jerusalem, all the manor of Cressynge, with the advowson of the church of the same manor, and also the manors of Egle and Witham." Queen Matilda, likewise, granted them the manor of Covele or Cowley in Oxfordshire, two mills in the same county, common of pasture in Shotover forest, and the church of Stretton in Rutland. Ralph de Hastings and William de Hastings also gave to the Templars, in the same reign, (A. D. 1152,) lands at Hurst and Wyxham in Yorkshire, afterwards formed into the preceptory of Temple Hurst. William Asheby granted them the estate whereon the house and church of Temple Bruere were afterwards erected; and the order continued rapidly to increase in power and wealth in England and in all parts of Europe, through the charitable donations of pious Christians.[*]

After the miserable failure of the second crusade, brother Everard des Barres, the Master of the Temple, returned to Paris, with his friend and patron Louis, the French king; and the Templars, deprived of their chief, were now left, alone and unaided, to withstand the victorious career of the fanatical Mussulmen. Their miserable situation is pourtrayed in a melancholy letter from the treasurer of the order, written to the Master, Everard des Barres, during his sojourn at the court of the king of France, informing him of the slaughter of the prince of Antioch and all his nobility. "We conjure you," says he, "to bring with you from beyond sea all our knights and serving brothers capable of bearing arms. Perchance, alas! with all your diligence, you may not find one of us alive. Use, therefore, all imaginable celerity; pray forget not the necessities of our house: they are such that no tongue can express them. It is also of the last importance to announce to the Pope, to the king of France, and to all the princes and prelates of Europe, the approaching desolation of the Holy Land, to the intent that they succor us in person, or send us subsidies."

The Master of the Temple, however, instead of proceeding to Palestine, abdicated his authority, and entered into the monastery of

---

[*] *Dugd. Monast.* vol. vii. p. 838; vol. ii. p. 820, 843, ed. 1830. Baronage, tom. i. p. 122.

Clairvaux, where he devoted the remainder of his days to the most rigorous penance and mortification. He was succeeded (A. D. 1151) by Bernard de Tremelay, a nobleman of an illustrious family in Burgundy, in France, and a valiant and experienced soldier.[*]

Shortly after his accession to power, the infidels crossed the Jordan, and advanced within sight of Jerusalem. Their banners waved on the summit of the Mount of Olives, and the warlike sound of their kettle-drums and trumpets was heard within the sacred precincts of the holy city. They encamped on the mount over against the Temple; and had the satisfaction of regarding from a distance the *Beit Allah*, or Temple of the Lord, their holy house of prayer; but in a night attack they were defeated with terrible slaughter, and were pursued all the way to the Jordan, five thousand of their number being left dead on the plain.

On the 20th of April, A. D. 1153, the Templars lost their great patron Saint Bernard, who died in the sixty-third year of his age. On his deathbed he wrote three letters in behalf of the order. The first was addressed to the patriarch of Antioch, exhorting him to protect and encourage the Templars, a thing which the holy abbot assures him will prove most acceptable to God and man. The second was written to Melesinda, queen of Jerusalem, praising her majesty for the favor shown by her to the brethren of the order; and the third, addressed to Brother André de Montbard, a Knight Templar, conveys the affectionate salutations of St. Bernard to the Master and brethren, to whose prayers he recommends himself.

The same year the Master of the Temple perished at the head of his knights whilst attempting to carry the important city of Ascalon by storm. Passing through a breach made in the walls, he penetrated into the centre of the town, and was there surrounded and overpowered. The dead bodies of the Master and his ill-fated knights were exposed in triumph from the walls; and, according to the testimony of an eye-witness, not a single Templar escaped.

De Tremelay was succeeded (A. D. 1154) by Brother Bertrand de Blanquefort, a knight of a noble family of Guienne, called by William of Tyre a pious and God-fearing man. On Tuesday, June 19, A. D. 1156, the Templars were drawn into an ambuscade whilst marching with Baldwin, king of Jerusalem, near Tiberias, three hundred of the brethren were slain on the field of battle, and eighty-seven fell into the hands of the enemy, among whom was Bertrand de Blanquefort himself, and Brother Odo, marshal of the kingdom. Shortly afterwards, a small band of them captured a large detachment of Saracens; and in a night attack on the camp of Noureddin, they compelled that famous chieftain to fly, without arms and half-naked, from the field of battle. In this last affair the name of Robert Mansel, an Englishman, and Gilbert de Lacy, preceptor of the Temple of Tripoli, are honorably mentioned.[†]

---

[*] *Will. Tyr.* lib. xvii. cap. 21, cap. 9.
[†] *Registr. epist.* apud *Martene*, tom. ii. col. 647.

The Knights Templars

The fiery zeal and warlike enthusiasm of the Templars were equalled, if not surpassed, by the stern fanaticism and religious ardour of the followers of Mahomet. "Noureddin fought," says his oriental biographer, "like the meanest of his soldiers, saying, 'Alas! it is now a long time that I have been seeking martyrdom without being able to obtain it.' The Imaum Koteb-ed-din, hearing him on one occasion utter these words, exclaimed, 'In the name of God do not put your life in danger, do not thus expose Islam and the Moslems. Thou art their stay and support, and if (but God preserve us therefrom) thou shouldest be slain, we are all undone.' 'Ah! Koteb-ed-deen,' said he, 'what hast thou said, who can save *Islam* and our country, but that great God who has no equal?' 'What,' said he, on another occasion, 'do we not look to the security of our houses against robbers and plunderers, and shall we not defend *religion*?'"* Like the Templars, Noureddin fought constantly with spiritual and with carnal weapons. He resisted the world and its temptations, by fasting and prayer, and by the daily exercise of the moral and religious duties and virtues inculcated in the Koran. He fought with the sword against the foes of Islam, and employed his whole energies, to the last hour of his life in the enthusiastic and fanatic struggle for the recovery of Jerusalem.† In his camp, all profane and frivolous conversation was severely prohibited; the exercises of religion were assiduously practiced, and the intervals of action were employed in prayer, meditation, and the study of the Koran. "The sword," says the prophet Mahomet, in that remarkable book, "is the key of heaven and of hell; a drop of blood shed in the cause of God, a night spent in arms, is of more avail than two months of fasting and of prayer. Whosoever falls in battle, his sins are forgiven him. At the day of judgment his wounds will be resplendent as vermillion, and odoriferous as musk, and the loss of limbs shall be supplied by the wings of angels and cherubims."

Among the many instances of the fanatical ardour of the Moslem warriors, are the following, extracted from the history of *Abu Abdollah Alwakidi*, Cadi of Bagdad. "Methinks," said a valiant Saracen youth, in the heat of battle—"methinks I see the black-eyed girls looking upon me, one of whom, should she appear in this world, all mankind would die for love of her; and I see in the hand of one of them a handkerchief of green silk, and a cap made of precious stones, and she beckons me, and calls out, Come hither quickly, for I love thee." With these words, charging the Christian host, he made havoc wherever he went, until at last he was struck down by a javelin. "It is not," said another dying Arabian warrior, when he embraced for the last time his sister and mother—"it is not the fading pleasure of this world that has prompted me to devote my life in the cause of *religion*, I seek the favor of God and his *apostle*, and I have heard from one of the companions of the prophet, that the spirits of the martyrs will be

---

* *Will. Tyr.* lib. xvii. cap. 27; lib. xviii. cap. 14; lib. xix. cap. 8.
† Keightley's Crusaders. The virtues of Noureddin are celebrated by the Arabic Historian *Ben-Schunah*, by *Azzeddin Ebn-al-athir*, by *Khondemir*, and in the work entitled, "The flowers of the two gardens," by *Omaddeddin Kateb*. See also *Will. Tyr.* lib. xx. cap. 33.

lodged in the crops of green birds who taste the fruits and drink of the waters of paradise. Farewell: we shall meet again among the groves and fountains which God has prepared for his elect."[*]

The Master of the Temple, Brother Bertrand de Blanquefort, was liberated from captivity at the instance of Manuel Comnenus, Emperor of Constantinople. After his release, he wrote several letters to Louis VII., king of France, describing the condition and prospects of the Holy Land: the increasing power and boldness of the infidels; and the ruin and desolation caused by a dreadful earthquake, which had overthrown numerous castles, prostrated the walls and defenses of several towns, and swallowed up the dwellings of the inhabitants. "The persecutors of the church," says he, "hasten to avail themselves of our misfortunes; they gather themselves together from the ends of the earth, and come forth as one man against the sanctuary of God."

It was during his mastership, that Geoffrey, the Knight Templar, and Hugh of Cæsarea, were sent on an embassy into Egypt, and had their famous interview with the Caliph. They were introduced into the palace of the Fatimites through a series of gloomy passages and glittering porticos, amid the warbling of birds and the murmur of fountains; the scene was enriched by a display of costly furniture and rare animals; and the long order of unfolding doors was guarded by black soldiers and domestic eunuchs. The sanctuary of the presence chamber was veiled with a curtain, and the vizier who conducted the ambassadors laid aside his scimitar, and prostrated himself three times on the ground; the veil was then removed, and they saw the Commander of the Faithful.[†]

Brother Bertrand de Blanquefort, in his letters to the king of France, gives an account of the military operations undertaken by the order of the Temple in Egypt, and of the capture of the populous and important city of Belbeis, the ancient Pelusium.[‡] During the absence of the Master with the greater part of the fraternity on that expedition, the sultan Noureddin invaded Palestine; he defeated with terrible slaughter the serving brethren and Turcopoles, or light horse of the order, who remained to defend the country, and sixty of the knights who commanded them were left dead on the plain. Amalric, king of Jerusalem, the successor of Baldwin the Third, in a letter "to his dear friend and father," Louis the Seventh, king of France, beseeches the good offices of that monarch in behalf of all the devout Christians of the Holy Land; "but above all," says he, "we earnestly entreat your Majesty constantly to extend to the utmost your favor and regard to the Brothers of the Temple, who continually render up their lives for God and the faith, and through whom we do the little that we are able to effect, for in them indeed, after God, is placed the entire reliance of all those in the eastern regions who tread in the right path."[§] The Master,

---

[*] *Alwakidi*, translated by Ockley, *Hist. Saracen. Cinnamus*, lib. iv. num. 22.
[†] His. de Saladin, per *M. Marin*, tome i. p. 120, 1. *Gibbon*, cap. 59.
[‡] *Hist. Franc. Script.* tom. iv. p. 692, 693. *Gesta Dei*, epist. xiv. p. 1178, 9.
[§] *Martene*, vet. Script., tom. ii. col. 846, 847, 883. *Gesta Dei*, tom. i. p. 1181-1184. *Duchesne*.

The Knights Templars

Brother Bertrand de Blanquefort, was succeeded, (A. D. 1167,) by Philip of Naplous, the first Master of the Temple who had been born in Palestine. He had been Lord of the fortresses of Krak and Montreal in Arabia Petræa, and took the vows and the habit of the order of the Temple after the death of his wife.[*]

We must now pause to take a glance at the rise of another great religio-military institution which, from henceforth, takes a leading part in the defense of the Latin kingdom. In the eleventh century, when pilgrimages to Jerusalem had greatly increased, some Italian merchants of Amalfi, who carried on a lucrative trade with Palestine, purchased of the Caliph *Monstasserbillah*, a piece of ground in the Christian quarter of the Holy City, near the church of the Resurrection, whereon two hospitals were constructed, the one being appropriated for the reception of male pilgrims, and the other for females. Several pious and charitable Christians, chiefly from Europe, devoted themselves in these hospitals to constant attendance upon the sick and destitute. Two chapels were erected, the one annexed to the female establishment being dedicated to St. Mary Magdalene, and the other to St. John the Eleemosynary, a canonized patriarch of Alexandria, remarkable for his exceeding charity. The pious and kind-hearted people who here attended upon the sick pilgrims, clothed the naked and fed the hungry, were called "The Hospitallers of St. John." On the conquest of Jerusalem by the Crusaders, these charitable persons were naturally regarded with the greatest esteem and reverence by their fellow-Christians from the west; many of the soldiers of the cross, smitten with their piety and zeal, desired to participate in their good offices, and the Hospitallers, animated by the religious enthusiasm of the day, determined to renounce the world, and devote the remainder of their lives to pious duties and constant attendance upon the sick. They took the customary monastic vows of obedience, chastity, and poverty, and assumed as their distinguishing habit a *black* mantle with a *white* cross on the breast. Various lands and possessions were granted them by the lords and princes of the Crusade, both in Palestine and in Europe, and the order of the hospital of St. John speedily became a great and powerful institution.

Gerard, a native of Provence, was at this period at the head of the society, with the title of "Guardian of the Poor." He was succeeded (A. D. 1118) by Raymond Dupuy, a knight of Dauphiné, who drew up a series of rules for the direction and government of his brethren. In these rules no traces are discoverable of the military spirit which afterwards animated the order of the Hospital of St. John. The first authentic notice of an intention on the part of the Hospitallers to occupy themselves with military matters, occurs in the bull of Pope Innocent the Second, dated A. D. 1130. This bull is addressed to the archbishops, bishops, and clergy of the church universal, and informs them that the Hospitallers then retained, at their own expense, a body of horsemen and foot soldiers, to defend the pilgrims

---

Hist. Franc. script. p. 698.
[*] *Will. Tyr.* lib. xxii. cap. 5.

in going to and returning from the holy places; the pope observes that the funds of the hospital were insufficient to enable them effectually to fulfill the pious and holy task, and he exhorts the archbishops, bishops, and clergy, to minister to the necessities of the order out of their abundant property. The Hospitallers consequently at this period had resolved to add the task of *protecting* to that of tending and relieving pilgrims.

After the accession (A. D. 1168) of Gilbert d'Assalit to the guardianship of the Hospital—a man described by De Vertot as "bold and enterprising, and of an extravagant genius"—a military spirit was infused into the Hospitallers, which speedily predominated over their pious and charitable zeal in attending upon the poor and the sick. Gilbert d'Assalit was the friend and confidant of Amalric, king of Jerusalem, and planned with that monarch a wicked invasion of Egypt in defiance of treaties. The Master of the Temple being consulted concerning the expedition, flatly refused to have anything to do with it, or to allow a single brother of the order of the Temple to accompany the king in arms: "For it appeared a hard matter to the Templars," says William of Tyre, "to wage war without cause, in defiance of treaties, and against all honor and conscience, upon a friendly nation, preserving faith with us, and relying on our own faith." Gilbert d'Assalit consequently determined to obtain for the king from his own brethren that aid which the Templars denied; and to tempt the Hospitallers to arm themselves generally as a great military society, in imitation of the Templars, and join the expedition to Egypt, Gilbert d'Assalit was authorized to promise them in the name of the king, the possession of the wealthy and important city of Belbeis, the ancient Pelusium, in perpetual sovereignty.

According to De Vertot, the senior Hospitallers were greatly averse to the military projects of their chief: "They urged," says he, "that they were a religious order, and that the church had not put arms into their hands to make conquests;" but the younger and more ardent of the brethren, burning to exchange the monotonous life of the cloister for the enterprise and activity of the camp, received the proposals of their superior with enthusiasm, and a majority of the chapter decided in favor of the plans and projects of their Guardian. They authorized him to borrow money of the Florentine and Genoese merchants, to take hired soldiers into the pay of the order, and to organize the Hospitallers as a great military society.

It was in the first year of the government of Philip of Naplous (A. D. 1168) that the king of Jerusalem and the Hospitallers marched forth upon their memorable and unfortunate expedition. The Egyptians were taken completely by surprise; the city of Belbeis was carried by assault, and the defenseless inhabitants were barbarously massacred. The cruelty and the injustice of the Christians, however, speedily met with condign punishment. The king of Jerusalem was driven back into Palestine; Belbeis was abandoned with precipitation; and the Hospitallers fled before the infidels in sorrow and disappointment to Jerusalem. There they vented their indignation and chagrin upon the unfortunate Gilbert d'Assalit, their superior, who had got the order into debt to the extent of 100,000 pieces of gold; they compelled him to resign his authority, and the unfortunate guardian of the hospital fled from Palestine to England, and was drowned in the Channel. From this period, however, the character of the order of the Hospital of St. John was entirely changed: the Hospitallers appear henceforth as a great military body; their superior styles himself Master, and leads in person the brethren into the field of battle. Attendance upon the poor and the sick still continued, indeed, one of the duties of the fraternity, but it must have been feebly exercised amid the clash of arms and the excitement of war.[*]

The Grand Master of the Temple, Philip of Naplous, resigned his authority after a short government of three years, and was succeeded (A. D. 1170) by Brother Odo de St. Amand, a proud and fiery warrior, of undaunted courage and resolution; having, according to William, Archbishop of Tyre, the fear neither of God nor of man before his eyes.[†] It was during his Grand Mastership (A. D. 1172) that the Knight Templar Walter du Mesnil slew an envoy or minister of the assassins. These were an odious religious sect, settled in the fastnesses of the mountains above Tripoli, and supposed to be descended from the Ismaelians of Persia. They devoted their souls and bodies in blind obedience to a chief who is called by the writers of the Crusades "the old man of the mountain," and were employed by him in the most extensive system of murder and assassination known in the history of the world. Both Christian and Moslem writers enumerate with horror the many illustrious victims that fell beneath their daggers. They assumed all shapes and disguises for the furtherance of their deadly designs, and carried, in general, no arms except a small poniard concealed in the folds of their dress, called in the Persian tongue *hassissin*, whence these wretches were called *assassins*, their chief the prince of the assassins; and the word itself, in all its odious import, has passed into most European languages.[‡]

Raimond, son of the count of Tripoli, had been slain by these fanatics whilst kneeling at the foot of the altar in the church of the Blessed Virgin at Carchusa or Tortosa; the Templars flew to arms to avenge his death; they penetrated into the fastnesses and strongholds of "the mountain chief," and at last compelled him to purchase peace by the payment of an annual tribute of two thousand crowns into the treasury of the order. In the ninth year of Amalric's reign, *Sinan Ben Suleiman*, imaun of the assassins, sent a trusty counselor to Jerusalem, offering, in the name of himself and his people, to embrace the Christian religion, provided the Templars would release them from the tribute money. The proposition was favorably received; the envoy was honorably entertained for some days, and on his departure he was furnished by the king with a guide and an escort to

---

[*] *Will. Tyr.* lib. xviii. cap. 4, 5. lib. xx. cap. 5. *Hoveden* in Hen. 2, p. 622. *De Vertot*, Hist. des Chevaliers de Malte, liv. ii. p. 150 to 161, ed. 1726.
[†] *Will. Tyr.* lib. xxi. cap. 29.
[‡] Académie des Inscriptions, tom. xvii. p. 127, 170.

conduct him in safety to the frontier. The Ismaelite had reached the borders of the Latin kingdom, and was almost in sight of the castles of his brethren, when he was slain by the Knight Templar Walter du Mesnil, who attacked the escort with a body of armed followers. The king of Jerusalem assembled the barons of the kingdom at Sidon to determine on the best means of obtaining satisfaction for the injury; and it was determined that two of their number should proceed to Odo de St. Amand to demand the surrender of the criminal. The haughty Master of the Temple bade them inform his majesty the king, that the members of the order were not subject to his jurisdiction, nor to that of his officers; that the Templars acknowledged no earthly superior except the pope; and that to the holy pontiff alone belonged the cognizance of the offence. He declared, however, that the crime should meet with due punishment: that he had caused the criminal to be arrested and put in irons, and would forthwith send him to Rome, but till judgment was given in his case, he forbade all persons of whatsoever degree to meddle with him.*

The Templars were now destined to meet with a more formidable opponent than any they had hitherto encountered in the field, one who was again to cause the *crescent* to triumph over the *cross*, and to plant the standard of the prophet upon the walls of the holy city. When the Fatimite caliph had received intelligence of king Amalric's invasion of Egypt, he sent the hair of his women, one of the greatest tokens of distress known in the East, to the pious Noureddin, who immediately despatched a body of troops to his assistance, headed by Sheerkoh, and his nephew, *Youseef-Ben-Acoub-Ben-Schadi* the famous Saladin. Sheerkoh died immediately after his arrival, and Youseef succeeded to his command, and was appointed vizier of the caliph. He had passed his youth in pleasure and debauchery, sloth and indolence, but as soon as he grasped the power of the sword, and obtained the command of armies, he renounced the pleasures of the world, and assumed the character of a saint. His dress was a coarse-woollen garment; water was his only drink; and he carefully abstained from everything disapproved of by the Mussulman religion. Five times each day he prostrated himself in public prayer, surrounded by his friends and followers, and his demeanor became grave, serious, and thoughtful. His nights were often spent in watching and meditation, he was diligent in fasting and in the study of the Koran, and his admiring brethren gave him the name of *Salah-ed-deen*, "Integrity of Religion," vulgarly called Saladin.

Having aroused the religious enthusiasm of the Moslems he proceeded to take vengeance upon the Christians for their perfidious invasion of Egypt. He assembled an army of forty thousand horse and foot, crossed the desert and besieged the fortified city of Gaza, which belonged to the Knights Templars, and was considered to be the key of Palestine towards Egypt. The luxuriant gardens, the palm and olive groves of this

---

* Adjecit etiam et alia *a spiritu superbiæ,* quo ipse plurimum abundabat, dictata, quæ præsenti narrationi non multum necessarium est interserere.—*Will. Tyr.* lib. xx. cap. 32.

city of the wilderness were destroyed by the wild cavalry of the desert, and the innumerable tents of the Arab host were thickly clustered on the neighboring sand-hills. The warlike monks of the Temple in their turn fasted and prayed, and invoked the aid of the God of battles; they made a desperate defense, and in an unexpected sally upon the enemy's camp, they performed such prodigies of valor, that Saladin, despairing of being able to take the place, abandoned the siege, and retired into Egypt.*

On the death of Noureddin, sultan of Damascus, (A. D. 1175,) Saladin raised himself to the sovereignty both of Egypt and of Syria. He again levied an immense army, crossed the desert, and planted the standard of Mahomet upon the sacred territory of Palestine. His forces were composed of twenty-six thousand light infantry, eight thousand horsemen, a host of archers and spearmen mounted on dromedaries, eighteen thousand common soldiers, and a body-guard of a thousand Mamlook emirs, clothed in yellow cloaks, worn over their shirts of mail. In the great battle fought near Ascalon, (Nov. 1, A. D. 1177,) Odo de St. Amand, the Master of the Temple, at the head of eighty of his knights, broke through the guard of Mamlooks, slew their commander, and penetrated to the imperial tent, from whence Saladin escaped with great difficulty, almost naked, upon a fleet dromedary. The year following, the Templars, in order to protect and cover the road leading from Damascus to Jerusalem, commenced the erection of a strong fortress on the northern frontier of the Latin kingdom, close to Jacob's ford on the river Jordan, at the spot where now stands *Djiss'r Beni Yakoob*, "the bridge of the sons of Jacob." Saladin advanced at the head of his forces to oppose the progress of the work, and the king of Jerusalem and all the chivalry of the Latin kingdom were gathered together in the plain to protect the Templars and their workmen. In a general action the entire army of the cross was defeated with immense slaughter. The Templars and the Hospitallers, with the count of Tripoli, stood firm on the summit of a small hillock, and for a long time presented a bold and undaunted front to the victorious enemy. The count of Tripoli at last cut his way through the infidels, and fled to Tyre; the Master of the Hospital, after seeing most of his brethren slain, swam across the Jordan, and fled, covered with wounds, to the castle of Beaufort; and the Templars after fighting with their accustomed zeal and fanaticism around the red-cross banner, which waved to the last over the field of blood, were all killed or taken prisoners, and the Master, Odo de St. Amand, fell alive into the hands of the enemy. Saladin then laid siege to the newly-erected fortress, which was defended by thick walls, flanked with large towers furnished with military engines, and after a gallant resistance on the part of the garrison, it was set on fire, and then stormed. "The Templars," says Abulpharadge, "flung themselves some into the fire, where they were burned, some cast themselves into the Jordan, some jumped down from the walls on to the rocks, and were dashed to pieces: thus were slain the

---

* *Will. Tyr.* lib. xx. xxi. xxii.

enemy." The fortress was reduced to a heap of ruins, and the enraged sultan, it is said, ordered all the Templars taken in the place to be sawn in two, excepting the most distinguished of the knights, who were reserved for a ransom, and were sent in chains to Aleppo. Saladin offered Odo de St. Amand his liberty in exchange for the freedom of his own nephew, who was a prisoner in the hands of the Templars; but the Master of the Temple haughtily replied, that he would never, by his example, encourage any of his knights to be mean enough to surrender, that a Templar ought either to vanquish or die, and that he had nothing to give for his ransom but his girdle and his knife. The proud spirit of Odo de St. Amand could but ill brook confinement; he languished and died in the dungeons of Damascus, and was succeeded (A. D. 1180) by Brother Arnold de Torroge, who had filled some of the chief situations of the order in Europe.

The affairs of the Latin Christians were at this period in a deplorable situation. Saladin encamped near Tiberias, and extended his ravages into almost every part of Palestine. His light cavalry swept the valley of the Jordan to within a day's march of Jerusalem, and the whole country as far as Panias on the one side, and Beisan, D'Jeneen, and Sebaste, on the other, was destroyed by fire and the sword. The houses of the Templars were pillaged and burnt; various castles belonging to the order were taken by assault; but the immediate destruction of the Latin power was arrested by some partial successes obtained by the Christian warriors, and by the skilful generalship of their leaders. Saladin was compelled to retreat to Damascus, after he had burnt Naplous, and depopulated the whole country around Tiberias. A truce was proposed, (A. D. 1184,) and as the attention of the sultan was then distracted by the intrigues of the Turcoman chieftains in the north of Syria, and he was again engaged in hostilities in Mesopotamia, he agreed to a suspension of the war for four years, in consideration of the payment by the Christians of a large sum of money.*

Immediate advantage was taken of this truce to secure the safety of the Latin kingdom. A grand council was called together at Jerusalem, and it was determined that Heraclius, the patriarch of the Holy City, and the Masters of the Temple and Hospital, should forthwith proceed to Europe, to obtain succor from the western princes. The sovereign mostly depended upon for assistance was Henry the Second, king of England, grandson of Fulk, the late king of Jerusalem, and cousin-german to Baldwin, the then reigning sovereign. Henry had received absolution for the murder of Saint Thomas à Becket, on condition that he should proceed in person at the head of a powerful army to the succor of Palestine, and should, at his own expense, maintain two hundred Templars for the defense of the holy territory. The patriarch and the two Masters landed in Italy, and after furnishing themselves with the letters of the pope, threatening the English monarch with the judgments of heaven if he did not forthwith perform the penance prescribed him, they set out for England. At Verona, the Master of

---

* *Will. Tyr.* lib. xx-xxii. *Abulpharadge* Chron. Syr. p. 379-381.

the Temple fell sick and died, but his companions proceeding on their journey, landed in safety in England at the commencement of the year 1185. They were received by the king at Reading, and throwing themselves at the feet of the English monarch, they with much weeping and sobbing saluted him in behalf of the king, the princes, and the people of the kingdom of Jerusalem. They explained the object of their visit, and presented him with the pope's letters, with the keys of the holy Sepulcher, of the tower of David, and of the city of Jerusalem, together with the royal banner of the Latin kingdom. Their eloquent and pathetic narrative of the fierce inroads of Saladin, and of the miserable condition of Palestine, drew tears from king Henry and all his court. The English sovereign gave encouraging assurances to the patriarch and his companions, and promised to bring the whole matter before the parliament, which was to meet the first Sunday in Lent.[*]

The patriarch, in the mean time, proceeded to London, and was received by the Knights Templars at the Temple in that city, the chief house of the order in Britain, where, in the month of February, he consecrated the beautiful Temple church, dedicated to the blessed Virgin Mary, which had just then been erected.[†]

[*] *Hemingford*, cap. 33. *Hoveden*, ad ann. 1185; *Radulph de Diceto*, p. 622-626. Concil. Mag. Brit. tom. iv, p. 788. *Matt. West.* ad ann. 185; *Guill. Neubr.* tom. i. lib. iii. cap. 12, 13.
[†] *Speed.* Hist. Britain, p. 506. A. D. 1185.

Chapter III.

Li fiere, li Mestre du Temple Qu'estoient rempli et ample D'Or et d'argent et de richesse, Et qui menoient tel noblesse, Ou sont-il? que sont devenu? Que tant ont de plait maintenu, Que nul a elz ne s'ozoit prendre Tozjors achetoient sans vendre Nul riche a elz n'estoit de prise; Tant va pot a eue qu'il brise.

Chron. à la suite du Roman de Favel.

The Knights Templars first established the chief house of their order in England, without Holborn Bars, on the south side of the street, where Southampton House formerly stood, adjoining to which Southampton Buildings were afterwards erected: and it is stated, that about a century and a half ago, part of the ancient chapel annexed to this establishment, of a circular form, and built of Caen stone, was discovered on pulling down some old houses near Southampton Buildings in Chancery Lane.* This first house of the Temple, established by Hugh de Payens himself, before his departure from England, on his return to Palestine, was adapted to the wants and necessities of the order in its infant state, when the knights, instead of lingering in the preceptories of Europe, proceeded at once to Palestine, and when all the resources of the society were strictly and faithfully forwarded to Jerusalem, to be expended in defense of the faith; but when the order had greatly increased in numbers, power, and wealth, and had somewhat departed from its original purity and simplicity, we find that the superior and the knights resident in London began to look abroad for a more extensive and commodious place of habitation. They purchased a large space of ground, extending from the White Friars westward to Essex House without Temple Bar, and commenced the erection of a convent on a scale of grandeur commensurate with the dignity and importance of the chief house of the great religio-military society of the Temple in Britain. It was called the *New* Temple, to distinguish it from the original establishment at Holborn, which came thenceforth to be known by the name of the *Old* Temple. This New Temple was adapted for the residence of numerous military monks and novices, serving brothers, retainers, and domestics. It contained the residence of the superior and of the knights, the cells and apartments of the chaplains and serving brethren, the council chamber where the chapters were held, and the refectory or dining-hall, which was connected, by a range of handsome cloisters, with

---

* *Stowe's* Survey. *Tanner*, Notit. Monast. *Dugd.* Orig. Jurid. *Herbert*, Antiq. Inns of Court.

the magnificent church, consecrated by the patriarch. Alongside the river extended a spacious pleasure ground for the recreation of the brethren, who were not permitted to go into the town without the leave of the Master. It was used also for military exercises and the training of horses.

The year of the consecration of the Temple Church, Geoffrey, the superior of the order in England, caused an inquisition to be made of the lands of the Templars in this country, and the names of the donors thereof,[*] from which it appears, that the larger territorial divisions of the order were then called bailiwicks, the principal of which were London, Warwic, Couele, Meritune, Gutinge, Westune, Lincolnscire, Lindeseie, Widine, and Eboracisire (Yorkshire). The number of manors, farms, churches, advowsons, demesne lands, villages, hamlets, windmills, and watermills, rents of assize, rights of common and free warren, and the amount of all kinds of property possessed by the Templars in England at the period of the taking of this inquisition, are astonishing. Upon the great estates belonging to the order, prioral houses had been erected, wherein dwelt the procurators or stewards charged with the management of the manors and farms in their neighborhood, and with the collection of the rents. These prioral houses became regular monastic establishments, inhabited chiefly by sick and aged Templars, who retired to them to spend the remainder of their days, after a long period of honorable service against the infidels in Palestine. They were cells to the principal house at London. There were also under them certain smaller administrations established for the management of the farms, consisting of a Knight Templar, to whom were associated some serving brothers of the order, and a priest who acted as almoner. The commissions or mandates directed by the Master of the Temple to the officers at the head of these establishments were called precepts, from the commencement of them, "*Præcipimus tibi,*" we enjoin or direct you, &c. &c. The knights to whom they were addressed were styled *Præceptores Templi*, or Preceptors of the Temple, and the districts administered by them *Præceptoria*, or preceptories.

*✠ANNO: AB·INCARNA
TIONE·DOMINI·Ɱ·CLXXXV.
DEDICATA✠hec·ECCLESIA·IN·hONO
RE·BEATE: MARIE·A·DNO·ERACLIO·DEI·GRA·
SCE·RESVRRECTIONIS·ECCLESIE· PATRI
ARCHA·IIII·IDVS·FEBRVARII·Q: EA·ANNATIM·
PETENTIB·DE·IINNCTA·SPENITENTIA·IX·DIES·INDVLSIT·*

The ancient inscription on the Temple Church as it stood over the door leading into the cloister.

---

* *Dugd.* Monast. Angl. vol vi. part ii. p. 820.

C. G. Addison
ON THE 10th OF FEBRUARY,
IN
THE YEAR FROM THE INCARNATION OF OUR LORD, 1185,
THIS CHURCH WAS CONSECRATED IN HONOR OF THE
BLESSED MARY BY THE LORD HERACLIUS,
BY
THE GRACE OF GOD PATRIARCH OF THE CHURCH OF THE
RESURRECTION, WHO
HATH GRANTED AN INDULGENCE OF SIXTY DAYS
TO THOSE YEARLY VISITING IT.

Translation of the inscription on the Temple Church, as it stood over the doorway leading into the cloister.

It will now be as well to take a general survey of the possessions and organization of the order both in Europe and Asia, "whose circumstances," saith William, archbishop of Tyre, writing from Jerusalem about the period of the consecration at London of the Temple Church, "are in so flourishing a state, that at this day they have in their convent (the Temple on Mount Moriah) more than three hundred knights robed in the white habit, besides serving brothers innumerable. Their possessions indeed beyond the sea, as well as in these parts, are said to be so vast, that there cannot now be a province in Christendom which does not contribute to the support of the aforesaid brethren, whose wealth is said to equal that of sovereign princes."[*]

The eastern provinces of the order were, 1. Palestine, the ruling province. 2. The principality of Antioch. 3. The principality of Tripoli. In Palestine the Templars possessed, in addition to the Temple at Jerusalem, the chief house of the order, and the residence of the Master, the fortified city of Gaza, the key of the kingdom of Jerusalem on the side next Egypt, which was granted to them in perpetual sovereignty, by Baldwin king of Jerusalem; also the Castle of Saphet, in the territory of the ancient tribe of Naphtali; the Castle of the Pilgrims, in the neighborhood of Mount Carmel; the Castle of Assur near Jaffa, and the house of the Temple at Jaffa; the fortress of Faba, or La Feue, the ancient Aphek, not far from Tyre, in the territory of the ancient tribe of Asher; the hill-fort Dok between Bethel and Jericho; the castles of La Cave, Marle, Citern Rouge, Castel Blanc, Trapesach, Sommelleria of the Temple, in the neighborhood of Acca, now St. John d'Acre; Castrum Planorum, and a place called Gerinum Parvum.[†] The Templars, moreover, purchased the castle of Beaufort and the city of Sidon; they also got into their hands a great part of the town of St. Jean d'Acre, where they erected a famous *temple*, and almost all the sea coast of Palestine was in the end divided between them and the Hospitallers of St. John. The principal houses of the Temple in the Province of Antioch were at Antioch itself, at Aleppo, and Haram; and in the Principality of Tripoli,

[*] *Will. Tyr.* lib. xii. cap. 7.
[†] *Will. Tyr.* lib. xx. cap. 21. *Rob. de Monte*, appen. ad chron. Sig. p. 631. *Marin, Sanut.* p. 221. *Bernard*, Thesaur. p. 768. *Matt. Par.* p. 142.

at Tripoli, Tortosa, the ancient Antaradus; Castel Blanc in the same neighborhood; Laodicea and Beyrout.

In the western province of Apulia and Sicily, the Templars possessed numerous houses, viz., at Palermo, Syracuse, Lentini, Butera, and Trapani. The house of the Temple at this last place has been appropriated to the use of some monks of the order of St. Augustin. In a church of the city is still to be seen the celebrated statue of the Virgin, which Brother Guerrege and three other Knights Templars brought from the East, with a view of placing it in the Temple Church on the Aventine hill in Rome, but which they were obliged to deposit in the island of Sicily. This statue is of the most beautiful white marble, and represents the Virgin with the infant Jesus reclining on her left arm; it is of about the natural height, and, from an inscription on the foot of the figure, it appears to have been executed by a native of the island of Cyprus, A. D. 733. The Templars possessed valuable estates in Sicily, around the base of Mount Etna, and large tracts of land between Piazza and Calatagirone, in the suburbs of which last place there was a Temple house, the church whereof, dedicated to the Virgin Mary, still remains. They possessed also many churches in the island, windmills, rights of fishery, of pasturage, of cutting wood in the forests, and many important privileges and immunities. The chief house was at Messina, where the Grand Prior resided.*

Upper and Central Italy also contained numerous preceptories of the order of the Temple, all under the immediate superintendence of the grand Prior or Preceptor of Rome. There were large establishments at Lucca, Milan, and Perugia, at which last place the arms of the Temple are still to be seen on the tower of the holy cross. At Placentia there was a magnificent and extensive convent, called Santa Maria del Tempio, ornamented with a very lofty tower. At Bologna there was also a large Temple house, and on a clock in the city is the following inscription, "*Magister Tosseolus de Miolâ me fecit ... Fr. Petrus de Bon, Procur. Militiæ Templi in curiâ Romanâ*, MCCCIII." In the church of St. Mary in the same place, which formerly belonged to the Knights Templars, is the interesting marble monument of Peter de Rotis, a priest of the order.

In the Province of Portugal, the military power and resources of the order were exercised in almost constant warfare against the Moors, and Europe derived essential advantage from the enthusiastic exertions of the warlike monks in that quarter against the infidels. In every battle, indeed, fought in the south of Europe, after the year 1130, against the enemies of the cross, the Knights Templars are to be found taking an active and distinguished part. They were extremely popular with all the princes and sovereigns of the great Spanish peninsula, and were endowed with cities, villages, lordships, and splendid domains. The Grand Prior or Preceptor of Portugal resided at the castle of Tomar. It is seated on the river Narboan, in Estremadura, and is still to be seen towering in gloomy magnificence on

---

* *Roccus Pyrrhus*, Sicil. Antiq. tom. iii. col. 1000, 1093, 4, 5, 6, 7, &c.

the hill above the town. The castle at present belongs to the order of Christ, and was lately one of the grandest and richest establishments in Portugal. It possessed a splendid library, and a handsome cloister, the architecture of which was much admired. The houses or preceptories of the Temple in the province of Castile and Leon were those of Cuenca, and Guadalfagiara; Tine and Aviles in the diocese of Oviedo, and Pontevreda in Galicia. In Castile alone the order is said to have possessed twenty-four bailiwicks.

In Aragon the Templars possessed the castles of Dumbel, Cabanos, Azuda, Granena, Chalonere, Remolins, Corbins, Lo Mas de Barbaran, Moncon, and Montgausi, with their territories and dependencies. They were lords of the cities of Borgia and Tortosa; they had a tenth part of the revenues of the kingdom, the taxes of the towns of Huesca and Saragossa, and houses, possessions, privileges, and immunities in all parts.* They possessed likewise lands and estates in the Balearic Isles, which were under the management of the Prior or Preceptor of the island of Majorca, who was subject to the Grand Preceptor of Aragon.

In Germany and Hungary the houses and preceptories most known were at Homburg, Assenheim, Rotgen in the Rhingau, Mongberg in the Marché of Brandenbourg, Nuitz on the Rhine, Tissia Altmunmunster near Ratisbon in Bavaria, Bamberg, Middleburgh, Hall, and Brunswick. The Templars possessed the fiefs of Rorich, Pausin and Wildenheuh in *Pomerania*, an establishment at Bach in *Hungary*, several lordships in *Bohemia* and *Moravia*, and lands, tithes, and large revenues, the gifts of pious German crusaders.† In Greece the Templars also possessed lands and establishments. Their chief house was at Constantinople, in the quarter called Ὁμόνοια, where they had an oratory dedicated to the holy martyrs Marin and Pentaleon.‡ In France the principal preceptories were at Besançon, Dole, Salins, à la Romagne, à la ville Dieu, Arbois in *Franche Comté*. Dorlesheim near Molsheim, where their still remains a chapel called Templehoff, Fauverney, where a chapel dedicated to the Virgin still preserves the name of the Temple, Des Feuilles, situate in the parish of Villett, near the chateau de Vernay, and Rouen, where there were two houses of the Temple; one of them occupied the site of the present *maison consulaire*, and the other stood in the street now called *La Rue des Hermites*. The preceptories and houses of the Temple in France, indeed, were so numerous, that it would be a wearisome and endless task to repeat the names of them. Between Joinville and St. Dizier may still be seen the remains of Temple Ruet, an old chateau surrounded by a moat; and in the diocese of Meaux are the ruins of the great manorial house of Choisy le Temple. Many interesting tombs are there visible, together with the refectory of the knights, which has been converted into a sheepfold. The chief house of the order for France, and also for Holland and the Netherlands, was the Temple at Paris, an extensive and magnificent

---

* *Mariana*, de. reb. Hist. lib. ii. cap. 23.
† Script. rer. Germ. tom. ii. col. 584.
‡ Constantinop. Christ. lib. iv. p. 157.

structure, surrounded by a wall and a ditch. It extended over all that large space of ground, now covered with streets and buildings, which lies between the Rue du Temple, the Rue St. Croix, and the environs de la Verrerie, as far as the walls and the fossés of the port du Temple. It was ornamented with a great tower, flanked by four smaller towers, erected by the Knight Templar Brother Herbert, almoner to the king of France, and was one of the strongest edifices in the kingdom.[*] Many of the modern streets of Paris which now traverse the site of this interesting structure, preserve in the names given to them some memorial of the ancient Temple. For instance, *La rue du Temple, La rue des fossés du Temple, Boulevard du Temple, Faubourg du Temple, rue de Faubourg du Temple, Vieille rue du Temple, &c., &c.*

J. Brandard, lith. W.H. Cubley, delt. M. &. N. Hanhart, Imp[t].
TOWER OF THE PRECEPTORY OF TEMPLE BRUERE,
LINCOLNSHIRE.

---

[*] Hist. Gen. de Languedoc. Hist. de la ville de Paris, tom. i. p. 174. Gall. christ. nov. tom. vi., tom. vii. col. 853.

C. G. Addison

All the houses of the Temple in Holland and the Netherlands were under the immediate jurisdiction of the Master of the Temple at Paris. The preceptories in these kingdoms were very numerous, and the property dependent upon them was of great value.

In England there were in bygone times the preceptories of Aslakeby, Temple Bruere, Egle, Malteby, Mere, Wilketon, and Witham, in *Lincolnshire.* North Feriby, Temple Hurst, Temple Newsom, Pafflete, Flaxflete, and Ribstane, in *Yorkshire.* Temple Cumbe, in *Somersetshire.* Ewell, Strode and Swingfield, near Dover, in *Kent.* Hadescoe, in *Norfolk.* Balsall and Warwick, in *Warwickshire.* Temple Rothley, in *Leicestershire.* Wilburgham Magna, Daney, and Dokesworth, in *Cambridgeshire.* Halston, in *Shropshire.* Temple Dynnesley, in *Hertfordshire.* Temple Cressing and Sutton, in *Essex.* Saddlescomb and Chapelay, in *Sussex.* Schepeley, in *Surrey.* Temple Cowley, Sandford, Bistelesham, and Chalesey, in *Oxfordshire.* Temple Rockley, in *Wiltshire.* Upleden and Garwy, in *Herefordshire.* South Badeisley, in *Hampshire.* Getinges, in *Worcestershire.* Giselingham and Dunwich, in *Suffolk.*

There were also several smaller administrations established, as before mentioned, for the management of the farms and lands, and the collection of rent and tithes. Among these were Liddele and Quiely in the diocese of Chichester; Eken in the diocese of Lincoln; Adingdon, Wesdall, Aupledina, Cotona, &c. The different preceptors of the Temple in England had under their management lands and property in every county of the realm.[*]

In *Leicestershire* the Templars possessed the town and the soke of Rotheley; the manors of Rolle, Babbegrave, Gaddesby, Stonesby, and Melton; Rothely wood, near Leicester; the villages of Beaumont, Baresby, Dalby, North and South Mardefeld, Saxby, Stonesby, and Waldon, with land in above *eighty* others! They had also the churches of Rotheley, Babbegrave, and Rolle; and the chapels of Gaddesby, Grimston, Wartnaby, Cawdwell, and Wykeham.[†]

In *Hertfordshire* they possessed the town and forest of Broxbourne, the manor of Chelsin Templars, (*Chelsin Templariorum,*) and the manors of Laugenok, Broxbourne, Letchworth, and Temple Dynnesley; demesne lands at Stanho, Preston, Charlton, Walden, Hiche, Chelles, Levecamp, and Benigho; the church of Broxbourne, two watermills, and a lock on the river Lea; also property at Hichen, Pyrton, Ickilford, Offeley Magna, Offeley Parva, Walden Regis, Furnivale, Ipolitz, Wandsmyll, Watton, Therleton, Weston, Gravele, Wilien, Leccheworth, Baldock, Datheworth, Russenden, Codpeth, Sumershale, Buntynford, &c., &c., and the Church of Weston.[‡]
In the county of *Essex* they had the manors of Temple Cressynge, Temple

---

[*] *Dugd.* Monast. Angl. vol. vi. part 2, p. 800 to 817. Concil. Magnæ Britanniæ, tom. iii. p. 333 to 382. Acta *Rymeri*, tom iii. p. 279, 288, 291, 295, &c.

[†] *Nichol's* Hist. of Leicestershire.

[‡] *Clutterbuck's* Hist. of Hertfordshire. Acta *Rymeri*, tom. iii. p. 133, 134. *Dodsworth*, MS. vol. xxxv.

Roydon, Temple Sutton, Odewell, Chingelford, Lideleye, Quarsing, Berwick, and Witham; the church of Roydon, and houses, lands, and farms, both at Roydon, at Rivenhall, and in the parishes of Prittlewall and Great and Little Sutton; an old mansion-house and chapel at Sutton, and an estate called Finchinfelde in the hundred of Hinckford.[*] In *Lincolnshire* the Templars possessed the manors of La Bruere, Roston, Kirkeby, Brauncewell, Carleton, Akele, with the soke of Lynderby, Aslakeby, and the churches of Bruere, Asheby, Akele, Aslakeby, Donington, Ele, Swinderby, Skarle, &c. There were upwards of thirty churches in the county which made annual payments, to the order of the Temple, and about forty windmills. The order likewise received rents in respect of lands at Bracebrig, Brancestone, Scapwic, Timberland, Weleburne, Diringhton, and a hundred other places; and some of the land in the county was charged with the annual payment of sums of money towards the keeping of lights eternally burning on the altars of the Temple church. William Lord of Asheby gave to the Templars the perpetual advowson of the church of Asheby in Lincolnshire, and they in return agreed to find him a priest to sing for ever twice a week in his chapel of St. Margaret.

In *Yorkshire* the Templars possessed the manors of Temple Werreby, Flaxflete, Etton, South Cave, &c.; the churches of Whitcherche Keluntune, &c.; numerous windmills and lands and rents at Nehus, Skelture, Pennel, and more than sixty other places besides. In *Warwickshire* they possessed the manors of Barston, Shirburne, Balshale, Wolfhey, Cherlecote, Herbebure, Stodleye, Fechehampstead, Cobington, Tysho and Warwick; lands at Chelverscoton, Herdwicke, Morton, Warwick, Hetherburn, Chesterton, Aven, Derset, Stodley, Napton, and more than thirty other places, the several donors whereof are specified in Dugdale's history of Warwickshire (p. 694) also the churches of Sireburne, Cardington, &c., and more than thirteen windmills. In 12 Hen. II., William Earle of Warwick built a new church for them at Warwick.[†] In *Kent* they had the manors of Lilleston, Hechewayton, Saunford, Sutton, Dartford, Halgel, Ewell, Cocklescomb, Strode, Swinkfield Mennes, West Greenwich, and the manor of Lydden, which now belongs to the archbishop of Canterbury; the advowsons of the churches of West Greenwich and Kingeswode juxta Waltham; extensive tracts of land in Romney marsh, and farms and assize rents in all parts of the county. In *Sussex* they had the manors of Saddlecomb and Shipley; lands and tenements at Compton and other places; and the advowsons of the churches of Shipley, Wodmancote, and Luschwyke.

In *Surrey* they had the manor farm of Temple Elfand or Elfant, and an estate at Merrow in the hundred of Woking. In *Gloucestershire*, the manors of Lower Dowdeswell, Pegsworth, Amford, Nishange, and five others which belonged to them wholly or in part, the church of Down

---

[*] *Morant's* Hist. Essex. *Rymer*, tom. iii. p. 290 to 294.
[†] Inquis. terrar. ut sup. *Peck's* MS. in Musseo Britannico, vol. iv. fol. 95. *Dodsworth*, MS. vol. xx. p. 65, 67. *Dugd.* Baron, tom. i. p. 70.

Ammey, and lands in Frampton, Temple Guting, and Little Rissington. In *Worcestershire*, the manor of Templars Lawern, and lands in Flavel, Temple Broughton, and Hanbury. In *Northamptonshire*, the manors of Asheby, Thorp, Watervill, &c., &c.; they had the advowson of the church of the manor of Hardwicke in Orlington hundred, and we find that "Robert Saunford, Master of the soldiery of the Temple in England," presented to it in the year 1238.[*] In *Nottinghamshire*, the Templars possessed the church of Marnham, lands and rents at Gretton and North Carleton; in *Westmoreland*, the manor of Temple Sowerby; in the Isle of Wight, the manor of Uggeton, and lands in Kerne. But it would be tedious further to continue with a dry detail of ancient names and places; sufficient has been said to give an idea of the enormous wealth of the order in this country, where it is known to have possessed some hundreds of manors, the advowson or right of presentation to churches innumerable, and thousands of acres of arable land, pasture, and woodland, besides villages, farm-houses, mills, and tithes, rights of common, of fishing, of cutting wood in forests, &c., &c. There were also several preceptories in Scotland and Ireland, which were dependent on the Temple at London.

The annual income of the order in Europe has been roughly estimated at six millions sterling! According to Matthew Paris, the Templars possessed *nine thousand* manors or lordships in Christendom, besides a large revenue and immense riches arising from the constant charitable bequests and donations of sums of money from pious persons.[†] The Templars, in imitation of the other monastic establishments, obtained from pious and charitable people all the advowsons within their reach, and frequently retained the tithe and the glebe in their own hands, deputing a priest of the order to perform divine service and administer the sacraments. The manors of the Templars produced them rent either in money, corn, or cattle, and the usual produce of the soil. By the custom in some of these manors, the tenants were annually to mow three days in harvest, one at the charge of the house, and to plough three days, whereof one at the like charge; to reap one day, at which time they should have a ram from the house, eight pence, twenty-four loaves, and a cheese of the best in the house, together with a pailful of drink. The tenants were not to sell their horse-colts if they were foaled upon the land belonging to the Templars, without the consent of the fraternity, nor marry their daughters without their licence. There were also various regulations concerning the cocks and hens and young chickens.

King Henry the Second, for the good of his soul and the welfare of his kingdom, granted the Templars a place situate on the river Fleet, near Bainard's Castle, with the whole current of that river at London, for erecting a mill; also a messuage near Fleet-street; the church of St.

---

[*] Monast. Angl. *Hasted.* Hist. Kent. *Manning's* Surrey. *Atkyn's* Gloucestershire; and see the references in *Tanner. Nash's* Worcestershire. *Bridge's* Northamptonshire, vol. ii. p. 100.
[†] *Thoroton's* Nottinghamshire. *Burn and Nicholson's* Westmoreland. *Worsley's* Isle of Wight. *Mat. Par.* p. 615, ed. Lond. 1640.

Clement, "quæ dicitur Dacorum extra civitatem Londoniæ;" and the churches of Elle, Swinderby and Skarle in Lincolnshire, Kingeswode juxta Waltham in Kent, the manor of Stroder in the hundred of Skamele, the vill of Kele in Staffordshire, the hermitage of Flikeamstede, and all his lands at Lange Cureway, a house in Brosal, and the market at Witham; lands at Berghotte, a mill at the bridge of Pembroke Castle, the vill of Finchinfelde, the manor of Rotheley, with its appurtenances, and the advowson of the church and its several chapels, the manor of Blalcolvesley, the park of Halshall, and three *fat bucks* annually, either from Essex or Windsor Forest. He likewise granted them an annual fair at Temple Bruere, and superadded many rich benefactions in Ireland.*

The Templars, in addition to their amazing wealth, enjoyed vast privileges and immunities within this realm. They were freed from all amerciaments in the Exchequer, and obtained the privilege of not being compelled to plead except before the king or his chief justice. By special grant from the kings of England, they enjoyed free warren in all their demesne lands, also the power of holding courts to judge their villains and vassals, and to try thieves and malefactors; they were relieved from all the customary feudal suits and services, from the works of parks, castles, bridges, the building of royal houses, and all other works; and also from waste regard and view of foresters, and from toll in all markets and fairs, and at all bridges, and upon all highways throughout the kingdom. They had also the chattels of felons and fugitives, and all waifs within their fee.†
In addition to the particular privileges conceded to them by the kings of England, the Templars enjoyed, under the authority of divers Papal bulls, various immunities and advantages, which gave great umbrage to the clergy. They were freed, as before mentioned, from the obligation of paying tithes, and might, with the consent of the bishop, receive them. No brother of the Temple could be excommunicated by any bishop or priest, nor could any of the churches of the order be laid under interdict except by virtue of a special mandate from the holy see. When any brother of the Temple, appointed to make charitable collections for the succor of the Holy Land, should arrive at a city, castle, or village, which had been laid under interdict, the churches, on their welcome coming, were to be thrown open, (once within the year,) and divine service was to be performed in honor of the Temple, and in reverence for the holy soldiers thereof. The privilege of sanctuary was thrown around their dwellings; and by various papal bulls it is solemnly enjoined that no person shall lay violent hands either upon the persons or the property of those flying for refuge to the Temple houses.‡

Sir Edward Coke, in the second part of the Institute of the Laws of England, observes, that "the Templars did so overspread throughout Christendome, and so exceedingly increased in possessions, revenues, and

---

* *Dugd.* Monast. Angl. p. 838.
† *Dugd.* Monast. p. 844.
‡ Acta *Rymeri*, tom. i. p. 30-32, 54, 298, 574, 575.

wealth, and specially in England, as you will wonder to reade in approved histories, and withall obtained so great and large privileges, liberties, and immunities for themselves, their tenants, and farmers, &c., as no other order had the like." He further observes, that the Knights Templars were *cruce signati*, and as the cross was the ensign of their profession, and their tenants enjoyed great privileges, they did erect crosses upon their houses, to the end that those inhabiting them might be known to be the tenants of the order, and thereby be freed from many duties and services which other tenants were subject unto; "and many tenants of other lords, perceiving the state and greatnesse of the knights of the said order, and withall seeing the great privileges their tenants enjoyed, did set up crosses upon their houses, as their very tenants used to doe, to the prejudice of their lords."

This abuse led to the passing of the statute of Westminster, the second, *chap. 33*, which recites, that many tenants did set up crosses or cause them to be set up on their lands in prejudice of their lords, that the tenants might defend themselves against the chief lord of the fee by the privileges of Templars, and enacts that such lands shall be forfeited to the chief lords or to the king. Sir Edward Coke observes, that the Templars were freed from tenths and fifteenths to be paid to the king; that they were discharged of purveyance; that they could not be sued for any ecclesiastical cause before the ordinary, *sed coram conservatoribus suorum privilegiorum*; and that of ancient time they claimed that a felon might take to their houses, having their crosses for his safety, as well as to any church. And concerning these conservers or keepers of their privileges, he remarks, that the Templars and Hospitallers "held an ecclesiasticall court before a canonist, whom they termed *conservator privilegiorum suorum*, which judge had indeed more authority than was convenient, and did dayly, in respect to the height of these two orders, and at their instance and direction, incroach upon and hold plea of matters determinable by the common law, for *cui plus licet quam par est, plus vult quam licet*; and this was one great mischiefe. Another mischiefe was, that this judge likewise at their instance, in cases wherein he had jurisdiction, would make general citations as *pro salute animæ*, and the like, without expressing the matter whereupon the citation was made, which also was against law, and tended to the grievous vexation of the subject."* To remedy these evils, another act of parliament was passed, prohibiting the Templars from bringing any man in plea before the keepers of their privileges, for any matter the knowledge whereof belonged to the king's court, and commanding such keepers of their privileges thenceforth to grant no citation at the instance of the Templars, before it be expressed upon what matter the citation ought to be made.†

---

* 2 Inst. p. 432, 465.
† Stat. Westr. 2, cap. 43, 13 Ed. I.

J. Brandard, lith. M. & N. Hanhart, Imp^{t}.
CHAPEL OF THE PRECEPTORY OF TEMPLE SWINGFIELD,
DOVER.

The Grand Master of the Temple ranked in Europe as a sovereign prince, and had precedence of all ambassadors and peers in the general councils of the church. He was elected to his high office by the chapter of the kingdom of Jerusalem, which was composed of all the knights of the East and of the West who could manage to attend. The western nations or provinces of the order were presided over by the provincial Masters, otherwise Grand Priors or Grand Preceptors, who were originally appointed by the Chief Master at Jerusalem, and were in theory mere trustees or bare administrators of the revenues of the fraternity, accountable to the treasurer-general at Jerusalem, and removable at the pleasure of the Chief Master. The superior of the Temple at London is always styled "Master of the Temple," and holds his chapters and has his officers corresponding to those of the Chief Master in Palestine. The latter, consequently, came to be denominated *Magnus Magister*, or Grand Master. The titles given indeed to the superiors of the different nations or provinces into which the order of the Temple was divided, are numerous and somewhat perplexing. In the East, these officers were known only, in the first instance, by the title of Prior, as Prior of England, Prior of France, Prior of Portugal, &c., and afterwards Preceptor of England, Preceptor of France, &c.; but in Europe they were called Grand Priors, and Grand Preceptors, to distinguish them from the Sub-priors and Sub-preceptors, and also Masters of the Temple. The Prior and Preceptor *of* England, therefore, and the Grand Prior, Grand Preceptor, and Master of the Temple *in* England, were one and the same person. There were also at the New Temple at London, in imitation of the establishment at the chief house in Palestine, in addition to the Master, the Preceptor of the Temple, the Prior of London, the Treasurer, and the Guardian of the church, who had three chaplains under him called readers.

The Master at London had his general and particular, or his ordinary and extraordinary chapters. The first were composed of the grand preceptors of Scotland and Ireland, and all the provincial priors and preceptors of the three kingdoms, who were summoned once a year to deliberate on the state of the Holy Land, to forward succor, to give an account of their stewardship, and to frame new rules and regulations for the management of the temporalities.[*] The ordinary chapters were held at the different preceptories, which the Master of the Temple visited in succession. In these chapters new members were admitted into the order; lands were bought, sold, and exchanged; and presentations were made by the Master to vacant benefices. Many of the grants and other deeds of these chapters, with the seal of the order of the Temple annexed to them, are to be met with in the public and private collections of manuscripts in this country. One of the most interesting and best preserved, is the Harleian charter, (83, c. 39,) in the British Museum, which is a grant of land made by Brother William de la More THE MARTYR, the last Master of the Temple in England, to the Lord Milo de Stapleton. It is expressed to be made by him, with the common consent and advice of his chapter, held at the Preceptory of Dynneslee, on the feast of Saint Barnabas the Apostle, and concludes, "In witness whereof, we have to this present indenture placed the seal of our chapter." A facsimile of this seal is given at the head of the present chapter. On the reverse of it is a man's head, decorated with a long beard, and surmounted by a small cap, and around it are the letters TESTIS SVM AGNI. The same seal is to be met with on various other indentures made by the Master and Chapter of the Temple.[†] The more early seals are surrounded with the words, Sigillum *Militis* Templi, "Seal of the *Knight* of the Temple;" as in the case of the deed of exchange of lands at Normanton in the parish of Botisford, in Leicestershire, entered into between Brother Amadeus de Morestello, Master of the chivalry of the Temple in England, and his chapter, of the one part, and the Lord Henry de Coleville Knight, of the other part. The seal annexed to this deed has the addition of the word *Militis*, but in other respects it is similar to the one above delineated.[‡]

The Master of the Temple in England sat in parliament as first baron of the realm, but that is to be understood among priors only. To the parliament holden in the twenty-ninth year of King Henry the Third, there was summoned sixty-five abbots, thirty-five priors, and the Master of the Temple.[§] The oath taken by the grand priors, grand preceptors, or provincial Masters in Europe, on their assumption of the duties of their high administrative office, was drawn up in the following terms:—"I *A. B.*,

[*] Concil. Mag. Brit. tom. ii. p. 335, 339, 340, 355, 356. Monast. Angl. p. 818.
[†] *Peck's* MS. in Museo Brittannico, vol. iv. p. 65.
[‡] *Nicholl's* Hist. Leicestershire, vol. iii. pl. cxxvii. fig. 947, p. 943; vol. ii. pl. v. fig. 13.
[§] Rot. claus. 49. H. III. m. xi. d. Acta *Rymeri*, tom. iii. p. 802.

Knight of the Order of the Temple, just now appointed Master of the knights who are in ——, promise to Jesus Christ my Savior, and to his vicar the sovereign pontiff and his successors, perpetual obedience and fidelity. I swear that I will defend, not only with my lips, but by force of arms and with all my strength, the mysteries of the faith; the seven sacraments, the fourteen articles of the faith, the creed of the Apostles, and that of Saint Athanasius; the books of the Old and the New Testament, with the commentaries of the holy fathers, as received by the church; the unity of God, the plurality of the persons of the holy Trinity; and the doctrine that Mary, the daughter of Joachim and Anna, of the tribe of Judah, and of the race of David, remained always a virgin before her delivery, during and after her delivery. I promise likewise to be submissive and obedient to the Master-general of the order, in conformity with the statutes prescribed by our father Saint Bernard; that I will at all times in case of need pass the seas to go and fight; that I will always afford succor against the infidel kings and princes; that in the presence of three enemies I will fly not, but cope with them, if they are infidels; that I will not sell the property of the order, nor consent that it be sold or alienated; that I will always preserve chastity; that I will be faithful to the king of ——; that I will never surrender to the enemy the towns and places belonging to the order; and that I will never refuse to the religious any succor that I am able to afford them; that I will aid and defend them by words, by arms, and by all sorts of good offices; and in sincerity and of my own free will I swear that I will observe all these things."[*]

Among the earliest of the Masters, or Grand Priors, or Grand Preceptors of England, whose names figure in history, is Richard de Hastings, who was at the head of the order in this country on the accession of King Henry the Second to the throne, (A. D. 1154,) and was employed by that monarch in various important negotiations. He was the friend and confidant of Thomas à Becket, and vainly endeavored to terminate the disputes between that haughty prelate and the king.[†] Richard de Hastings was succeeded by Richard Mallebeench, who confirmed a treaty of peace and concord which had been entered into between his predecessor and the abbot of Kirkested; and the next Master of the Temple appears to have been Geoffrey son of Stephen, who received the patriarch Heraclius as his guest at the new Temple on the occasion of the consecration of the Temple church. He styles himself "*Minister* of the soldiery of the Temple in England."[‡]

In consequence of the high estimation in which the Templars were held, and the privilege of sanctuary enjoyed by them, the Temple at London came to be made "a storehouse of treasure." The wealth of the king, the nobles, the bishops, and of the rich burghers of London, was

---

[*] L'Histoire des Cisteaux, *Chrisost Henriques*, p. 479.
[†] *Lord Littleton's* Life of Henry II. tom. ii. p. 356. *Hoveden*, 453. *Chron. Gervasii*, p. 1386, apud X. script.
[‡] *Lansdowne* MS. 207 E. fol. 467. Ibid. fol. 201.

generally deposited therein, under the safeguard and protection of the military friars. The money collected in the churches and chapels for the succor of the Holy Land was also paid to the treasurer of the Temple, to be forwarded to its destination: and the treasurer was at different times authorized to receive the taxes imposed upon the moveables of the ecclesiastics, also the large sums of money extorted by the rapacious popes from the English clergy, and the annuities granted by the king to the nobles of the kingdom.[*] The money and jewels of Hubert de Burgh, earl of Kent, the chief justiciary, and at one time governor of the king and kingdom of England, were deposited in the Temple, and when that nobleman was disgraced and committed to the Tower, the king attempted to lay hold of the treasure. Matthew Paris gives the following curious account of the affair:—"It was suggested," says he, "to the king, that Hubert had no small amount of treasure deposited in the New Temple, under the custody of the Templars. The king accordingly, summoning to his presence the Master of the Temple, briefly demanded of him if it was so. He indeed, not daring to deny the truth to the king, confessed that he had money of the said Hubert, which had been confidentially committed to the keeping of himself and his brethren, but of the quantity and amount thereof he was altogether ignorant. Then the king endeavored with threats to obtain from the brethren the surrender to him of the aforesaid money, asserting that it had been fraudulently subtracted from his treasury. But they answered to the king, that money confided to them in trust they would deliver to no man without the permission of him who had intrusted it to be kept in the Temple. And the king, since the above-mentioned money had been placed under their protection, ventured not to take it by force. He sent, therefore, the treasurer of his court, with his justices of the Exchequer, to Hubert, who had already been placed in fetters in the Tower of London, that they might exact from him an assignment of the entire sum to the king. But when these messengers had explained to Hubert the object of their coming, he immediately answered that he would submit himself and all belonging to him to the good pleasure of his sovereign. He therefore petitioned the brethren of the chivalry of the Temple that they would, in his behalf, present all his keys to his lord the king, that he might do what he pleased with the things deposited in the Temple. This being done, the king ordered all that money, faithfully counted, to be placed in his treasury, and the amount of all the things found to be reduced into writing and exhibited before him. The king's clerks, indeed, and the treasurer acting with them, found deposited in the Temple gold and silver vases of inestimable price, and money and many precious gems, an enumeration whereof would in truth astonish the hearers."[†]

The kings of England frequently resided in the Temple, and so also did the haughty legates of the Roman pontiffs, who there made contributions in the name of the pope upon the English bishoprics.

---

[*] Acta *Rymeri*, tom. i. p. 442, 4, 5. *Wilkins*. Concilia, tom. ii. p. 230.
[†] *Matt. Par.* p. 381.

The Knights Templars

Matthew Paris gives a lively account of the exactions of the nuncio Martin, who resided for many years at the Temple, and came there armed by the pope with powers such as no legate had ever before possessed. "He made," says he, "whilst residing at London in the New Temple, unheard of extortions of money and valuables. He imperiously intimated to the abbots and priors that they must send him rich presents, desirable palfreys, sumptuous services for the table, and rich clothing; which being done, that same Martin sent back word that the things sent were insufficient, and he commanded the givers thereof to forward him better things, on pain of suspension and excommunication."[*]

The convocations of the clergy and the great ecclesiastical councils were frequently held at the Temple, and laws were there made by the bishops and abbots for the government of the church and monasteries in England.[†]

---

[*] *Matt. Par.* p. 253, 645.
[†] *Wilkins.* Concilia Magnæ Britanniæ, tom. ii. p. 19, 26, 93, 239, 253, 272, 292.

Chapter IV.

"The foes of the Lord break into his holy city, even into that glorious tomb where the virgin blossom of Mary was wrapt up in linen and spices, and where the first and greatest flower on earth rose up again."—*S. Bernardi*, epist. cccxxii.

The Grand Master, Arnold de Torroge, who died on his journey to England, as before mentioned, was succeeded by Brother Gerard de Riderfort.[*]

On the 10th of the calends of April, a month after the consecration by the patriarch Heraclius of the Temple church, the grand council or parliament of England, composed of the bishops, earls, and barons, assembled in the house of the Hospitallers at Clerkenwell in London. It was attended by William king of Scotland and David his brother, and many of the counts and barons of that distant land. The august assembly was acquainted, in the king's name, with the object of the solemn embassy just sent to him from Jerusalem, and with the desire of the royal penitent to fulfill his vow and perform his penance; but the barons were at the same time reminded of the old age of their sovereign, of the bad state of his health, and of the necessity for his presence in England. They accordingly represented to King Henry that the solemn oath taken by him on his coronation was an obligation antecedent to the penance imposed on him by the pope; that by that oath he was bound to stay at home and govern his dominions, and that, in their opinion, it was more wholesome for the king's soul to defend his own country against the barbarous French, than to desert it for the purpose of protecting the distant kingdom of Jerusalem.[†]

Fabian, in his chronicle, gives the following quaint account of the king's answer to the patriarch, taken from the Chron. Joan Bromton: "Lasteley the kynge gaue answere, and sayde that he myghte not leue hys lande wythoute kepynge, nor yet leue yt to the praye and robbery of Frenchemen. But he wolde gyue largely of hys own to such as wolde take upon theym that vyge. Wyth thys answere the patryarke was dyscontente, and sayde, 'We seke a man, and not money; welnere euery crysten regyon sendyth unto us money, but no land sendyth to us a prince. Therefore we aske a prynce that nedeth money, and not money that nedeth a prynce.' But the kynge layde for hym suche excuses, that the patryarke departed from

---

[*] *Muratori* script. rer. Ital. p. 792. *Cotton* MS. Nero E. vi. p. 60, fol. 466.
[†] *Radulph de Diceto*, p. 626. *Matt. Par.* ad ann. 1185. *Hoveden*, p. 636, 637.

hym dyscontentyd and comforteless, whereof the kynge beynge aduertysed, entendynge somwhat to recomforte hym with pleasaunte words, followed hym to the see syde. But the more the kynge thought to satysfye hym with hys fayre speche, the more the patryarke was dyscontentyd, in so myche that at the last he sayde unto hym, 'Hytherto thou haste reygned gloryously, but here after thou shalt be forsaken of hym whom thou at thys tyme forsakeste. Thynke on hym what he hath gyuen to thee, and what thou haste yelden to him agayne: howe fyrste thou were false unto the kynge of Fraunce, and after slewe that holy man Thomas of Caunterburye, and lastely thou forsakeste the proteccyon of Crystes faith.' The kynge was amoued wyth these wordes, and sayde unto the patryarke, 'Though all the men of my lande were one bodye, and spake with one mouth, they durste not speke to me such wordys.' 'No wonder,' sayde the patryarke, 'for they loue thyne and not the; that ys to meane, they loue thy goodes temporall, and fere the for losse of promocyon, but they loue not thy soule.' And when he hadde so sayde, he offeryd hys hedde to the kynge, sayenge, 'Do by me ryghte as thou dyddest by that blessed man Thomas of Caunterburye, for I had leur to be slayne of the, then of the Sarasyns, for thou art worse than any Sarasyn.' But the kynge kepte hys paycence, and sayde, 'I may not wende oute of my lande, for myne own sonnes wyll aryse agayne me whan I were absente.' 'No wonder,' sayde the patryarke, 'for of the deuyll they come, and to the deuyll they shall go,' and so departyd from the kynge in great ire.'[*]

According to Roger de Hoveden, however, the patriarch, on the 17th of the calends of May, accompanied King Henry into Normandy, where a conference was held between the sovereigns of France and England concerning the proposed succor to the Holy Land. Both monarchs were liberal in promises and fair speeches; but as nothing short of the presence of the king of England, or of one of his sons, in Palestine, would satisfy the patriarch, that haughty ecclesiastic failed in his negotiations and returned in disgust and disappointment to the Holy Land. On his arrival at Jerusalem with intelligence of his ill success the greatest consternation prevailed amongst the Latin Christians: and it was generally observed that the true cross, which had been recovered from the Persians by the Emperor Heraclius, was about to be lost under the pontificate, and by the fault of a patriarch of the same name. A cotemporary writer of Palestine tells us that the patriarch was a very handsome person, and, in consequence of his beauty, the mother of the king of Jerusalem fell in love with him, and made him archbishop of Cæsarea. He then describes how he came to be made patriarch, and how he was suspected to have poisoned the archbishop of Tyre. After his return from Rome he fell in love with the wife of a haberdasher who lived at Naplous, twelve miles from Jerusalem. He went to see her very often, and, not long after the acquaintanceship commenced, the husband died. Then the patriarch brought the lady to Jerusalem, clothed

---

[*] The above passage is almost literally translated from the *Chron. Joan. Bromton*, abbatis Jornalensis, script. X. p. 1144, ad ann. 1185.

her in rich apparel, bought her a house, and furnished her with an elegant retinue.*

Baldwin the fourth, who was the reigning sovereign of the Latin kingdom at the period of the departure of the patriarch Heraclius and the Grand Master of the Temple for Europe, was afflicted with a frightful leprosy, which rendered it unlawful for him to marry, and he was consequently deprived of all hope of having an heir of his body to inherit the crown. Sensible of the dangers and inconvenience of a female succession, he selected William V. marquis of Montferrat, surnamed "Long-sword," as a husband for his eldest sister Sibylla. Shortly after his marriage the marquis of Montferrat died, leaving by Sibylla an infant son named Baldwin. Sibylla's second husband was Guy de Lusignan, a nobleman of a handsome person, and descended of an ancient family of Poitou in France. Her choice was at first approved of by the king, who received his new brother-in-law with favor, loaded him with honors, and made him regent of the kingdom. Subsequently, through the intrigues of the count of Tripoli, the king was induced to deprive Guy de Lusignan of the regency, and to set aside the claims of Sibylla to the throne, in favor of her son the young Baldwin, who was then about five years of age. He gave orders for the coronation of the young prince, and resigned his authority to the count of Tripoli, who was appointed regent of the kingdom during the minority of the sovereign, whilst all the fortresses and castles of the land were committed to the safe keeping of the Templars and Hospitallers. The youthful Baldwin was carried with vast pomp to the great church of the Holy Sepulcher, and was there anointed and crowned by the patriarch in the presence of the Grand Masters of the Temple and the Hospital. According to ancient custom he was taken, wearing his crown, to the Temple of the Lord, to make certain offerings, after which he went to the Temple of Solomon, where the Templars resided, and was entertained at dinner, together with his barons, by the Grand Master of the Temple and the military friars. Shortly after the coronation (A. D. 1186) the ex-king, Baldwin IV., died at Jerusalem, and was buried in the church of the Resurrection, by the side of Godfrey de Bouillon, and the other Christian kings. His death was followed, in the short space of seven months, by that of the infant sovereign Baldwin V., and Sibylla thus became the undoubted heiress to the throne. The count of Tripoli refused, however, to surrender the regency, accusing Sibylla of the horrible and improbable crime of poisoning her own child. But Gerard de Riderfort, the Grand Master of the Temple, invited her to repair to Jerusalem, and gave orders for the coronation. He sent letters, in the queen's name, to the count of Tripoli and the rebellious barons who had assembled with their followers in arms at Naplous, (the ancient Shechem,) requiring them to attend at the appointed time to do homage, and take the oath of allegiance, but the barons sent back word that they intended to remain where they were; and they

---

* Contin. hist. apud *Martene*, tom. v. col. 606.

despatched two Cistercian abbots to the Grand Master of the Temple, and the patriarch Heraclius, exhorting them for the love of God and his holy apostles to refrain from crowning Isabella countess of Jaffa, as long as she remained the wife of Guy de Lusignan. They represented that the latter had already manifested his utter incapacity for command, both in the field and in the cabinet; that the kingdom of Jerusalem required an able general for its sovereign; and they insisted that Sibylla should be immediately divorced from Guy de Lusignan, and should choose a husband better fitted to protect the country and undertake the conduct of the government.

As soon as this message had been received, the Grand Master of the Temple directed the Templars to take possession of all the gates of the city of Jerusalem, and issued strict orders that no person should be allowed to enter or withdraw from the Holy City without an express permission from himself. Sibylla and Guy de Lusignan were then taken, guarded by the Templars, to the great church of the Resurrection, where the patriarch Heraclius and all his clergy were in readiness to receive them. The crowns of the Latin kingdom were kept in a large chest in the treasury, fastened with two locks. The Grand Master of the Temple kept the key of one of these locks, and the Grand Master of the Hospital had the other. On their arrival at the church, the key of the Grand Master of the Temple was produced, but the key of the Grand Master of the Hospital was not forthcoming, nor could that illustrious chieftain himself anywhere be found. Gerard de Riderfort and Heraclius at last went in person to the Hospital, and after much hunting about they found the Grand Master, and immediately demanded the key in the queen's name.

The powerful Superior of the Hospitallers at first refused to produce it, but being pressed by many arguments and entreaties, he at last took out the key and flung it upon the ground, whereupon the patriarch picked it up, and proceeding to the treasury, speedily produced the two crowns, one of which he placed upon the high altar of the church of the Resurrection, and the other by the side of the chair upon which the countess of Jaffa was seated. Heraclius then performed the solemn ceremony of the coronation, and when he had placed the crown on the queen's head, he reminded her that she was a frail and feeble woman, but ill fitted to contend with the toil and strife in which the beleaguered kingdom of Palestine was continually involved, and he therefore exhorted her to make choice of some person to govern the kingdom in conjunction with herself; whereupon her majesty, taking up the crown which had been placed by her side, and calling for her husband, Guy de Lusignan, thus addressed him:—"Those whom God hath joined, let no man put asunder. Sire, receive this crown, for I know none more worthy of it than yourself." And immediately Guy de Lusignan was crowned king of Jerusalem, and received the blessing of the patriarch.

Great was the indignation of the count of Tripoli and the barons, when they received intelligence of these events. They raised the standard of revolt, and proclaimed the princess Isabella, the younger sister of Sibylla, who had been married, at the early period of eight years, to

Humphrey de Thoron, queen of Jerusalem. As soon as Humphrey de Thoron heard of the proceedings of the count of Tripoli and the barons, he hurried with the princess to Jerusalem, and the two, throwing themselves at the feet of the king and queen, respectfully tendered to them their allegiance. This loyal and decisive conduct struck terror and dismay into the hearts of the conspirators, most of whom now proceeded to Jerusalem to do homage; whilst the count of Tripoli, deserted by his adherents, retired to the strong citadel of Tiberias, of which place he was the feudal lord, and there remained, proudly defying the royal power.[*]

The king at first sought to avail himself of the assistance of the Templars against his rebellious vassal, and exhorted them to besiege Tiberias; but they refused, as it was contrary to their oaths, and the spirit of their institution, for them to undertake an aggressive warfare against any Christian prince. The king then gave orders for the concentration of an army at Nazareth; the count of Tripoli prepared to defend Tiberias, and it appears unquestionable that he sent to Saladin for assistance, and entered into a defensive and independent alliance with that monarch. The citadel of Tiberias was a place of great strength, the military power of the count was very considerable, and the friends of the king, foreseeing that the infidels would not fail to take advantage of a civil war, earnestly besought his majesty to offer terms of reconciliation to his powerful vassal. It was accordingly agreed that the Grand Masters of the Temple and the Hospital should proceed with the archbishop of Tyre, the Lord Balian d'Ibelin, and the Lord Reginald of Sidon, to Tiberias, and attempt to bring back the count to his allegiance. These illustrious personages set out from Jerusalem, and slept the first night at Naplous, of which town Balian d'Ibelin was the feudal lord, and the next day they journeyed on towards Nazareth. As they drew near that place, the Grand Master of the Temple proceeded to pass the night at a neighboring fortress of the Knights Templars, called "the castle of La Feue," and was eating his supper with the brethren in the refectory of the convent, when intelligence was brought to him that a strong corps of the Mussulman cavalry, under the command of Malek al Afdal, one of Saladin's sons, had crossed the Jordan at sunrise, and was marching through the territories of the count of Tripoli.

The chronicle of the Holy Land, written by Radolph, abbot of the monastery of Coggleshale in Essex, forms the most important and trustworthy account now in existence of the conquest of Jerusalem by Saladin, for the writer was, as he tells us, an eye-witness of all the remarkable events he relates. Radolph was an English monk of the Cistercian order, and a man of vast learning and erudition. He went on a pilgrimage to Palestine, and was there on the breaking out of the war which immediately preceded the loss of the Holy City. He was present at the

---

[*] Contin. Hist. *Will. Tyr.* apud *Martene*, tom. v. col. 585, 593-596. This valuable old chronicle appears to have been written by a resident in Palestine. It was translated into Latin by Francis Piper and published by Muratori inter rer Italicar. script. tom. vii. as the chronicle of Bernard the treasurer. Assizes de Jerusalem, cap. 287, 288.

siege of Jerusalem, and was wounded by an arrow, "which," says the worthy abbot, "pierced through the nose of the relator of these circumstances; the wood was withdrawn, but a part of the iron barb remains to this day." His chronicle was published in 1729, by the fathers Martene and Durand, in their valuable collection of ancient chronicles and manuscripts. It commences in the year 1187, and finishes in 1191.

As soon as the Grand Master of the Temple heard that the infidels had crossed the Jordan and were ravaging the Christian territories, he sent messengers to a castle of the Templars called "The Convent of Caco," situate four miles distant from La Feue, commanding all the knights that could be spared from the garrison at that place to mount and come to him with speed. The knights had retired to rest when the messengers arrived, but they arose from their beds, and at midnight they were encamped with their horses around the walls of the castle of La Feue. The next morning, as soon as it was light, the Grand Master, at the head of ninety of his knights, rode over to Nazareth, and was joined at that place by the Grand Master of the Hospital and forty knights of the garrison of Nazareth. The Templars and Hospitallers were accompanied by four hundred of their foot soldiers, and the whole force, under the command of the two Grand Masters, amounted to about six hundred men. With this small but valiant band, they set out in quest of the infidels, and had proceeded about seven miles from Nazareth in the direction of the Jordan, when they came suddenly upon a strong column of Mussulman cavalry amounting to several thousand men, who were watering their horses at the brook Kishon. Without waiting to count the number of their enemies, the Templars raised their war cry, unfolded the blood-red banner, and dashed into the midst of the astonished and terrified Mussulmen, dealing around them, to use the words of Abbot Coggleshale, "death and damnation." The infidels, taken by surprise, were at first thrown into confusion, discomfited, and slaughtered; but when the smallness of the force opposed to them became apparent, they closed in upon the Templars, overwhelmed them with darts and missiles, and speedily thinned their ranks with a terrific slaughter. An eye-witness tells us that the military friars were to be seen bathed with blood and sweat; trembling with fatigue; with their horses killed under them, and with their swords and lances broken, closing with the Mussulman warriors, and rolling headlong with them in the dust. Some tore the darts with which they had been transfixed from their bodies, and hurled them back with a convulsive effort upon the enemy; and others, having lost all their weapons in the affray, clung around the necks of their opponents, dragged them from their horses, and endeavored to strangle them under the feet of the combatants. Jacqueline de Mailly, Marshal of the Temple, performed prodigies of valor. He was mounted on a white horse, and clothed in the white habit of his order, with the blood-red cross, the symbol of martyrdom, on his breast; he became, through his gallant bearing and demeanor, an object of admiration, even to the Moslems. Radolph compares the fury and the anger of this warlike monk, as he looked around him upon his slaughtered brethren, to the wrath of the lioness who has lost her whelps; and his position and demeanor in the midst of the throng of infidels, he likens to that of the wild boar when surrounded by dogs whom he is tearing with his tusks. Every blow of this furious man, says the worthy abbot, "despatched an infidel to hell;" but with all his valor Jacqueline de Mailly was slain.

In this bloody battle perished the Grand Master of the Hospital and all the Templars excepting the Grand Master, Gerard de Riderford, and two of his knights, who broke through the dense ranks of the Moslems, and made their escape to Nazareth. The Mussulmen severed the heads of the slaughtered Templars from their bodies, and attaching them with cords to the points of their lances, they marched off in the direction of Tiberias. This disastrous engagement was fought on Friday, the 1st of May, the feast of St. James and St. Philip. "In that beautiful season of the year," says Abbot Coggleshale, "when the inhabitants of Nazareth were wont to seek the rose and the violet in the fields, they found only the sad traces of carnage, and the lifeless bodies of their slaughtered brethren. With mourning and great lamentation they carried them into the burial-ground of the blessed Virgin Mary at Nazareth, crying aloud, 'Daughters of Galilee, put on your mourning clothes, and ye daughters of Zion, bewail the misfortunes that threaten the kings of Judah.'"

Whilst this bloody battle was being fought, the Lord Balian d'Ibelin was journeying with another party of Templars from Naplous to join the Grand Master at Nazareth, and the following interesting account is given of their march towards that place. "When they had travelled two miles, they came to the city of Sebaste. It was a lovely morning, and they determined to march no further until they had heard mass. They accordingly turned towards the house of the bishop and awoke him up, and informed him that the day was breaking. The bishop accordingly ordered an old chaplain to put on his clothes and say mass, after which they hastened forwards. Then they came to the castle of La Feue, (a fortress of the Templars,) and there they found, outside the castle, the tents of the convent of Caco pitched, and there was no one to explain what it meant. A varlet was sent into the castle to inquire, but he found no one within but two sick people who were unable to speak. Then they marched towards Nazareth, and after they had proceeded a short distance from the castle of La Feue, they met a brother of the Temple on horseback, who galloped up to them at a furious rate, calling out, 'Bad news, bad news;' and he informed them how that the Master of the Hospital had had his head cut off, and how of all the brothers of the Temple there had escaped but three, the Master of the Temple and two others, and that the knights whom the king had placed in garrison at Nazareth, were all taken and killed." "If Balian d'Ibelin," says the chronicler, "had marched straight to Nazareth, with his knights, instead of halting to hear mass at Sebaste, he would have been in time to have saved his brethren from slaughter." As it was, he arrived just in time to hear the funeral service read over their dead bodies by William, archbishop of Tyre.*

The Knights Templars

The Grand Master of the Temple, who was at Nazareth, suffering severely from his wounds, hastened to collect together a small force at that place to open the communications with Tiberias, which being done, the Lord Balian d'Ibelin and the archbishop of Tyre proceeded to that place to have their interview with the count of Tripoli. The Grand Master accompanied them as far as the hill above the citadel, but not liking to trust himself into the power of the count, he then retraced his steps to Nazareth. Both the Moslem and the Christian writers agree in asserting that the count of Tripoli had at this period entered into an alliance with Saladin; nevertheless, either smitten with remorse for his past conduct, or moved by the generous overtures of the king, he consented to do homage and become reconciled to his sovereign, and for this purpose immediately set out from Tiberias for Jerusalem. The interview and reconciliation between the king and the count took place at Joseph's well, near Naplous, in the presence of the Templars and Hospitallers, and the bishops and barons. The count knelt upon one knee and did homage, whereupon the king raised him up and kissed him, and they then both returned together to Naplous to take measures for the protection of the country.

Saladin, on the other hand, was concentrating together a large army and rapidly maturing his plans for the reconquest of the Holy City—the long-cherished enterprise of the Mussulmen. Whilst discord and dissensions had been gradually undermining the strength of the Christian empire, Saladin had been carefully extending and consolidating his power. He had reduced the various independent chieftains of the north of Syria to submission to his throne and government; he had conquered the cities of Mecca and Medina, and the whole of Arabia Felix; and his vast empire now extended from Tripoli, in Africa, to the Tigris, and from the Indian Ocean to the mountains of Armenia. The Arabian writers enthusiastically recount his pious exhortations to the true believers to arm in defense of Islam, and describe with vast enthusiasm his glorious preparations for the holy war. Bohadin, son of Sjeddadi, his friend and secretary, and great biographer, before venturing upon the sublime task of describing his famous and sacred actions, makes a solemn confession of faith, and offers up praises to the one true God. "Praise be to God," says he, "who hath blessed us with *Islam*, and hath led us to the understanding of the true faith beautifully put together, and hath befriended us; and, through the intercession of our prophet, hath loaded us with every blessing. I bear witness that there is no God but that one great God who hath *no partner*, (a testimony that will deliver our souls from the smoky fire of hell,) that Mohammed is his *servant* and *apostle*, who hath opened unto us the gates of the right road to salvation. These solemn duties being performed, I will begin to write concerning the victorious *defender of the faith*, the tamer of the followers of the cross, the lifter up of the standard of justice and equity, the saviour of the world and of religion, Saladin Aboolmodaffer Joseph,

---

* *Rad. Cogg.* apud *Martene*, tom. v. col. 550-552. Contin. Hist., ib. col. 599, 600.

the son of Job, the son of Schadi, Sultan of the Moslems, ay, and of Islam itself; the deliverer of the holy house of God (the Temple) from the hands of the idolaters, the servant of two holy cities, whose tomb may the Lord moisten with the dew of his favor, affording to him the sweetness of the fruits of the faith."[*]

Crowds of Mussulmen from all parts of Asia crowded round the standard of Saladin, and the caliph of Bagdad and all the imauns put up daily prayers for the success of his arms. After protecting the return of the caravan from Mecca, Saladin marched to Ashtara, probably the Ashtaroth Karnain of scripture, belonging to the tribe of Manasseh, not far from Damascus. He was there met by his son, *Al Malek al Afdal*, "Most excellent Prince," and *Moh-hafferoddin ibn Zinoddin*, with the army under their command. Being afterwards joined by the forces of *Al Mawsel*, commanded by *Màsûd al Zaf'arâni, Maredin*, and *Hamah*, he reviewed his army, first on the hill called Tel Taisel, and afterwards at Ashtara, the place of general rendezvous. Whilst completing his preparations at this place, Saladin received intelligence of the reconciliation of the count of Tripoli with the king of Jerusalem, and he determined instantly to lay siege to Tiberias. For this purpose, on Friday the 17th of the month Rabi, he advanced in three divisions upon Al Soheira, a village situate at the northern end of the Lake of Tiberias, where he encamped for the night. The next day he marched round to the western shore of the lake, and proceeded towards Tiberias in battle array. On the 21st Rabi, he took the town by storm, put all who resisted to the sword, and made slaves of the survivors. The place was then set on fire and reduced to ashes. The countess of Tripoli retired with the garrison into the citadel, and from thence she sent messengers to her husband and the king of Jerusalem, earnestly imploring instant succor.

The king had pitched his tents at Sepphoris, and all the chivalry of the Latin kingdom were hastening to join his standard and make a last effort in defense of the tottering kingdom of Jerusalem. The Templars and Hospitallers collected together a strong force from their different castles and fortresses,[†] and came into the camp with the holy cross which had been brought from the church of the Resurrection, to be placed in the front of the Christian array. The count of Tripoli joined them with the men of Tripoli and Galilee. Prince Reginald of Mount Royal, made his appearance at the head of a body of light cavalry. The Lord Balian of Naplous came in with all his armed retainers, and Reginald, Lord of Sidon, marched into the camp with the men from the sea coast.

The Grand Master of the Temple had brought with him the treasure which had been sent to the Templars by the king of England, to be employed in the defense of the Holy Land, in expiation of the murder of St. Thomas à Becket, and it was found very acceptable in the exhausted condition of the Latin treasury. Whilst the Christian forces were

---

[*] *Bohadin ib'n Sjeddadi*, apud *Schultens*, ex. MS. Arab. Pref.
[†] *Rad. Cogg.* col. 552, 553. *Abulfed.* Chron. Hejir. 582.

assembling at Sepphoris, Saladin sent forward a strong corps of cavalry, which ravaged and laid waste all the country around the brook Kishon, from Tiberias to Bethoron, and from the mountains of Gilboa and Jezreel to Nazareth. From all the eminences nought was to be seen but the smoking ruins of the villages, hamlets, and scattered dwellings of the Christian population. The whole country, before the very noses of the warriors of the cross, was enveloped in flame and smoke, and the Christian camp was filled with fugitives who had fled with terror before the merciless swords of the Moslems. To complete the misfortunes of the Latins, the king was irresolute and continually giving contradictory commands, and the Christian chieftains, having lost all confidence in their leader, and despairing of being able to contend with success against the vast power of Saladin, seemed to be preparing for a retreat to the sea coast, rather than for a desperate struggle with the infidels for the preservation of Jerusalem. Upon this ground only can be explained the long delay of the Christian army at Sepphoris. This place, the ancient capital of Galilee, is situate between Nazareth and Acre, and an army could at any time secure an easy and safe retreat from it to the port of the last-named city. Here, then, the Christians remained, quietly permitting Saladin to occupy a strong position from whence he could pour his vast masses of cavalry into the great plain of Esdraelon, and open for himself a direct road to the Holy City, either through the valley of the Jordan, or through the great plain along the bases of the mountains of Gilboa.

When the messengers from the countess of Tripoli arrived in the Christian camp, with intelligence that Saladin had burnt and stormed the town of Tiberias, and that the countess had retired into the citadel, the king called a council of war. This council assembled in the royal tent, on the evening of the 2nd of July, A. D. 1187, and there were present at it, Gerard de Riderfort, the Grand Master of the Temple, the newly-elected Grand Master of the Hospital, the archbishop of Tyre, the count of Tripoli, Balian d'Ibelin, lord of Naplous, and nearly all the bishops and barons of Palestine. The count of Tripoli, although his capital was in flames, his territories spoiled by the enemy, and his countess closely besieged, advised the king to remain inactive where he was; but the Grand Master of the Temple, hearing this advice, rose up in the midst of the assembly, and stigmatized the count as a traitor, urging the king instantly to march to the relief of Tiberias. The barons, however, sided with the count of Tripoli, and it was determined that the army should remain at Sepphoris. The council broke up; each man retired to his tent, and the king went to supper. But the Grand Master of the Temple, agitated by a thousand conflicting emotions, could not rest. At midnight he arose and sought the presence of the king. He reproached him for remaining in a state of inaction at Sepphoris, whilst the enemy was ravaging and laying waste all the surrounding country, and reducing the Christian population to a state of hopeless bondage. "It will be an everlasting reproach to you, sire," said he, "if you quietly permit the infidels to take before your face an important

Christian citadel, which you ought to feel it your first duty to defend. Know that the Templars will sooner tear the white mantle from their shoulders, and sell all that they possess, than remain any longer quiet spectators of the injury and disgrace that have been brought upon the Christian arms."

Moved by the discourse of the Grand Master, the king consented to march to the relief of Tiberias, and at morning's dawn the tents of the Templars were struck, and the trumpets of the order sounded the advance. In vain did the count of Tripoli and the barons oppose this movement, the king and the Templars were resolute, and the host of the cross soon covered, in full array, the winding road leading to Tiberias. The count of Tripoli insisted upon leading the van of the army, as the Christian forces were marching through his territories, and the Templars consequently brought up the rear. The patriarch Heraclius, whose duty it was to bear the holy cross in front of the Christian array, had remained at Jerusalem, and had confided his sacred charge to the bishops of Acre and Lidda, a circumstance which gave rise to many gloomy forebodings amongst the superstitious soldiers of Christ.

As soon as Saladin heard of the advance of the Christian army, he turned the siege of the citadel of Tiberias into a blockade, called in his detachments of cavalry, and hastened to occupy all the passes and defiles of the mountains leading to Tiberias. The march of the infidel host, which amounted to 80,000 horse and foot, over the hilly country, is compared by an Arabian writer, an eye-witness, to mountains in movement, or to the vast waves of an agitated sea. Saladin encamped on the hills beyond Tiberias, resting his left wing upon the lake, and planting his cavalry in the valleys. When the Latin forces had arrived within three miles of Tiberias, they came in sight of the Mussulman army, and were immediately assailed by the light cavalry of the Arabs. During the afternoon of that day a bloody battle was fought. The Christians attempted, but in vain, to penetrate the defiles of the mountains; and when the evening came they found that they had merely been able to hold their ground without advancing a single step. Instead of fighting his way, at all hazards, to the lake of Tiberias, or falling back upon some position where he could have secured a supply of water, the king, following the advice of the count of Tripoli, committed the fatal mistake of ordering the tents to be pitched. "When the Saracens saw that the Christians had pitched their tents," says the chronicler, "they came and encamped so close to them that the soldiers of the two armies could converse together, and not even a cat could escape from the Christian lines without the knowledge of the Saracens." It was a sultry summer's night, the army of the cross was hemmed in amongst dry and barren rocks, and both the men and horses, after their harassing and fatiguing march, threw themselves on the parched ground, sighing in vain for water. During the livelong night, not a drop of that precious element touched their lips, and the soldiers arose exhausted and unrefreshed, for the toil, and labor, and fierce warfare of the ensuing day.

The Knights Templars

At sunrise the Templars formed in battle array in the van of the Christian army, and prepared to open a road through the dense ranks of the infidels to the lake of Tiberias. An Arabian writer, who witnessed the movement of their dense and compact columns at early dawn, speaks of them as "terrible in arms, having their whole bodies cased with triple mail." He compares the noise made by their advancing squadrons to the *loud humming of bees!* and describes them as animated with "a flaming desire of vengeance."* Saladin had behind him the lake of Tiberias, his infantry was in the centre, and the swift cavalry of the desert was stationed on either wing, under the command of *Faki-ed-deen* (teacher of religion). The Templars rushed, we are told, like lions upon the Moslem infidels, and nothing could withstand their heavy and impetuous charge. "Never," says an Arabian doctor of the law, "have I seen bolder or more powerful soldiers; none more to be feared by the believers in the true faith." Saladin set fire to the dry grass and dwarf shrubs which lay between both armies, and the wind blew the smoke and the flames directly into the faces of the military friars and their horses. The fire, the noise, the gleaming weapons, and all the accompaniments of the horrid scene, have given full scope to the descriptive powers of the oriental writers. They compare it to the last judgment; the dust and the smoke obscured the face of the sun, and the day was turned into night. Sometimes gleams of light darted like the rapid lightning amid the throng of combatants; then you might see the dense columns of armed warriors, now immoveable as mountains, and now sweeping swiftly across the landscape like the rainy clouds over the face of heaven. "The sons of paradise and the children of fire," say they, "then decided their terrible quarrel; the arrows rustled through the air like the wings of innumerable sparrows, the sparks flew from the coats of mail and the glancing sabres, and the blood spurting forth from the bosom of the throng deluged the earth like the rains of heaven."... "The avenging sword of the true believers was drawn forth against the infidels; the faith of the *unity* was opposed to the faith of the *trinity*, and speedy ruin, desolation, and destruction, overtook the miserable sons of baptism!"

The lake of Tiberias was two miles distant from the Templars, and ever and anon its blue and placid waters were to be seen calmly reposing in the bright sun-beams, or winding gracefully amid the bosom of the distant mountains; but every inch of the road was fiercely contested; the expert archers of the Mussulmen lined all the eminences, and the thirsty soil was drenched with the blood of the best and bravest of the Christian warriors. After almost superhuman exertions, the Templars and Hospitallers halted, and sent to the king for succor. At this critical juncture the count of Tripoli, who had always insisted on being in the van, and whose conduct, from first to last, had been most suspicious, dashed with a few followers through a party of Mussulmen, who opened their ranks to let him pass, and fled in safety to Tyre. The flight of this distinguished nobleman gave rise to a

---

* *Muhammed, F. Muhammed, N. Koreisg. Ispahan*, apud *Schultens*, p. 18.

sudden panic, and the troops that were advancing to the support of the Templars were driven in one confused mass upon the main body. The military friars, who rarely turned their backs upon the enemy, maintained, alone and unaided, a short, sharp, and bloody conflict, which ended in the death or captivity of every one of them excepting the Grand Master of the Hospital, who clove his way from the field of battle, and reached Ascalon in safety, but died of his wounds the day after his arrival.

The Christian soldiers now gave themselves up to despair; the infantry, which was composed principally of the native population of Palestine, men taken from the plough and the pruning-hook, crowded together in disorder and confusion, around the bishops and the holy cross. They were so wedged together that they were unable to act against the enemy, and they refused to obey their leaders. Brother Terric, Grand Preceptor of the Temple, who had been attached to the person of the king, the Lord Reginald of Sidon, Balian d'Ibelin, lord of Naplous, and many of the lesser barons and knights, collected their followers together, rushed over the rocks, down the mountain sides, pierced through the enemies' squadrons, and leaving the infantry to their fate, made their escape to the sea coast. The Arab cavalry dashed on, and surrounding, with terrific cries, the trembling and unresisting foot soldiers, they mowed them down with a frightful carnage.

In vain did the bishops of Ptolemais and Lidda, who supported with difficulty the Holy Cross in the midst of the disordered throng, attempt to infuse into the base-born peasantry some of that daring valor and fiery-religious enthusiasm which glowed so fiercely in the breasts of the Moslems. The Christian fugitives were crowded together like a flock of sheep when attacked by dogs, and their bitter cries for mercy ever and anon rent the air, between the loud shouts of Allah *acbar*—"God is victorious." The Moslem chieftains pressed into the heart of the throng, and cleft their way towards the Holy Cross; the bishop of Ptolemais was slain, the bishop of Lidda was made captive, and the cross itself fell into the hands of the infidels. The king of Jerusalem, the Grand Master of the Temple, the Marquis of Montferrat, the Lord Reginald de Chatillon, and many other nobles and knights, were at the same time taken prisoners and led away into captivity. "Alas, alas," says Abbot Coggleshale, "that I should have lived to have seen in my time these awful and terrible calamities." When the sun had sunk to rest, and darkness had put an end to the slaughter, a crowd of Christian fugitives, who survived the long and frightful carnage, attempted to gain the summit of Mount Hittin, in the vain hope of escaping from the field of blood, under cover of the obscurity of the night. But every pass and avenue were strictly watched, and when morning came they were found cowering on the elevated summit of the mountain. They were maddened with thirst and exhausted with watching, but despair gave them some energy; they availed themselves with success of the strength of their position, and in the first onslaught the Moslems were repulsed. The sloping sides of Mount Hittin were covered with dry grass and thistles, which had been scorched and killed by the hot summer's sun, and the Moslems again resorted to the expedient of setting fire to the parched vegetation. The heat of a July sun, added to that of the raging flames, soon told with fearful effect upon the weakened frames of the poor Christian warriors, who were absolutely dying with thirst; some threw away their arms and cast themselves upon the ground; some cried for mercy, and others calmly awaited the approach of death.

The Moslem appetite for blood had at this time been slaked; feelings of compassion for the misfortunes of the fallen had arisen in their breasts, and as resistance had now ceased in every quarter of the field, the lives of the fugitives on Mount Hittin were mercifully spared. Thus ended the memorable battle of Tiberias, which commenced on the afternoon of the 3rd of July, and ended oh the morning of Saturday, the 5th. The multitude of captives taken by the Moslems was enormous; cords could not be found to bind them, the tent ropes were all used for the purpose, but were insufficient, and the Arabian writers tell us, that on seeing the dead, one would have thought that there could have been no prisoners, and on seeing the prisoners, that there could be no dead. "I saw," says the secretary and companion of Saladin, who was present at this terrible fight, and is unable to restrain himself from pitying the disasters of the vanquished—"I saw the mountains and the plains, the hills and the valleys, covered with their dead. I saw their fallen and deserted banners sullied with dust and with blood. I saw their heads broken and battered, their limbs scattered abroad, and the blackened corpses piled one upon another like the stones of the builders. I called to mind the words of the Koran, 'The infidel shall say, What am I but *dust*?'... I saw thirty or forty tied together by one cord. I saw in one place, guarded by one Mussulman, two hundred of these famous warriors gifted with amazing strength, who had but just now walked forth amongst the mighty: their proud bearing was gone: they stood naked with downcast eyes, wretched and miserable.... The lying infidels were now in the power of the true believers. Their king and their cross were captured, that cross before which they bow the head and bend the knee; which they bear aloft and worship with their eyes; they say that it is the identical wood to which the God whom they adore was fastened. They had adorned it with fine gold and brilliant stones; they carried it before their armies; they all bowed towards it with respect. It was their first duty to defend it; and he who should desert it would never enjoy peace of mind. The capture of this cross was more grievous to them than the captivity of their king. Nothing can compensate them for the loss of it. It was their God; they prostrated themselves in the dust before it, and sang hymns when it was raised aloft!"

As soon as all fighting had ceased on the field of battle, Saladin proceeded to a tent, whither, in obedience to his commands, the king of Jerusalem, Gerard de Riderfort, the Grand Master of the Temple, and Reginald de Chatillon had been conducted. This last nobleman had greatly distinguished himself in various daring expeditions against the caravans of pilgrims travelling to Mecca, and had become on that account particularly obnoxious to the pious Saladin. The sultan, on entering the tent, ordered a bowl of sherbet, the sacred pledge amongst the Arabs of hospitality and security, to be presented to the fallen monarch of Jerusalem, and to the Grand Master of the Temple; but when Reginald de Chatillon would have drunk thereof, Saladin prevented him, and reproaching the Christian nobleman with perfidy and impiety, he commanded him instantly to acknowledge the prophet whom he had blasphemed, or to be prepared to meet the death he had so often deserved. On Reginald's refusal, Saladin struck him with his scimitar, and he was immediately despatched by the guards. Bohadin, Saladin's friend and secretary, an eye-witness of the scene, gives the following account of it: "Then Saladin told the interpreter to say thus to the king, 'It is thou, not I, who givest drink to this man!' Then the sultan sat down at the entrance of the tent, and they brought Prince Reginald before him, and after refreshing the man's memory, Saladin said to him, 'Now then, I myself will act the part of the defender of Mohammed!' He then offered the man the Mohammedan faith, but he refused it; then the king struck him on the shoulder with a drawn scimitar, which was a hint to those that were present to do for him; so they sent his soul to *hell*, and cast out his body before the tent door!"

The next day Saladin proceeded in cold blood to enact the grand concluding tragedy. The warlike monks of the Temple and of the Hospital, the bravest and most zealous defenders of the Christian faith, were, of all the warriors of the cross, the most obnoxious to zealous Mussulmen, and it was determined that death or conversion to Mahometanism should be the portion of every captive of either order, excepting the Grand Master of the Temple, for whom it was expected a heavy ransom would be given. Accordingly, on the Christian Sabbath, at the hour of sunset, the appointed time of prayer, the Moslems were drawn up in battle array under their respective leaders. The Mamlook emirs stood in two ranks clothed in yellow, and, at the sound of the holy trumpet, all the captive knights of the Temple and of the Hospital were led on to the eminence above Tiberias, in full view of the beautiful lake of Gennesareth, whose bold and mountainous shores had been the scene of so many of their Savior's miracles. There, as the last rays of the sun were fading away from the mountain tops, they were called upon to deny him who had been crucified, to choose God for their Lord, Islam for their faith, Mecca for their temple, the Moslems for their brethren, and Mahomet for their prophet. To a man they refused, and were all decapitated in the presence of Saladin by the devout zealots of his army, and the doctors and expounders of the law. An oriental historian, who was present, says that Saladin sat with a smiling countenance viewing the execution, and that some of the executioners cut off the heads with a degree of dexterity that excited great applause. "Oh," say Omad'eddin Muhammed, "how beautiful an ornament is the blood of the infidels sprinkled over the followers of the faith and the true religion!"[*]

---

[*] *Omad'eddin Kateb*, in the book called Fatah. Extraits Arabes, *Michaud. Radulph Coggleshale*. Chron. Terr. Sanct. apud *Martene*, tom. v. col. 552 to 559. Contin. Hist. ib. col.

The Knights Templars

If the Mussulmen displayed a becoming zeal in the decapitation and annihilation of the infidel Templars, these last manifested a no less praiseworthy eagerness for martyrdom by the swords of the unbelieving Moslems. The Knight Templar, Brother Nicolas, strove vigorously, we are told, with his companions to be the first to suffer, and with great difficulty accomplished his purpose. It was believed by the Christians, in accordance with the superstitious ideas of those times, that heaven testified its approbation by a visible sign, and that for three nights, during which the bodies of the Templars remained unburied on the field, celestial rays of light played around the corpses of those holy martyrs.

Immediately after this fatal battle, the citadel of Tiberias surrendered to Saladin, and the countess of Tripoli was permitted to depart in safety in search of her fugitive husband. There was now no force in the Latin kingdom capable of offering the least opposition to the victorious career of the infidels, and Saladin, in order that he might overrun and subjugate the whole country with the greatest possible rapidity, divided his army into several bodies, which were to proceed in different directions, and assemble at last under the walls of Jerusalem. One strong column, under the command of Malek el Afdal, proceeded to attack La Feue or Faba, the castle of the Knights Templars. Nearly all the garrison had perished in the battle of Tiberias, and after a short conflict the infidels walked into the fortress, over the dead bodies of the last of its defenders. From thence they crossed the great plain to Sebaste, and entered the magnificent church erected by the empress Helena, over the prison in which St. John the Baptist was beheaded, and over the humble grave where still repose the remains of St. John and of Zacharias and Elizabeth his parents. The terrified bishop and clergy had removed all the gold and silver vessels from the altars and the rich copes and vestments of the priests, to conceal them from the cupidity of the Moslems, whereupon these last caused the bishop to be stripped naked and beaten with rods, and led away all his clergy into captivity. The wild Turcoman and Bedouin cavalry then dashed up the beautiful valley of Succoth to Naplous, the ancient Shechem; which they found deserted and desolate; the inhabitants had abandoned their dwellings and fled to Jerusalem, and the Mussulmen planted their banners upon the gray battlements of the castle, and upon the lofty summit of Mount Gerizim. They then pitched their tents around the interesting well where our Savior spoke with the woman of Samaria, and pastured their cavalry in the valley where Joseph's brethren were feeding their flocks when they sold him to the wandering Ishmaelites. Here they remained to gather some tidings of the operations of their fellow-soldiers on the other side of the Jordan, and then proceeded to ravage and lay waste all the country between Naplous and Jerusalem, "continuing," says Abbot Coggleshale, "both by night and by day to slaughter every living thing that they met."

602—608. *Bohadin*, p. 70. *Jac. de Vitr.* cap. xciv. *Abulfeda*, cap. 27. *Abulpharag.* Chron. Syr. p. 399, 401, 402. Gesta Dei, tom. i. p. 1150, 1. *Vinisauf.* apud *Gale*, p. 15.

The column which was to proceed through the valley of the Jordan, entered the great plain of Esdraelon by Mount Thabor, and taking the direction of Nain and Endor to Jezreel, they crossed the mountains of Gilboa to Beisan, and descended the valley of the Jordan, as far as Jericho. Thence they proceeded to lay siege to a solitary castle of the Templars, seated upon that celebrated mountain where, according to tradition, our Savior was tempted by the Devil with the visionary scene of "all the kingdoms of the world, and the glory of them." In this castle the Templars maintained a garrison, for the protection of the pilgrims who came to bathe in the Jordan, and visit the holy places in the neighborhood of Jericho. From the toppling crag, whereon it was seated, the eye commanded an extensive view of the course of the Jordan, until it falls into the Dead Sea, also of the eastern frontier of the Latin kingdom, and of the important passes communicating with Jerusalem. The place was called *Maledoim*, or "the Red Mountain," on account of the blood that had been shed upon the spot. Fifty Tyrian dinars had been offered by Saladin, for the head of every Knight Templar that was brought him, and the blood-thirsty infidels surrounded the doomed castle eager for the reward. The whole garrison was put to the sword, and the place was left a shapeless ruin. The infidels then marched off in the direction of Jerusalem, and laid waste all the country between Jericho and the Holy City. They pitched their tents at Bethany, upon the spot where stood the houses of Simon the leper, and of Mary Magdalene and Martha, and they destroyed the church built over the house and tomb of Lazarus. The wild Arab cavalry then swept over the Mount of Olives; they took possession of the church constructed upon the summit of that sacred edifice, and extended their ravages up to the very gates of Jerusalem.

In the mean time Saladin's valiant brother Saifeddin, "sword of the faith," had crossed the desert from Egypt, to participate in the plunder and spoil of the Christian territories. He laid waste all the country from Daron and Gerar to Jerusalem. In front of his fierce warriors were to be seen the long bands of mournful captives tied together by the wrists, and behind them was a dreary desert, soaked with Christian blood. Saifeddin had besieged the strong town of Mirabel, and placed his military engines in position, when the terrified inhabitants sent a suppliant deputation to implore his clemency. He agreed to spare their lives in return for the immediate surrender of the place, and gave them an escort of four hundred Mussulmen, to conduct them in safety to Jerusalem. Accompanied by their wives and little ones, the miserable Christians cast a last look upon their once happy homes, and proceeded on their toilsome journey to the Holy City. On their arrival at an eminence, two miles from Jerusalem, their Arabian escort left them, and immediately afterwards a party of Templars dashed through the ravine, charged the retiring Moslems, and put the greater part of them to the sword.

The great Saladin, on the other hand, immediately after the battle of Tiberias, hastened with the main body of his forces to Acre, and the terrified inhabitants threw open their gates at his approach. From thence he swept the whole sea coast to Jaffa, reducing all the maritime towns, excepting the city of Tyre, which manfully resisted him. The savage Turcomans from the north, the predatory Bedouins, the fanatical Arabians, and the swarthy Africans, hurried across the frontiers, to share in the spoil and plunder of the Latin kingdom. Radolph, our worthy abbot of Coggleshale, one of those who fled before the ruthless swords of the infidels, gives a frightful picture of the aspect of the country. He tells us that the whole land was covered with dead bodies, rotting and putrifying in the scorching sun-beams. At early morning you might see the rich and stately church, with the bright and happy dwellings scattered around it, the blooming garden, the silvery olive grove, and the rich vineyard; but the fading rays of the evening sun would fall on smoking masses of shapeless ruins, and on a dreary and solitary desert. The holy abbot mourns over the fall of Nazareth, and the desecration by the infidels of the magnificent church of the Holy Virgin at that place. Sidon, Caiphas, Sepphoris, Nazareth, Cæserea, Jaffa, Lidda, and Rama, successively fell into the hands of the Moslems; the inhabitants were led away into captivity, and the garrisons were put to the sword. The infidels laid waste all the country about Mount Carmel and Caiphas, and they burnt the celebrated church of Elias, on the mountain above the port of Acre, which served as a beacon for navigators.

The government of the order of the Temple, in consequence of the captivity of the Grand Master Gerard de Riderfort, who was detained in prison, with Guy, king of Jerusalem, at Damascus, devolved upon Brother Terric, the Grand Preceptor of Jerusalem, who addressed letters to all the brethren in the west, imploring aid and assistance. One of these letters was duly received by Brother Geoffrey, Master of the Temple at London, as follows:—"Brother Terric, Grand Preceptor of the poor house of the Temple, and every poor brother, and the whole convent, now, alas! almost annihilated, to all the preceptors and brothers of the Temple, to whom these letters shall come, salvation through him to whom our fervent aspirations are addressed, through him who causeth the sun and the moon to reign marvellous.

"The many and great calamities wherewith the anger of God, excited by our manifold sins, hath just now permitted us to be afflicted, we cannot for grief unfold to you, neither by letters nor by our sobbing speech. The infidel chiefs having collected together a vast number of their people, fiercely invaded our Christian territories, and we, assembling our battalions, hastened to Tiberias to arrest their march. The enemy having hemmed us in among barren rocks, fiercely attacked us; the holy cross and the king himself fell into the hands of the infidels, the whole army was cut to pieces, two hundred and thirty of our knights were beheaded, without reckoning the sixty who were killed on the 1st of May. The Lord Reginald of Sidon, the Lord Ballovius, and we ourselves, escaped with vast difficulty from that miserable field. The pagans, drunk with the blood of our Christians, then marched with their whole army against the city of Acre, and took it by storm. The city of Tyre is at present fiercely besieged, and neither by night nor by day do the infidels discontinue their furious assaults. So great is the multitude of them, that they cover like ants the whole face of the country from Tyre to Jerusalem, and even unto Gaza. The holy city of Jerusalem, Ascalon, and Tyre, and Beyrout, are yet left to us and to the Christian cause, but the garrisons and the chief inhabitants of these places, having perished in the battle of Tiberias, we have no hope of retaining them without succor from heaven and instant assistance from yourselves."* Saladin, on the other hand, sent triumphant letters to the caliph. "God and his *angels*," says he, "have mercifully succored Islam. The infidels have been sent to feed the *fires* of *hell*! The cross is fallen into our hands, around which they fluttered like the moth round a light; under whose shadow they assembled, in which they boldly trusted as in a wall; the cross, the centre and leader of their pride, their superstition, and their tyranny.".…

Saladin pursued his rapid conquests along the sea coast to the north of Acre, and took by storm several castles of the Templars. After a siege of six days, the strong fortress of Tebnin, on the road to Beirout, was taken by assault, the garrison was put to the sword, and the fortifications were razed to the ground. On the 22nd, Jomada, the important city of Beirout, surrendered to Saladin, and shortly afterwards the castles of Hobeil and Bolerum. The old chronicle published by Martene, has the following strange passage concerning the last named castle. "To this castle belonged the lady whom the count of Tripoli refused to give up to Gerard de Riderfort, the Grand Master of the Temple, whence arose the great quarrel between them, which caused the loss of the Holy Land." After the reduction of all the maritime towns between Acre and Tripoli, Saladin ordered his different detachments to concentrate before Jerusalem, and hastened in person to the south to complete the conquest of the few places which still resisted the arms of the Mussulmen. He sat down before Ascalon, and whilst preparing his military engines for battering the walls, he sent messengers to the Templars at Gaza, representing to them that the whole land was in his power, that all further efforts at resistance were useless, and offering them their lives and a safe retreat to Europe, if they would give up to him the important fortress committed to their charge. But the military friars sent back a haughty defiance to the victorious sultan, and recommended him to take Ascalon before he ventured to ask for the surrender of Gaza. The season was now advancing—vague rumors were flying about of stupendous preparations in Europe for the recovery of Palestine, and Saladin was anxious to besiege and take Jerusalem ere the winter's rains commenced. When, therefore, his military engines were planted under the walls of Ascalon, he once more, as the place was strong, summoned the inhabitants to surrender, and they then agreed to capitulate

---

* *Hoveden*, rer. Angl. script. post Bedam, p. 636, 637. Chron. *Gervas.* ib. col. 1562.

on receiving a solemn promise from Saladin that he would forthwith set at liberty the king of Jerusalem and the Grand Master of the Temple, and would respect both the persons and the property of the inhabitants. These terms were acceded to, and on the 4th of September the gates of Ascalon were thrown open to the infidels.[*]

The inhabitants of this interesting city appear to have been much attached to their king, Guy de Lusignan, and his queen Sibylla. They had received them when they came from Jerusalem, as fugitives from the wrath of Baldwin IV., and protected them against the power of that monarch. The sultan imposed such conditions upon the prisoners as were necessary for his own security. They were to quit Palestine never more to return, and were in the mean time, until a fitting opportunity for their embarkation to Europe could be found, to take up their abode at Naplous, under the surveillance of the Moslem garrison. Immediately after the capture of Ascalon, Saladin pitched his tents beneath the walls of Gaza, the great fortress of the Knights Templars. He had been repulsed by the military friars with great loss in a previous attack upon this important station, and he now surrounded it with his numerous battalions, thirsting for vengeance. The place surrendered after a short siege; the fortifications were demolished, but the fate of the garrison has not been recorded.

Having subjugated all the country bordering upon the sea coast, Saladin moved forward in great triumph towards the sacred city of Jerusalem. He encamped the first night at Bersabee, the ancient Beersheba, around the well digged by Abraham, in the land of the Philistines, and on the spot where Abraham delivered the seven ewe lambs, and made the covenant with Abimelech, and planted a grove, and called "on the name of the Lord, the everlasting God." The next day Saladin marched towards Bethlehem, halting on the way before a castle of the Hospitallers, which he summoned to surrender, but in vain. Leaving a party of horse to watch the place, he pitched his tents the same evening around Bethlehem, and the next morning at sunrise, the Moslem soldiers might be seen pouring into the vast convent and the magnificent church erected by the empress Helena and her son Constantine, over the sacred spot where the Saviour of the world was born. They wandered with unbounded admiration amid the unrivalled Corinthian colonnade, formed by a quadruple row of forty ancient columns, which support a barn-roof constructed of the cedar of Lebanon. They paused to admire the beautiful mosaics which covered the lofty walls, the richly carved screen on either side of the high altar, and the twenty-five imperial eagles. Saladin was present in person, and no serious disorders appear to have been committed. The inhabitants of the town had all fled to Jerusalem, with whatever property they could carry with them, and in the afternoon, after establishing a garrison in the place, the sultan commenced his march towards the Holy City.

---

[*] Contin. Hist. col. 611. *Jac. de Vitr.* cap. xc. *Vinisauf,* p. 257. *Michaud,* Extr.

C. G. Addison

At the hour of sunset, when the bells of the churches of Jerusalem were tolling to vespers, the vast host of Saladin crowned in dark array the bleak and desolate eminences which surround the city of David. The air was rent with the loud Mussulman shouts *El Kods, El Kods*—"The Holy City, the Holy City!" and the green and yellow banners of the prophet, and the various colored emblems of the Arabian tribes, were to be seen standing out in bold relief upon the lofty ridges of the hills, and gleaming brightly in the last trembling rays of the setting sun. The Arabian writers descant with enthusiasm upon the feelings experienced by their countrymen on beholding "the long lost sister of Mecca and Medina," on gazing once more upon the swelling domes of the Mosque of Omar, and on the sacred eminence from whence, according to their traditions, "Mahomet ascended from earth to heaven." It must have been, indeed, a strange, and an awful scene. The Moslem host took up their stations around the Holy City at the very hour when the followers both of the Christian and Mahometan religion were wont to assemble to offer up their prayers to the one Great God, the common Father of us all. On the one hand, you might hear the sound of the sweet vesper bells from the towers of the Christian churches wafted softly upon the evening breeze, the hoarse chant of the monks and priests, and the loud swelling hymn of praise; while on the other, over all the hills and eminences around Jerusalem, stole the long shrill cry of the muezzins, loudly summoning the faithful to their evening devotions. Within the walls, for one night at least, the name of Christ was invoked with true piety and fervent devotion; while without the city, the eternal truth and the Moslem fiction were loudly proclaimed, "There is but one God, and *Mahomet* is his apostle."

That very night, when the Mussulmen had finished their prayers, and ere darkness spread its sable shroud over the land, the loud trumpets of Saladin summoned the Christians to surrender "the house of God" to the arms of the faithful: but the Christians returned for answer, that, please God, the Holy City should *not* be surrendered. The next morning at sunrise, the terrified inhabitants were awakened by the clangor of horns and drums, the loud clash of arms, and the fierce cries of the remorseless foe. The women and children rushed into the churches, and threw themselves on their knees before the altars, weeping and wailing, and lifting up their hands to heaven, whilst the men hastened to man the battlements. The Temple could no longer furnish its hundreds and thousands of brave warriors for the defense of the holy sanctuary of the Christians; a few miserable knights, with some serving brethren, alone remained in its now silent halls and deserted courts. For fifteen days did the Christians successfully resist the utmost efforts of the enemy; the monks and the canons, the bishops and the priests, took arms in defense of the Holy Sepulcher, and lined in warlike array the dark gray battlements and towers of Jerusalem. But the Mussulman archers soon became so numerous and so expert, that the garrison durst not show themselves upon the walls "Their arrows fell," says our worthy countryman, abbot

Coggleshale, one of the brave defenders of the place, "as thick as hail upon the battlements, so that no one could lift a finger above the walls without being maimed. So great indeed was the number of the wounded, that it was as much as all the doctors of the city and of the Hospital could do to extract the weapons from their bodies. The face of the narrator of these events was lacerated with an arrow which pierced right through his nose; the wooden shaft was withdrawn, but a piece of the iron head remains there to this day."*

Jerusalem was crowded with fugitives who had been driven into the Holy City from the provinces. The houses could not contain them, and the streets were filled with women and children, who slept night after night upon the cold pavement. At the expiration of a fortnight, Saladin finding his incessant attacks continually foiled, retired from the walls, and employed his troops in the construction of military engines, stationing ten thousand cavalry around the city to intercept fugitives, and prevent the introduction of supplies. When his engines were completed, he directed all his efforts against the northern wall of the city, which extends between St. Stephen's gate and the gate of Jaffa. Ten thousand soldiers were attached to the military engines, and were employed day and night in battering the fortifications. Barefoot processions of women, monks, and priests were made to the holy Sepulcher, to implore the Son of God to save his tomb and his inheritance from impious violation. The females, as a mark of humility and distress, cut off their hair and cast it to the winds; and the ladies of Jerusalem made their daughters do penance by standing up to their necks in tubs of cold water placed upon Mount Calvary. But it availed nought, "for our Lord Jesus Christ," says the chronicler, "would not listen to any prayer that they made, for the filth, the luxury, and the adultery which prevailed in the city did not suffer prayer or supplication to ascend before God."

To prevent the garrison from attempting to break the force of the battering-rams, Saladin constructed vast mangonels and machines, which cast enormous stones and flaming beams of timber, covered with pitch and naptha, upon the ramparts, and over the walls into the city. He moreover employed miners to sap the foundations of the towers, and on the 16th of October the angle of the northern wall, where it touches the valley of Gehinnon, was thrown down with a tremendous crash. The appalling intelligence spread through the city, and filled every heart with mourning. Friends embraced one another as it were for the last time; mothers clung to their little ones, anticipating with heart-rending agony the fearful moment when they would be torn from them for ever; and the men gazed around in gloomy silence, appalled and stupefied. Young mothers might be seen carrying their babes in their arms to Mount Calvary, and placing them before the altars of the church of the Resurrection, as if they thought that the sweet innocence of these helpless objects would appease the wrath of

---

* *Rad. Cogg.* col. 567, 568.

heaven. The panic-stricken garrison deserted the fortifications, but the infidels fortunately deferred the assault until the succeeding morning. During the night attempts were made, but in vain, to organize a strong guard to watch the breach. "With my own ears," says abbot Coggleshale, "I heard it proclaimed, between the wall and the counterscarp, by the patriarch and the chief men of the city, that if fifty strong and valiant foot soldiers would undertake to guard for one night only the angle which had been overthrown, they should receive fifty golden bezants; but none could be found to undertake the duty."

In the morning a suppliant deputation proceeded to Saladin to implore his mercy, but ere they reached the imperial tent the assault had commenced, and twelve banners of the prophet waved in triumph upon the breach. The haughty sultan accordingly refused to hear the messengers, and dismissed them, declaring that he would take Jerusalem from the Franks as they had taken it from the Moslems, that is say, *sword in hand.* But some spirit of resistance had at last been infused into the quailing garrison, the few Templars and Hospitallers in Jerusalem manned the breach, and in a desperate struggle the Moslems were repulsed, and the standards of the prophet were torn down from the walls. The messengers then returned to Saladin, and declared that if he refused to treat for the surrender of Jerusalem, the Christians would set fire to the Temple or Mosque of Omar, would destroy all the treasures they possessed in the city, and massacre their Moslem prisoners. The announcement of this desperate determination, which was accompanied with the offer of a very considerable ransom, induced Saladin to listen to terms, and a treaty was entered into with the Christians to the following effect. The Moslems were immediately to be put into possession of all the gates of Jerusalem, and the liberty and security of the inhabitants were to be purchased in the following manner. Every man was to pay to Saladin ten golden bezants as a ransom, every woman five, and every child under seven years was to pay one bezant.

When these terms, so disgraceful to the Christian negotiators, were known in the Holy City, nothing could exceed the grief and indignation of the poorer classes of people, who had no money wherewith to pay the ransom, and had consequently been delivered up to perpetual bondage by their richer Christian brethren. All resistance on their part, however, to the treaty was then hopeless; the poor had been betrayed by the rich; the infidels were already in possession of the tower of David, and their spears were gleaming in the streets of the Holy City. It is recorded to the praise of the few Templars and Hospitallers who were then in Jerusalem, that they spent all the money they possessed in ransoming their poor Christian brethren, whom they escorted in safety to Tripoli. The number of those who, being unable to pay the ransom, were reduced to a state of hopeless slavery, is estimated at fourteen thousand, men, women, and children. They were sold in the common slave-markets, and distributed through all the Mussulman countries of Asia. The women became the concubines and the handmaids of their masters, and the children were educated in the Mohammedan faith.

The Arabian writers express their astonishment at the number of the Christian captives, and give a heart-rending account of their sorrows and misfortunes. One of them tells us that he saw in his native village a fair European woman, bright as the morning star, who had two beautiful children. She seldom spoke, but remained the live-long day absorbed in melancholy contemplation; there was, says he, such a sweetness and gentleness in her deportment, that it made one's heart ache to see her. "When I was at Aleppo," says the historian, Azz'eddin Ali Ibn-Al'atsyr, who fought in Saladin's army, and was present at the battle of Tiberias, "I had for a slave one of the Christian women taken at Jaffa. She had with her a little child, about a year old, and many a bitter tear did she shed over this tender infant. I did my best to comfort her, but she exclaimed, 'Alas, sir, it is not for this child that I weep; I had a husband and two sisters, and I know not what has become of them. I had also six brothers, all of whom have perished.' This is the case of one person only. Another day I saw at Aleppo a Christian slave accompanying her master to the house of a neighbor. The master knocked at the door, and another Frank woman came to open it; the two females immediately give a loud cry; they rush into each other's arms; they weep; they sit down on the ground and enter into conversation. They were two sisters who had been sold as slaves to different masters, and had been brought without knowing it to the same town."*

Thus fell the holy city of Jerusalem, eighty-eight years after its conquest by Godfrey de Bouillon and the crusaders. Our excellent chronicler, Radolph, abbot of Coggleshale, who was redeemed from bondage by payment of the ten golden bezants, throws a pitying glance upon the misfortunes and miseries of the poor captives, but attributes the fall of Jerusalem, and all the calamities consequent thereon, to the sins and iniquities of the inhabitants. "They honored God," says he, "with their lips, but their hearts were far from him." He speaks of the beautiful women who thronged Jerusalem, and of the general corruption of the city, and exclaims, in the words of the prophet, "The Lord hath said unto the heathen, Go ye up against her walls and destroy, take away her battlements, for they are not the Lord's."

Immediately after the surrender of the city (October 11, A. D. 1187) the Moslems rushed to the Temple in thousands. "The imauns and the doctors and expounders of the wicked errors of Mahomet," says Abbot Coggleshale, "first ascended to the Temple of the Lord, called by the infidels *Beit Allah*, (the house of God,) in which, as a place of prayer and religion, they place their great hope of salvation. With horrible bellowings they proclaimed the law of Mahomet, and vociferated, with polluted lips, Allah *acbar*—Allah *acbar* (God is victorious). They defiled all the places

---

* *Ibn-Alatsyr.* Extraits par *M. Michaud.* Bib. des Croisaides, p. 464.

that are contained within the Temple; i. e. the place of the presentation, where the mother and glorious Virgin Mary delivered the Son of God into the hands of the just Simeon; and the place of the confession, looking towards the porch of Solomon, where the Lord judged the woman taken in adultery. They placed guards that no Christian might enter within the seven atria of the Temple; and as a disgrace to the Christians, with vast clamor, with laughter and with mockery, they hurled down the golden cross from the pinnacle of the building, and dragged it with ropes throughout the city, amid the exulting shouts of the infidels and the tears and lamentations of the followers of Christ." When every Christian had been removed from the precincts of the Temple, Saladin proceeded with vast pomp to say his prayers in the *Beit Allah*, the holy house of God, or "Temple of the Lord," erected by the Caliph Omar. He was preceded by five camels laden with rose-water, which he had procured from Damascus, and he entered the sacred courts to the sound of martial music, and with his banners streaming in the wind. The *Beit Allah*, "the Temple of the Lord," was then again consecrated to the service of one God and his prophet Mahomet; the walls and pavements were washed and purified with rose-water; and a pulpit, the labor of Noureddin, was erected in the sanctuary.*

The following account of these transactions was forwarded to Henry the Second, king of England. "To the beloved Lord Henry, by the grace of God, the illustrious king of the English, duke of Normandy and Guienne, and count of Anjou, Brother Terric, formerly Grand Preceptor of the house of the Temple at Jerusalem, sendeth greeting,—salvation through him who saveth kings. Know that Jerusalem, with the citadel of David, hath been surrendered to Saladin. The Syrian Christians, however, have the custody of the holy Sepulcher up to the fourth day after Michaelmas, and Saladin himself hath permitted ten of the brethren of the Hospital to remain in the house of the hospital for the space of one year, to take care of the sick.... Jerusalem, alas, hath fallen; Saladin hath caused the cross to be thrown down from the summit of the Temple of the Lord, and for two days to be publicly kicked and dragged in the dirt through the city. He then caused the Temple of the Lord to be washed within and without, upwards and downwards, with rose-water, and the law of Mahomet to be proclaimed throughout the four quarters of the Temple with wonderful clamor...."†

Bohadin, Saladin's secretary, mentions as a remarkable and happy circumstance, that the holy city was surrendered to the sultan of most pious memory, and that God restored to the faithful their sanctuary on the 27th of the month Regeb, on the night of which very day their most glorious prophet Mahomet performed his wonderful nocturnal journey from the Temple of the Lord, through the seven heavens, to the throne of God. He also describes the sacred congregation of the Mussulmen gathered together in the Temple and the solemn prayer offered up to God; the shouting and

---

* *Rad. Cogg.* col. 570-573. Contin. Hist. Bell. Sacr. col. 614, 615, 621. *Bohadin*, cap. xxxvi. and the Arab Extracts, apud *Schultens*, cap. xxvii. p. 42, 43.
† *Hoveden*, Rer. Angl. script. post Bedam, p. 645, 646.

the sounds of applause, and the voices lifted up to heaven, causing the holy buildings to resound with thanks and praises to the most bountiful Lord God. He glories in the casting down of the golden cross, and exults in the very splendid triumph of Islam. Saladin restored the sacred area of the Temple to its original condition under the first Mussulman conquerors of Jerusalem. The ancient Christian church of the Virgin (the mosque *Al Acsa*, and "Temple of Solomon") was washed with rose-water, and was once again dedicated to the religious services of the Moslems. On the western side of this venerable edifice the Templars had erected, according to the Arabian writers, an immense building in which they lodged, together with granaries of corn and various offices, which enclosed and concealed a great portion of the edifice. Most of these were pulled down by the sultan to make a clear and open area for the resort of the Mussulmen to prayer. Some new erections placed between the columns in the interior of the structure were taken away, and the floor was covered with the richest carpets. "Lamps innumerable," says Ibn Alatsyr, "were suspended from the ceiling; verses of the Koran were again inscribed on the walls; the call to prayer was again heard; the bells were silenced; the exiled faith returned to its ancient sanctuary; the devout Mussulmen again bent the knee in adoration of the one only God, and the voice of the imaun was again heard from the pulpit, reminding the true believers of the resurrection and the last judgment."[*]

The Friday after the surrender of the city, the army of Saladin, and crowds of true believers, who had flocked to Jerusalem from all parts of the East, assembled in the Temple of the Lord to assist in the religious services of the Mussulman sabbath. Omad, Saladin's secretary, who was present, gives the following interesting account of the ceremony, and of the sermon that was preached. "On Friday morning at daybreak," says he, "everybody was asking whom the sultan had appointed to preach. The Temple was full; the congregation was impatient; all eyes were fixed on the pulpit; the ears were on the stretch; our hearts beat fast, and tears trickled down our faces. On all sides were to be heard rapturous exclamations of 'What a glorious sight! What a congregation! Happy are those who have lived to see the resurrection of Islam.' At length the sultan ordered the judge (doctor of the law) *Mohieddin Aboulmehali-Mohammed* to fulfill the sacred function of imaun. I immediately lent him the black vestment which I had received as a present from the caliph. He then mounted into the pulpit and spoke. All were hushed. His expressions were graceful and easy, and his discourse was eloquent and much admired. He displayed the virtue and sanctity of Jerusalem; he spoke of the purification of the Temple; he alluded to the silence of the bells, and to the flight of the infidel priests. In his prayer he named the caliph and the sultan, and terminated his discourse with that chapter of the Koran in which God orders justice and good works. He then descended from the pulpit, and

---

[*] *Bohadin* apud *Schultens*, cap. 36. *Abulfeda*, ib. cap. xxvii. p. 43. *Wilken* Comment. p. 148.

prayed in the Mihrab. Immediately afterwards a sermon was preached before the congregation."

This sermon was delivered by *Mohammed Ben Zeky*. "Praise be to God," saith the preacher, "who by the power of his might hath raised up Islamism on the ruins of polytheism; who governs all things according to his will; who overthroweth the devices of the infidels, and causeth the *truth* to triumph! I praise God, who hath succored his elect, who hath rendered them victorious and crowned them with glory, who hath purified his holy house from the filthiness of idolatry.... I bear witness that there is no God but that one great God who standeth *alone* and hath no *partner*; sole, supreme, eternal; who begetteth not and is not begotten, and hath *no equal*. I bear witness that Mahomet is his servant, his envoy, and his prophet, who hath dissipated doubts, confounded polytheism, and put down *lies*! O men, declare ye the blessings of God, who hath restored to you this holy city, after it has been left in the power of the infidels for a hundred years. This *holy house* of the Lord hath been built, and its foundations have been established, for the glory of God. This sacred spot is the dwelling-place of the prophets, the *kebla* (place of prayer) towards which you turn at the commencement of your religious duties, the birth-place of the saints, the scene of the revelation. It is thrice holy, for the angels of God spread their wings over it. This is that blessed land of which God hath spoken in his sacred book. In this house of prayer, Mahomet prayed with the angels who approach God. It is to this spot that all fingers are turned after the two holy places. This conquest, O men, hath opened unto you the gates of heaven; the angels rejoice, and the eyes of the prophets glisten with joy." The preacher proceeds, in a high strain of enthusiasm, to enlarge upon the merits of the holy war. "The holy war, the holy war!" says he, "is better than religious worship; it is the noblest of your occupations. Aid God, and he will assist you; protect the Lord, and he will protect you; remember him, and he will have you in remembrance; do good to him, and he will do good to you. Cut off the branches of iniquity; purify the earth from unbelievers, and destroy the nations who have excited the wrath of God and his apostle, &c...."[*]

Omad informs us that the marble altar and chapel which had been erected over the sacred rock in the Temple of the Lord, or Mosque of Omar, was removed by Saladin, together with the stalls for the priests, the marble statues, and all the abominations which had been placed in the venerated building by the Christians. The Mussulmen discovered with horror that some pieces of the holy stone or rock had been cut off by the Franks, and sent to Europe. Saladin caused it to be immediately surrounded by a grate of iron. He washed it with rose-water, and Malek-Afdel covered it with magnificent carpets. Saladin, in his famous letter to the caliph, giving an account of the conquest of Jerusalem, exclaims—"God hath at length turned towards the supporters of the true faith; he hath let loose his

---

[*] Khotbeh, or sermon of *Mohammed Ben Zeky*.—*Michaud*, Extraits Arabes.

wrath against the infidels, and hath driven them from his sanctuary.... The infidels have erected churches in the holy city, and the great houses of the Templars and Hospitallers. In these structures are rich marbles and many precious things. Thy servant hath restored the Mosque Al-Acsa to its ancient destination. He hath appointed imauns to celebrate divine service, and on the 14th chaaban they preached, the *khotbeh* (sermon). The heavens are rent with joy and the stars dance with delight. The word of God hath been exalted, and the tombs of the prophets, which the infidel hath defiled, have been purified."* Saladin restored the fortifications of Jerusalem; he founded several schools, and converted the great house of the Hospitallers into a college. He then quitted the Holy City to pursue his military operations in the field.

The Templars still maintained themselves in some of the strongest castles of Palestine, and the maritime city of Tyre continued to resist all the attacks of the Moslems. This important sea-port was preserved to the Christians by the valor and military talents of the young Conrad, marquis of Montferrat, who digged a ditch across the isthmus which connects Tyre with the main land, repaired the fortifications and planted catapults and balistæ in boats, so as to command the only approach to the town. Saladin proceeded in person to Tyre, to conduct the operations against this important place. He was on horseback from morn till night, and was assisted by his sons, his brother, and his nephew, all of whom commanded in the field under the eye of the sultan, and animated the troops by their example. The following account of the state of affairs in Palestine is contained in a letter from Brother Terric, Grand Preceptor of the Temple, and Treasurer General of the order, to Henry the Second, king of England. "The brothers of the hospital of Belvoir as yet bravely resist the Saracens; they have captured two convoys, and have valiantly possessed themselves of the munitions of war and provisions which were being conveyed by the Saracens from the fortress of La Feue. As yet, also, Carach, in the neighborhood of Mount Royal, Mount Royal itself, the Temple of Saphet, the hospital of Carach, Margat, and Castellum Blancum, and the territory of Tripoli, and the territory of Antioch, resist Saladin.... From the feast of Saint Martin, up to that of the circumcision of the Lord, Saladin hath besieged Tyre incessantly, by night and by day, throwing into it immense stones from thirteen military engines. On the vigils of St. Silvester, the Lord Conrad, the marquis of Montferrat, distributed knights and foot soldiers along the wall of the city, and having armed seventeen galleys and ten small vessels, with the assistance of the house of the Hospital and the brethren of the Temple, he engaged the galleys of Saladin, and vanquishing them he captured eleven, and took prisoners the great admiral of Alexandria and eight other admirals, a multitude of the infidels being slain. The rest of the Mussulman galleys, escaping the hands of the Christians, fled to the army of Saladin, and being run aground by his command, were

---

* *Michaud*, Pieces justificatives, No. ix. 485.

set on fire and burnt to ashes. Saladin himself, overwhelmed with grief, having *cut off the ears and the tail of his horse*, rode that same horse through his whole army in the sight of all. Farewell!"[*] Tyre continued to be valiantly defended until the winter had set in, and then the disappointed sultan, despairing of taking the place, burnt his military engines and retired to Damascus.

The king of Jerusalem, and the Grand Master of the Temple, who had, as before mentioned, been residing at Naplous, under the surveillance of Saladin's officers, were now set at full liberty, pursuant to the treaty of Ascalon, on the understanding that they would immediately proceed to Tyre and embark for Europe. Queen Sibylla, who was in Jerusalem at the time of its surrender to Saladin, had been permitted to join her royal husband at Naplous, and the king, the queen, and the Grand Master of the Temple, consequently proceeded together to Tyre. On their arrival at that place, they found the gates shut against them. The young Conrad declared, that as the city had been preserved solely by the swords of himself and his followers, it justly belonged to him, and that neither the king nor the queen of Jerusalem any longer possessed authority within it. Cruelly repelled from Tyre, the king and queen, with their infant children, the Grand Master of the Temple, and the patriarch Heraclius, proceeded to Antioch.

As soon as the winter rains had subsided, Saladin took the field, and attempted to reduce various strong castles of the Templars and Hospitallers. The most formidable of these were the castles of Saphet and Kowkab (the star); the one belonging to the order of the Temple, and the other to the order of the Hospital of Saint John. Saphet is one of the four holy cities of the Talmud, and is held in peculiar veneration by the Jews. The castle of the Templars crowned the summit of a lofty mountain, along the sides of which extended the houses and churches of the town. It was the strongest fortress possessed by the order in Palestine. From the ramparts the eye ranged over a rich prospect of luxuriant vineyards and smiling villages, and embraced a grand panoramic view of lofty mountains. Through the valley below rolled the Jordan; to the southward extended the vast blue expanse of the lake of Tiberias; and in the north-east the snowy summits of Anti-Lebanon might be seen piercing the skies. This important fortress commanded the greater part of Galilee; it had always been a great check upon the incursions of the infidels, and was considered one of the bulwarks of the Latin kingdom. Saladin's exertions, consequently, for the capture of the place were strenuous and incessant. He planted a large body of troops around it, under the command of his brother Saifeddin; but the season was not far enough advanced for their operations to be carried on with any chance of success. The tents of the besiegers were blown off the mountain by the furious whirlwinds, and the operation of the military engines was impeded by heavy rains. The Templars made continued sallies upon the works, burnt the military engines, butchered the soldiers in their

---

[*] *Hoveden*, p. 646. Contin. Hist. col. 623. *Ibn-Alatsyr*, p. 474-477.

sleep, and harassed them with incessant alarms in the dead of night. The siege was consequently turned into a blockade, and Saladin drew off the greater part of his forces to attack the Christian possessions in the principality of Antioch. He divided his army into several detachments, which were sent in different directions, with orders to ravage all the neighboring country, drive away the oxen, sheep, and cattle, and collect the booty together in the plain of the Orontes, along the banks of the lake of Kades. He crossed the vast mountain ranges which extend between the Orontes and the sea-coast, and appeared in arms before the gates of Tripoli. Strenuous preparations had been made to receive him, and the sultan contented himself with reconnoitering the place and examining its defenses; having done which, he directed his march upon Tortosa. The Grand Master of the Temple, who was anxiously watching Saladin's movements, immediately threw himself into the strong castle of the Templars at that place, and prepared to defend the town; but the fortifications were weak, the inhabitants were panic-stricken, and the Templars, after a short struggle, were compelled to abandon the city, and retire behind their fortifications. There they maintained a fierce and bloody contest with the Moslems, and during the various assaults and sallies the town was set on fire and burnt to the ground. Bohadin gives a fearful account of the destruction by fire of the great cathedral church, and of the roaring and crackling of the flames as they burst through the huge cedar beams and timbers of the roof. He says that thousands of faithful Mussulmen gathered around the vast and venerable pile, and raised exulting shouts as they witnessed the progress of the fire, lifting up their voices to heaven, and returning thanks to the most bountiful Lord God!

Having failed in all his attempts to take the castle of the Templars, Saladin drew off his forces, leaving the once populous and flourishing town of Tortosa a dreary desert. He then besieged and took the city of Gabala, and then approached in warlike array the far-famed Laodicea. The panic-stricken inhabitants refused to defend the town, and abandoned the fortifications, but some Templars and other knights, throwing themselves into the citadel with their followers, boldly resisted the attacks of the infidels. After a desperate defense a capitulation was signed, the garrison marched out with all the honors of war, and the banners of Islam were then planted upon the towers and battlements. Both Ibn Alatsyr and Bohadin give an enthusiastic description of the town and its environs. They speak of its noble harbor, its beautiful houses, elegant villas, rich marbles, luxuriant gardens, and shady groves. All these became the prey of the fierce Mussulman soldiery, who committed great excesses. They broke to pieces the choice specimens of ancient sculpture, considering them hated evidences of idolatry; they stripped all the churches of their ornaments, and sold the sacred vestments of the priests. From Laodicea, Saladin marched to Sohioun or Sekyun, a fortress of prodigious strength, situate amongst the mountains midway between Gabala and the Orontes. It was almost entirely surrounded by a deep precipitous ravine, the sides of which were in many places perpendicular. After a siege of five days, a part of the Mussulman soldiers clambered over some rocks which were thought to be inaccessible, climbed the outer wall of the town, and opened the gates to their companions; the second and third walls were then carried by assault, and the citadel surrendered after a short siege. Many other important cities and castles speedily fell into the hands of the victorious Saladin. Among these were the city of Bakas, or Bacas, on the banks of the Orontes, and the castle of Al Shokhr, which was connected with the town by a bridge over the river; the castle of Al Jahmàhûnîn, near Gabala; Blatanous, near Antioch; Sarminiah, or Sarmaniya, a fortress, a day's journey N. E. of Aleppo; and many other places of note. All the towns and castles between Sarminiah and Gabala surrendered to the Moslems. "Glory be to God," says Ibn Alatsyr, "who hath made easy that which appeared to be difficult."

Saladin then recrossed the Orontes, and laid siege to Berzyeh, or Borzya, a fortress which commanded the high road from Antioch to Emesa, or Hems, and was, therefore, a place of very great importance. During a very hot day, when the garrison had been fighting from sunrise till noon, Saladin suddenly called up his reserve, placed himself at their head, scaled the fortifications, and entered the town sword in hand. The houses were set on fire, the streets were drenched with blood, and all the inhabitants who escaped the general massacre, were made slaves. From Berzyeh, Saladin marched down the vast and fertile plain of the Orontes, to the famous iron bridge over that river, about six or seven miles from Antioch, with a view of besieging the strong castle of the Knights Templars, called Derbazâc, or Darbêsak. On the 8th Regeb, having collected his forces together, and procured a vast number of powerful military engines, he moved forward and invested the place. The walls were surrounded with wooden towers, filled with expert archers, who swept the battlements with their arrows. Under cover of these towers, battering-rams were placed in position, and a vast breach was made in the walls. Saladin's body-guard moved forward to the assault, supported by crowds of archers on either flank, but the Templars filled up the breach with their bodies, and after a bloody contest the Mussulmen were driven back, leaving the ground covered with their dead. The Templars repaired the breach, and the sultan shifted his ground of attack. Hurdles covered with raw hides were advanced against the walls, and an expert party of miners were employed, under cover of these hurdles, to undermine a huge tower, which was considered to be the key of the fortifications. The tower was so well and strongly built, that it resisted for a length of time all the efforts of the miners; they dug away a great part of the foundations, and the tower appeared, says Ibn Alatsyr, to be suspended in the air. At last, however, it fell with a tremendous crash, carrying along with it into the ditch a vast portion of the walls on either side, so that a large yawning gap was opened in the fortifications. Again the Mussulmen rushed to the assault with loud shouts, and again they were hurled back by the stout arms of the Templars, leaving the heaps of stone, and the vast masses of shattered walls around them, crimsoned with the blood of their best men. Bohadin, who witnessed the assault, declares that he never saw such an obstinate defense. As soon as any one of the Templars fell, another, he tells us, would immediately take his place, and thus they remained upon the breach immoveable as a rock. At last, it was agreed that if the fortress was not succored by the prince of Antioch, within a given period, the Templars should surrender it, and march out with their arms in their hands. No succor arrived by the appointed time, and the place was consequently given up to the Mussulmen.*

Immediately after the surrender of Darbêsak, Saladin marched upon Bagras, a town situate at the foot of Mount Al Locam, and pushed on his advanced guard to the environs of the vast and populous city of Antioch, but he contented himself with the mere sight of the place, and declined to undertake the siege of it. He remained for some time in observation before the city, and sent out detachments in different directions to lay waste the surrounding country, and collect spoil. The population of Antioch was estimated at 150,000 souls: nearly all the surviving Templars of the principality were collected together within the walls, under the command of their valiant Grand Master, and the Prince Bohemond was at the head of a numerous and well-organized force, fully prepared for a desperate struggle in defense of his rich and princely city. Saladin consequently preferred entering into a truce to continuing the war, and concluded a treaty with Bohemond, whereby a suspension of arms was agreed upon for the term of eight months, to commence from the first of the approaching month of November, and it was stipulated that all the Moslem prisoners detained in Antioch should be set at liberty. Saladin then returned by the valley of the Orontes to Damascus, and his troops became very impatient to be dismissed to their homes for the winter, but he reminded them of the brevity and uncertainty of human life, told them that there was plenty of work before them, and that they ought not to leave for to-morrow that which could be done to-day. He accordingly set out from Damascus at the head of a large body of forces, and proceeded to lay siege to Saphet, the strong and important castle of the Knights Templars. Bohadin accompanied the sultan, and gives an interesting account of his incessant exertions for the capture of the place. During a windy and tempestuous night, he superintended the planting of five besieging engines. To every soldier he allotted a specific task, and turning to his secretary he said, "Let us not go to bed to-night, until these five engines are completed." Every now and then messengers came in to narrate the progress of the work, and Saladin spent the intermediate time in cheerful converse with his friend. The night was dark and long, the weather miserably wet and cold, and the ground covered with mud. Bohadin ventured to address some observations to his royal master, upon the imprudence of exposing himself to the

---

* Ipse meis vidi oculis, uno eorum cadente, alter mox eundem locum occuparet, immotique, perstarent ad instar muri. *Bohadin* apud *Schultens*, p. 85. *Michaud*, Extraits, p. 487, 488.

inclemency of the season, and to so much watching and fatigue, but the pious sultan reminded him of the words of the prophet, "The fire of hell shall not prevail against the eye that wakes and watches in the service of God, and the eye that weeps through fear of God."

The Templars manfully defended themselves, and their brethren in Tyre made an attempt to send them succor. Two hundred valiant and determined soldiers set out from that city, and marched through the country by night, sheltering themselves in the day-time in caverns and solitary places amongst the mountains. They reached Saphet, and attempted to conceal themselves in the neighborhood of the castle, until they could find an opportunity of communicating with their beleaguered brethren. Unfortunately one of their number strayed from his place of concealment, and was seen by a Mussulman emir, who immediately called out a strong guard, searched the neighborhood, and took the whole party prisoners. They were brought into Saladin's presence and condemned to death; but before the sentence was carried into execution negotiations were entered into for the surrender of Saphet. The Templars in the fortress were ill provided with provisions; they had now lost all hope of succor, and they agreed to surrender, on condition that they should be permitted to march out with their arms to Tyre, in company with the prisoners whom Saladin had just taken. These terms were acceded to, and the fortifications of the strong castle of Saphet were speedily demolished by the infidels.[*]

In the mean time all Europe had been thrown into consternation by the dismal intelligence of the fall of Jerusalem. Public prayers were put up in the churches, and fasts were ordered, as in times of great national calamities. Pope Urban III. is said to have died of grief, and the cardinals made a solemn resolution to renounce all kinds of diversions and pleasures, to receive no presents from any one who had causes depending in the court of Rome, and never to mount a horse as long as the Holy Land was trodden under foot by the infidels. Pope Gregory VIII. addressed apostolical letters to the sovereigns, bishops, nobles, and people of all Christian countries, painting in pathetic terms the miserable disasters of the Latin Christians, the capture of the holy cross, the slaughter of the Templars and Hospitallers, and the fall of Jerusalem, and exhorting all faithful Christians immediately to assume the cross, and march to the deliverance of the Holy City. Crowds of armed pilgrims again quitted the shores of Europe for Palestine, and the Templars, obedient to the pressing calls of their brethren, hurried from their preceptories to the seaports of the Mediterranean, and embarked in the ships of Genoa, Pisa, and Venice. The Grand Master of the Temple, and the king of Jerusalem, placed themselves at the head of the newly arrived battalions, and established their head quarters at Ras el Ain, a small village on the main land opposite Tyre. Many valiant Templars from the Temple at London, and the different preceptories of England, Scotland, and Ireland, joined their chief, and brought with them arms,

---

[*] *Ibn Alatsyr*, ut sup. p. 479-484, 492. *Bohadin*, cap. 41-44, 48, 49.

horses, clothing, and munitions of war, with a vast amount of treasure, which had been collected in the churches. They were the bearers likewise of a large sum of money which had been sent by king Henry the Second for the defense of Tyre. This money was delivered to the Grand Master, but as the siege of Tyre had been raised before its arrival, and the young Conrad claimed the sovereignty of the city, and set up his authority in opposition to that of the king of Jerusalem, Gerard de Riderfort very properly refused to deliver the money into his hands; whereupon Conrad wrote letters filled with bitter complaints to the archbishop of Canterbury and to king Henry.*

At the commencement of the summer, the king and the Grand Master took the field at the head of an army of 9,000 men, and marched along the coast with the intention of laying siege to the important city of Acre. Saladin wrote to all the governors of the Moslem provinces, requiring them to join him without delay, and directed his army to concentrate at Sepphoris. From thence he marched to Keruba, and then moved in order of battle to Tel Kaisan, where the plain of Acre begins. The city of Acre had been regularly invested for some days previous to his arrival, and after reconnoitering the position of the Christian army, he encamped, extending his left wing to Al Nahr Al Halu, "the sweet river," and his right to Tel Al'Ayâdhiya, in such a manner, that the besiegers themselves became the besieged. He then made a sudden attack upon the weakest part of the Christian camp, broke through the lines, penetrated to the gate of Acre, called Karàkûsh, which he entered, and threw into the city a reinforcement of 5,000 warriors, laden with arms, provisions, clothing, and everything necessary for the defense of the place. Having accomplished this bold feat, Saladin made a masterly retreat to his camp at Tel Al'Ayâdhiya.

On the 4th of October, the newly-arrived warriors from Europe, eager to signalize their prowess against the infidels, marched out of their intrenchments to attack Saladin's camp. The holy gospels, wrapped in silk, were borne by four knights on a cushion, before the king of Jerusalem, and the patriarch Heraclius and the western bishops appeared at the head of the Christian forces with crucifixes in their hands, exhorting them to obtain the crown of martyrdom in defense of the Christian faith. The Templars marched in the van, and led the assault; they broke through the right wing of the Mussulman army, which was commanded by Saladin's nephew, and struck such terror into the hearts of the Moslems, that some of them fled, without halting, as far as Tiberias. The undisciplined masses of the Christian army, however, thinking that the day was their own, rushed heedlessly on after the infidels, and penetrating to the imperial tent, abandoned themselves to pillage. The Grand Master of the Temple, foreseeing the result, collected his knights and the forces of the order around him. The infidels rallied, they were led on by Saladin in person, and the Christian army would have been annihilated but for the Templars. Firm

---

* *Radulph de Diceto*, apud X. script. p. 642.

and immoveable, they presented for the space of an hour an unbroken front to the advancing Moslems, and gave time for the discomfited and panic-stricken crusaders to recover from their terror and confusion; but ere they had been rallied, and had returned to the charge, the Grand Master Gerard de Riderfort, was slain; he fell, pierced with arrows, at the head of his knights, the seneschal of the order shared the same fate, and more than half the Templars were numbered with the dead.[*]

To Gerard de Riderfort succeeded (A. D. 1189) the Knight Templar, Brother Walter.[†] Never did the flame of enthusiasm burn with fiercer or more destructive power than at this famous siege of Acre. Nine pitched battles were fought, with various fortune, in the neighborhood of Mount Carmel, and during the first year of the siege a hundred thousand Christians are computed to have perished. The tents of the dead, however, were replenished by new-comers from Europe; the fleets of Saladin succored the town, the Christian ships brought continual aid to the besiegers, and the contest seemed interminable. Saladin's exertions in the cause of the prophet were incessant. The Arab authors compare him to a mother wandering with desperation in search of her lost child, to a lioness who has lost its young. "I saw him," says his secretary Bohadin, "in the fields of Acre afflicted with a most cruel disease, with boils from the middle of his body to his knees, so that he could not sit down, but only recline on his side when he entered into his tent, yet he went about to the stations nearest to the enemy, arranged his troops for battle, and rode about from dawn till eve, now to the right wing, then to the left, and then to the centre, patiently enduring the severity of his pain." Having received intelligence of the mighty preparations which were being made in Europe for the recovery of Jerusalem, and of the march of the emperor Frederick Barbarossa through Hungary and Greece to Constantinople, with a view of crossing the Hellespont, into Asia, Saladin sent orders to the governors of Senjâr, Al Jazîra, Al Mawsel, and Arbel, ordering them to attend him with their troops, and directed his secretary Bohadin to proceed to the caliph Al Nâssr Deldin'illah, at Bagdad, humbly to request the Mussulman pontiff to use his spiritual authority and influence to induce all the Moslem nations and tribes to heal their private differences and animosities, and combine together against the Franks, for the defense of Islam. Bohadin was received with the greatest distinction and respect by the caliph and the whole divan at Bagdad, and whilst the pope was disseminating his apostolical letters throughout Christendom, calling upon the western nations to combine together for the triumph of the CROSS, the Mussulman pontiff was addressing, from the distant city of Bagdad, his pious exhortations to all true believers, to assemble under the holy banners of the prophet, and shed their blood in defense of *Islam*.

---

[*] *Vinisauf* apud *Gale* XV. script, vol. 2. p. 270. *Rad. Cogg.* col. 574. Gesta Dei, tom. 1, part 2, p. 1165. *Radulph de Diceto* col. 649.
[†] *Ducange*, Gloss, tom. vi. p. 1036. Cotton MS. Nero E. vi. p. 60, fol. 466.

The Knights Templars

Shortly after the commencement of the new year, (586, Hejir which began Feb. 9th, A. D. 1190,) Saladin collected his troops together, to raise the siege of Acre. He moved from Al Kherûba to Tel Al Ajûl, where he pitched his camp. He was there joined by his son Al Malek, Al Daher Gayâtho'ddîn Gâzi, the governor of Aleppo, with a select body of cavalry, and by Mohaffero'ddîn I'Bn Zinoddin, with his light horse. The Templars and the crusaders, during the winter, had not been idle; they had dug trenches around their camp, thrown up ramparts, and fortified their position in such a way that it would have been difficult, says the Arabian writer, for even a bird to get in. They had, moreover, filled up the ditch around the town, and constructed three enormous towers, the largest of which was much higher than the walls, was sixty cubits in length, and could contain from five to six hundred warriors, with a proper quantity of arms and military engines. These towers were covered with the raw hides of oxen soaked in vinegar and mud, to render them incombustible; they were strengthened from top to bottom with bands of iron, and were each divided into five platforms or galleries filled with soldiers and military engines. They were rolled on wheels to the walls, and the Templars and the crusaders were about to descend from the platforms and galleries upon the battlements of the city, when the towers, and all the warriors upon them, were consumed by some inextinguishable inflammable composition, discharged out of brass pots by a brazier from Damascus. "We were watching," says Bohadin, who was standing in the Moslem camp by Saladin's side, "with intense anxiety the movements of the soldiers upon the towers, and thought that the city must inevitably be taken, when suddenly we saw one of them surrounded with a blaze of light, which shot up into the skies; the heavens were rent with one joyous burst of acclamation from the sons of Islam, and in another instant another tower was surrounded with raging flames and clouds of black smoke, and then the third; they were ignited one after the other in the most astonishing and surprising manner, with scarce an interval of a minute between them. The sultan immediately mounted his horse, and ordered the trumpets to sound to arms, exclaiming with a loud voice, in the words of the prophet, 'When the gate of good fortune is thrown open, delay not to enter in.'"

At the commencement of the summer Saladin detached a considerable portion of his forces to the north, to oppose the progress of the German crusaders and Templars, who were advancing from Constantinople, under the command of the emperor Frederic Barbarossa. These advancing Templars were the especial favorites of Barbarossa, and after his melancholy death, from the effects of a cold bath in the river Cydnus, they formed part of the body-guard of his son the duke of Suabia.

In the month of July the Templars suffered severe loss in another attack upon Saladin's camp. The Christian soldiery, deceived by the flight of the Mussulmen, were again lured to the pillage of their tents, and again defeated by the main body of Saladin's army, which had been posted in reserve. The Templars were surrounded by an overpowering force, but they fought their way through the dense ranks of the infidels to their own camp, leaving the plain of Acre strewed with the lifeless bodies of the best and bravest of their warriors. "The enemies of God," says Bohadin, "had the audacity to enter within the camp of the lions of Islamism, but they speedily experienced the terrible effects of the divine indignation. They fell beneath the sabres of the Mussulmen as the leaves fall from the trees during the tempests of autumn. Their mangled corpses, scattered over the mountain side, covered the earth even as the branches and boughs cover the hills and valleys when the woodsman lops the forest timber." "They fell," says another Arabian historian, "beneath the swords of the sons of Islam as the wicked will fall, at the last day, into the everlasting *fire* of *hell*. Nine rows of the dead covered the earth between the sea-shore and the mountains, and in each row might be counted the lifeless bodies of at least one thousand warriors."

The Moslem garrison continued manfully to defend the town; they kept up a constant communication with Saladin, partly by pigeons, partly by swimmers, and partly by men in small skiffs, who traversed the port in secresy, by favor of the night, and stole into the city. At one period the besieged had consumed nearly all their provisions, and were on the point of dying with famine, when Saladin hit upon the following stratagem, for the purpose of sending them a supply. He collected together a number of vessels at Beirout laden with sacks of meal, cheese, onions, sheep, rice, and other provisions. He disguised the seamen in the Frank habit, put crosses on their pendants, and covered the decks of the vessels with hogs. In this way the little fleet sailed safely through the blockading squadron of the Christians, and entered the port of Acre. On another occasion Saladin sent 1,000 *dinars* to the garrison, by means of a famous diver named Isa; the man was unfortunately drowned during his passage to the city, but the money, being deposited in three bladders, tied to his body, was a few days afterwards thrown ashore near the town, and reached the besieged in safety. At the commencement of the winter the garrison was again reduced to great straits for want of food, and was on the point of surrendering, when three vessels from Egypt broke through the guard-ships of the Christians, and got safely into the harbor with a copious supply of provisions, munitions of war, and everything requisite to enable the city to hold out until the ensuing spring.

To prevent the further introduction of succors by sea, the crusaders endeavored to take possession of the tower of Flies, a strong castle, built upon a rock in the midst of the sea at the mouth of the harbor, which commanded the port. The Templars employed one of their galleys upon this service, and crowds of small boats, filled with armed men, military engines, and scaling-ladders, were brought against the little fortress, but without effect. The boats and vessels were set on fire by the besieged and reduced to ashes, and after losing all their men, the Christians gave over the attempt. On the land side, the combats and skirmishes continued to be incessant. Wooden towers, and vast military machines, and engines, were constantly erected by the besiegers, and as constantly destroyed by the sallies and skilful contrivances of the besieged. The Templars, on one occasion, constructed two battering machines of a new invention, and most enormous size, and began therewith furiously to batter the walls of the town, but the garrison soon destroyed them with fire-darts, and beams of timber, pointed with red-hot iron.*

At the commencement of the next year, (587, Hejir. which began Jan. 29th, A. D. 1191,) a tremendous tempest scattered the fleet of the crusaders, and compelled their ships to take refuge in Tyre. The sea being open, Saladin hastily collected some vessels at Caiphas, threw a fresh body of troops into Acre, and withdrew the exhausted garrison, which had already sustained so many hardships and fatigues in defense of the town. This exchange of the garrison was most happily timed, for almost immediately after it had been effected, the walls of the city were breached, and preparations were made for an assault. The newly-arrived troops, however, repulsed the assailants, repaired the walls, and once more placed the city in a good posture of defense. The scarcity and famine in the Christian camp continued to increase, and a vast many of the crusaders, utterly unable to withstand the hardships and difficulties of their position, deserted to Saladin, embraced the Mohammedan faith, and were employed by him, at their own request, in cruising off the coast against their quondam friends. Bohadin tells us that they met with vast success in their employment. On board one of their prizes was found a silver table, and a great deal of money and plate, which the captors brought to the sultan, the 13th Dhu'lhajja, but Saladin returned the treasure to them, saying, that it was a sufficient satisfaction to him and the Moslems, to see that the Franks pillaged and plundered one another with such alacrity.

Famine and disease continued to make frightful ravages amongst the crusaders. The duke of Suabia, Baldwin, archbishop of Canterbury, the patriarch Heraclius, four archbishops, twelve bishops, forty counts, and five hundred other nobles and knights, besides common soldiers, fell victims to the malady. From two to three hundred persons died daily, and the survivors became unequal to the task of burying the dead. The trenches which the Christians had dug for their protection, now became their graves. Putrefying corpses were to be seen floating upon the sea, and lining the sea-shore, and the air was infected with an appalling and intolerable effluvia. The bodies of the living became bloated and swollen, and the most trifling wounds were incurable. In addition to all this, numbers of the poorer class of people died daily from starvation. The rich supported themselves for a time upon horse-flesh, and Abbot Coggleshale tells us, that a dinner off the entrails of a horse cost 10d. Bones were ground to powder, mixed with water, and eagerly devoured, and all the shoes, bridles, and saddles, and old leather in the camp, were boiled to shreds, and greedily eaten.

* *Bohadin*, cap. 55-58, 75-84. *Ibn Alat.* ut sup. p. 499, 500, 510-514. *Vinisauf*, apud *Gale* XV. script. cap. 58-60. *D'Herbelot*, Bib. Orient, p. 743.

Queen Sibylla, who appears to have been sincerely attached to the unpopular husband she had raised to the throne, was present in the Christian camp with four infant daughters. She had wandered with the king, Guy de Lusignan, from one place to another, ever since his liberation from captivity, and had been his constant companion through all the horrors, trials, and anxieties of the long siege of Acre. Her delicate frame, weakened by sorrow and misfortune, was unable to contend with the many hardships and privations of the Christian camp. She fell a victim to the frightful epidemic which raged amongst the soldiers, and her death was speedily followed by that of her four children. The enemies of the king now maintained that the crown of the Latin kingdom had descended upon Isabella, the younger sister of Sibylla, and wife of Humphrey de Thoron, Lord of Montreal, or Mount Royal; but the latter seemed to think otherwise, and took no steps either to have his wife made queen, or himself king. The enterprising and ambitious Conrad, Marquis of Montferrat, accordingly determined to play a bold game for the advancement of his own fortunes. He paid his addresses to Isabella, and induced her to consent to be divorced from Humphrey de Thoron, and take him for her husband. He went to the bishop of Beauvais, and persuaded that prelate to pronounce the divorce, and immediately after it had been done, he carried off Isabella to Acre, and there married her. As soon as the nuptials had been performed, Conrad caused himself and his wife to be proclaimed king and queen of Jerusalem, and forthwith entered upon the exercise of certain royal functions. He went to the Christian camp before Acre, and his presence caused serious divisions and dissensions amongst the crusaders. The king, Guy de Lusignan, stood upon his rights; he maintained that, as he had been once a king, he was always a king, and that the death of his wife could not deprive him of the crown which he had solemnly received, according to the established usage of the Latin kingdom. A strong party in the camp declared themselves in his favor, and an equally strong party declared in favor of his rival, Conrad, who prepared to maintain his rights, sword in hand. The misfortunes of the Christians appeared, consequently, to have approached their climax. The sword, the famine, and the pestilence, had successively invaded their camp, and now the demon of discord came to set them one against the other, and to paralyze all their exertions in the Christian cause.[*]

---

[*] *Rad. Cogg.* col. 557. *Vinisauf,* cap. 64, 74. L'Art de Verif. tom. 4, p. 59, ed. 1818.

Chapter V.

"Therefore, friends, As far as to the Sepulcher of Christ (Whose soldier now under whose blessed cross We are impressed and engag'd to fight,) Forthwith a power of English shall we levy Whose arms were moulded in their mother's womb, To chase these pagans, in those holy fields, Over whose acres walked those blessed feet, Which, fourteen hundred years ago, were nail'd, For our advantage, on the bitter cross."

In the mean time the crusade continued to be preached with great success in Europe. William, archbishop of Tyre, had proceeded to the courts of France and England, and had represented in glowing colors the miserable condition of Palestine, and the horrors and abominations which had been committed by the infidels in the holy city of Jerusalem. The English and French monarchs laid aside their private animosities, and agreed to fight under the same banner against the infidels, and towards the close of the month of May, in the second year of the siege of Acre, the royal fleets of Philip Augustus and Richard Cœur de Lion floated in triumph in the bay of Acre. The Templars had again lost their Grand Master, and Brother Robert de Sablè, or Sabloil, a valiant knight of the order, who had commanded a division of the English fleet on the voyage out, was placed (A. D. 1191) at the head of the fraternity.[*] The Templars performed prodigies of valor; "Their name and reputation, and the fame of their sanctity," says James of Vitry, bishop of Acre, "like a chamber of perfume sending forth a sweet odor, were diffused throughout the entire world, and all the congregation of the saints will recount their battles and glorious triumphs over the enemies of Christ; knights, indeed, from all parts of the earth, dukes, and princes, after their example, casting off the shackles of the world, and renouncing the pomps and vanities of this life, for Christ's sake, hastened to join them, and to participate in their holy profession and religion." They carried before them, at this time, to battle, "a bipartite banner of black and white, which they call *beauseant*, that is to say, in the Gallic tongue, *bienseant*, because they are fair and favorable to the friends of Christ, but black and terrible to his enemies."[†]

Saladin had passed the winter on the heights of Schaferan and Keruba. His vast army had been thinned and weakened by incessant

---

[*] Hist. de la maison de Sablè, liv. vi. chap. 5. p. 174, 175. Cotton MS. Nero, E. vi. p. 60. folio 466, where he is called Robert de Sambell. L'Art de Verif. tom. v. p. 347.
[†] *Jac. de Vitr.* Gesta Dei, cap. 65.

watching, by disease, and continual battles, and he himself was gradually sinking under the effects of a dreadful disease, which baffled all the skill of his medical attendants, and was gradually drawing him towards the grave. But the proud soul of the great chieftain never quailed; nor were his fire and energy at any time deadened. As soon as he heard of the arrival of the two powerful Christian monarchs, he sent envoys and messengers throughout all Mussulman countries, earnestly demanding succor, and on the Mussulman sabbath, after prayers had been offered up to God for the triumph of his arms, and the deliverance of Islam, he caused to be read, in all the mosques letters to the following effect;—

"In the name of God, the most *merciful* and *compassionate*. To all devout Believers in the one only God, and his prophet Mahomet, our Master. The armies of the infidels, numerous as the stars of heaven, have come forth from the remote countries situate beyond Constantinople, to wrest from us those conquests which have gladdened the hearts of all who put their trust in the Koran, and to dispute with us the possession of that holy territory whereon the Caliph Omar, in bygone days, planted the sacred standard of the Prophet. O men, prepare ye to sacrifice your lives and fortunes in defense of *Islam*. Your marches against the infidels, the dangers you encounter, the wounds you receive, and every minute action, down to the fording of a river, are they not written in the book of God? Thirst, hunger, fatigue, and death, will they not obtain for you the everlasting treasures of heaven, and open to your gaze the delicious groves and gardens of Paradise? In whatsoever place ye remain, O men, death hath dominion over you, and neither your houses, your lands, your wives, your children, nor the strongest towers, can defend you from his darts. Some of you, doubtless, have said one to another, Let us not go up to fight during the heat of summer; and others have exclaimed, Let us remain at home until the snow hath melted away from the mountain tops; but is not the fire of hell more terrible than the heats of summer, and are not its torments more insupportable than the winter's cold? Fear God, and not the *infidels*; hearken to the voice of your chief, for it is Saladin himself who calls you to rally around the standard of *Islam*. If you obey not, your families will be driven out of Syria, and God will put in their places a people better than you. Jerusalem, the holy, the sister of Medina and Mecca, will again fall into the power of the idolaters, who assign to God a son, and raise up an equal to the Most High. Arm yourselves then, with the buckler and the lance, scatter these children of fire, the wicked sons of hell, whom the sea hath vomited forth upon our shores, repeating to yourselves these words of the Koran, 'He who abandoneth his home and family to defend our holy religion, shall be rewarded with happiness, and with many friends.'"[*]

The siege of Acre was now pressed with great vigour; the combined fleets of France and England completely deprived the city of all supplies by sea, and the garrison was reduced to great straits. The sultan despaired

---

[*] *Michaud*, Hist. des Croisades, tom. ii. p. 383, 384.

of being able to save the city, and was sick, Bohadin tells us, both in mind and body. He could neither eat nor drink. At night he would lie down upon the side of the hill Aladajia, and indulge in some broken slumbers, but at morning's dawn he was on horseback, ordering his brazen drum to be sounded, and collecting his army together in battle array. At last letters were received, by means of pigeons, announcing that the garrison could hold out no longer. "Saladin gazed," says Bohadin, "long and earnestly at the city, his eyes were suffused with tears, and he sorrowfully exclaimed, '*Alas for Islam!*'" On the morning of the 12th of July, (A. D. 1191,) the kings of France and England, the Christian chieftains, and the Turkish emirs with their green banners, assembled in the tent of the Grand Master of the Temple, to treat for the surrender of Acre; and on the following day the gates were thrown open to the exulting warriors of the cross. The Templars took possession of their ancient quarters by the side of the sea, and mounted a large red-cross banner upon the tower of the Temple. They possessed themselves of three extensive localities along the sea-shore, and the Temple at Acre from thenceforth became the chief house of the order. Richard Cœur de Lion took up his abode with the Templars whilst Philip Augustus resided in the citadel.

By the terms of the surrender of Acre, the inhabitants were to pay a ransom of two hundred thousand pieces of gold for their lives and liberties; two thousand noble and five hundred inferior Christian captives were to be set at liberty, and the true cross, which had been taken at the battle of Tiberias, was to be restored to the Latin clergy. Two months were accorded for the performance of these conditions. I'Bn Alatsyr, who was then in Saladin's camp, tells us that Saladin had collected together 100,000 pieces of gold, that he was ready to deliver up the two thousand five hundred Christian captives, and restore the true cross, but his Mamlook emirs advised him not to trust implicitly to the good faith of the Christian adventurers of Europe for the performance of their part of the treaty, but to obtain from the Templars, of whose *regard for their word, and reverence for the sanctity of an oath*, the Moslems had, he tells us, a high opinion, a solemn undertaking for the performance, by the Christians, of the stipulations they had entered into. Saladin accordingly sent to the Grand Master of the Temple, to know if the Templars would guarantee the surrender to him of all the Moslem prisoners, if the money, the Christian captives, and the true cross, were sent to them; but the Grand Master declined giving any guarantee of the kind. The doubts about the agreement, and the delay in the execution of it, kindled the fierce indignation of the English monarch, and Richard Cœur de Lion led out all his prisoners, 2,000 in number, into the plain of Acre, and caused them all to be beheaded in sight of the sultan's camp!* During his voyage from Messina to Acre, king Richard had revenged himself on Isaac Comnenus, the ruler of the island of Cyprus, for an insult offered to the beautiful Berengaria,

---

* *Bohadin*, cap. 95-110, 112. *I'Bn Alat.* p. 520. *Bohadin*, cap. 115. Contin. Hist. col. 634, 635.

princess of Navarre, his betrothed bride. He had disembarked his troops, stormed the town of Limisso, and conquered the whole island; and shortly after his arrival at Acre he sold it to the Templars for 300,000 livres d'or.[*]

On the 21st of August, (A. D. 1191,) the Templars joined the standard of king Richard, and left Acre for the purpose of marching upon Jerusalem, by way of the sea-coast. They crossed the river Belus, and pitched their tents on its banks, where they remained for three days, to collect all the troops together. The most copious and authentic account of their famous march by the side of the king of England, through the hostile territories of the infidels, is contained in the history of king Richard's campaign, by Geoffrey de Vinisauf, who accompanied the crusaders on their expedition, and was an actor in the stirring events he describes.[†] On Sunday, the 25th of August, the Templars, under the conduct of their Grand Master, and the crusaders, under the command of king Richard, commenced their march towards Cæsarea. The army was separated into three divisions, the first of which was led by the Templars, and the last by the Hospitallers. The baggage moved on the right of the army, between the line of march and the sea, and the fleet, loaded with provisions, kept pace with the movements of the forces, and furnished them daily with the necessary supplies. Saladin, at the head of an immense force, exerted all his energies to oppose their progress, and the march to Jaffa formed one perpetual battle. Vast masses of cavalry hovered upon their flanks, cut off all stragglers, and put every prisoner that they took to death. The first night after leaving the Belus, the Templars and the crusaders encamped along the banks of the brook Kishon, around some wells in the plain between Acre and Caiphas. The next day they forded the brook, fought their way to Caiphas, and there halted for one day, in order that the reluctant crusaders, who were lingering behind at Acre, might come on and join them. On Wednesday, September 28, at dawn of day, they prepared to force the passes and defiles of Mount Carmel. All the heights were covered with dense masses of Mussulmen, who disputed the ground inch by inch. The Templars placed themselves in the van of the Christian army, and headed the leading column, whilst the cavalry of the Hospitallers protected the rear. They ascended the heights through a dense vegetation of dry thistles, wild vines, and prickly shrubs, drove the infidels before them, crossed the summit of Mount Carmel, and descending into the opposite plain, encamped for the night at the pass by the sea-shore, called "the narrow way," about eight miles from Caiphas. Here they recovered possession of a solitary tower, perched upon a rock overhanging the pass, which had been formerly built by the Templars, but had for some time past been in the hands of the Saracens. After lingering at this place an entire day, waiting the arrival of the fleet and the barges, laden with provisions, they recommenced their march (Friday, the 13th of August) to Tortura, the

---

[*] Contin. Hist. col. 633. *Trivet* ad ann. 1191. Chron. de S. Denis, lib. ii. cap. 7.
[†] Itinerarium regis Anglorum Ricardi et aliorum in terram Hierosolymorum auctore *Gaufrido de Vinisauf. Gale's* scriptores Historiæ Anglicanæ, tom. ii. p. 247-429.

ancient Dora, about seven miles distant. The Grand Master of the Temple, and his valiant knights, were, as usual, in the van, forcing a passage through the dense masses of the Moslems. The country in every direction around their line of march, was laid waste, and every day the attacks became more daring. The military friars had hitherto borne the brunt of the affray, but on the march to Tortura, they suffered such heavy loss, that king Richard determined the next day to take the command of the van in person, and he directed them to bring up the rear.

On the fifth day from their leaving the river Belus, the Templars and the crusaders approached the far-famed Cæsarea, where St. Paul so long resided, and where he uttered his eloquent oration before king Agrippa and Felix. But the town was no longer visible; the walls, the towers, the houses, and all the public buildings, had been destroyed by command of Saladin, and the place was left deserted and desolate. The Templars pitched their tents on the banks of the Crocodile river, the *flumen crocodilon* of Pliny, having been five days in performing the journey from the river Belus, a distance of only thirty-six miles. The army halted at Cæsarea during the whole of Sunday, the 1st of September, and high mass was celebrated by the clergy with great pomp and solemnity, amid the ruins of the city. On Monday, the 2nd of September, the tents of the Templars were struck at morning's dawn, and they commenced their march, with the leading division of the army, for the city of Jaffa, which is about thirty miles distant from Cæsarea. They forded the Crocodile river, and proceeded on their journey through a long and narrow valley, torn by torrents, and filled with vast masses of rock, which had been washed down from the heights by the winter rains. They had the sea on their right, and on their left, a chain of craggy eminences. Every advantage was taken by the enemy of the irregularity of the ground; the Mussulman archers lined the heights, and vast masses of cavalry were brought into action, wherever the nature of the country admitted of their employment. The Christian warriors were encumbered with their heavy armor and military accoutrements, which were totally unfit for the burning climate, yet they enthusiastically toiled on, perseveringly overcoming all obstacles.

Bohadin speaks with admiration of the valiant and martial bearing of the warriors of the cross, and of their fortitude and patient endurance during the long and trying march from Acre to Jaffa. "On the sixth day," says he, "the sultan rose at dawn as usual, and heard from his brother that the enemy were in motion. They had slept that night in suitable places about Cæsarea, and were now dressing and taking their food. A second messenger announced that they had begun their march; our brazen drum was sounded, all were alert, the sultan came out, and I accompanied him: he surrounded them with chosen troops, and gave the signal for attack. The archers were drawn out, and a heavy shower of arrows descended, still the enemy advanced.... Their foot soldiers were covered with thick-strung pieces of cloth, fastened together with rings, so as to resemble coats of mail. I saw with my own eyes several who had not one or two, but *ten darts sticking in their backs*! and yet marched on with a calm and cheerful step, without any trepidation. They had a division of infantry in reserve, to protect those who were weary, and look after the baggage. When any portion of their men became exhausted and gave way through fatigue or wounds, this division advanced and supported them. Their cavalry in the mean time kept together in close column, and never moved away from the infantry, except when they rushed to the charge. In vain did our troops attempt to lure them away from the foot soldiers; they kept steadily together in close order, protecting one another and slowly forcing their way with wonderful perseverance."

After a short march of only eight miles from Cæsarea, the Templars pitched their tents on the banks of the Nahr al Kasab, a small river, called by Geoffrey de Vinisauf "*the dead river*." Here they remained two nights, waiting for the fleet. On the 4th of September they resumed their march through a desert country which had been laid waste in every direction by command of Saladin. Finding their progress along the shore impeded by the tangled thickets, they quitted the plain and traversed the hills which run parallel with the sea. Their march was harassed by incessant charges of cavalry. The Templars brought up the rear of the army, and lost so many horses during the day, that they were almost driven to despair. At nightfall they descended to the beach, and encamped on the banks of a salt creek, close by the village of Om Khaled, near the ruins of the ancient Apollonias, having performed a march of five miles. The next morning, being Thursday, the 5th of September, the Templars set out at sunrise from the salt creek in battle array, having received intelligence that Saladin had prepared an ambuscade in the neighboring forest of Arsoof, and intended to hazard a general engagement. Scouts were sent on into the forest, who reported that the road was clear; and the whole army, ascending a slight rising ground, penetrated through the wood, and descended into the plain of Arsur or Arsoof. Through the midst of this plain rolls a mountain torrent, which takes its rise in the mountains of Ephraim, and on the opposite side of the stream Saladin had drawn up his army in battle array. The Templars encamped for the night on the right bank of the stream, having during the day marched nine miles.

On Saturday, the 7th of November, king Richard, having completed all his arrangements for a general engagement, drew up his army at dawn. The Templars again formed the first division, and were the first to cross the mountain torrent, and drive in Saladin's advanced guard. They were followed by Guy, king of Jerusalem, who was at the head of the division of Poitou, and then by the main body of the army under the personal conduct of king Richard. Geoffrey de Vinisauf tells us, that on all sides, far as the eye could reach, from the sea-shore to the mountains, nought was to be seen but a forest of spears, above which waved banners and standards innumerable. The wild Bedouins, the children of the desert, with skins blacker than soot, mounted on their fleet Arab mares, coursed with the rapidity of lightning over the vast plain, and darkened the air with clouds of missiles. They advanced to the attack with horrible screams and bellowings, which, with the deafening noise of the trumpets, horns, cymbals, and brazen kettle-drums, produced a clamor that resounded through the plain, and would have drowned even the thunder of heaven. King Richard received the attack in close and compact array, strict orders having previously been given that all the soldiers should remain on the defensive until two trumpets had been sounded in the front, two in the centre, and two in the rear of the army, when they were in their turn to become the assailants. The ferocious Turks, the wild Bedouins, and the swarthy Æthiopians, gathered around the advanced guard of the Templars, and kept up a distant and harassing warfare with their bows and arrows, whilst the swift cavalry of the Arabs dashed down upon the foot soldiers as if about to overwhelm them, then suddenly checking their horses, they wheeled off to the side, raising clouds of smothering, suffocating dust, which oppressed and choked the toiling warriors. The baggage moved on between the army and the sea, and the Christians thus continued slowly to advance under the scorching rays of an autumnal sun. "They moved," says Vinisauf, "inch by inch; it could not be called walking, for they were pushing and hacking their way through an overpowering crowd of resisting foes." Emboldened by their passive endurance, the Moslems approached nearer, and began to ply their darts and lances. The Marshall of the Hospital then charged at the head of his knights, without waiting for the signal, and in an instant the action became general. The clash of swords, the ringing of armor, and the clattering of iron clubs and flails, as they descended upon the helmets and bucklers of the European warriors, became mingled with the groans of the dying, and with the fierce cries of the wild Bedouins. Clouds of dust were driven up into the skies, and the plain became covered with banners, lances, and all kinds of arms, and with emblems of every color and device, torn and broken, and soiled with blood and dust. Cœur de Lion was to be seen everywhere in the thickest of the fight, and after a long and obstinate engagement the infidels were defeated; but amid the disorder of his troops Saladin remained on the plain without lowering his standard or suspending the sound of his brazen kettle-drums; he rallied his forces, retired upon Ramleh, and prepared to defend the mountain passes leading to Jerusalem. The Templars pushed on to Arsoof, and pitched their tents before the gates of the town.

On Monday, September 9th, the Christian forces moved on in battle array to Jaffa, the ancient Joppa, about eight miles from Arsoof. The Templars brought up the rear of the army; and after marching about five miles, they reached the banks of the Nahr el Arsoof, or river of Arsoof, which empties itself into the sea, about three miles from Jaffa, and pitched their tents in a beautiful olive grove on the sea-shore. Saladin laid waste all the country around them, drove away the inhabitants, and carried off all the cattle, corn, and provisions. The towns of Cæsarea, Ramleh, Jaffa, Ascalon, and all the villages, had been set on fire and burnt to ashes, and all the castles and fortresses within reach of the crusading army were dismantled and destroyed. Among these last were the castles of St. George, Galatia, Blancheward, Beaumont, Belvoir, Toron, Arnald, Mirabel, the castle of the plain, and many others. Every place, indeed, of strength or refuge was utterly destroyed by command of the inexorable Saladin. Bohadin tells us that the sultan mourned grievously over the destruction of the fair and beautiful city of Ascalon, saying to those around him, "By God, I would sooner lose my sons than touch a stone of this goodly city, but what God wills, and the good of Islam requires, must be done." The walls and fortifications of Ascalon were of great extent and stupendous strength, and an army of thirty thousand men was employed for fourteen days in the work of demolition. "The weeping families were removed from their houses, amid the most heart-rending confusion and misery," says Bohadin, "that I ever witnessed." Thousands of men were employed in dashing down the towers and the walls, and throwing the stones into the ditches and into the adjoining sea, and thousands were occupied in carrying away property and the contents of the public granaries and magazines. But ere half the effects had been removed, the impatient sultan ordered the town to be set on fire, "and soon," says Bohadin, "the raging flames were to be seen, tearing through the roofs, and curling around the minarets of the mosques." The great tower of the Hospitallers was the only edifice that resisted the flames and the exertions of the destroyers. It stood frowning in gloomy and solitary magnificence over the wide extended scene of ruin. "We must not depart," said Saladin, "until yon lofty tower has been brought low," and he ordered it to be filled with combustibles and set on fire. "It stood," says Bohadin, "by the sea-side, and was of amazing size and strength. I went into it, and examined it. The walls and the foundations were so solid, and of such immense width, that no battering machines could have produced the slightest effect upon them." Every heart was filled with sorrow and mourning at the sight of the scorched and blackened ruins of the once fair and beautiful Ascalon. "The city," says Bohadin, "was very elegant, and, in truth, exquisitely beautiful; its stupendous fortifications and lofty edifices possessed a majesty and grandeur which inspired one with awe."*

Ascalon, once the proudest of the five satrapies of the lords of the Philistines, is now uninhabited. The walls still lie scattered in huge fragments along the sea-shore, mixed with columns and broken pillars, which are wedged in among them, and amid the confused heaps of ruin which mark the site of the ancient city, not a single dwelling is now visible. "The king shall perish from Gaza," saith the prophet, "and Ascalon shall *not be inhabited.*"

On the 16th of October Cœur de Lion wrote a letter to Saladin, exhorting him to put an end to the holy war; but he demanded, as the price of peace, the restitution of Jerusalem, of Palestine, and the true cross.

---

* Erat autem perelegans ea et per sane venusta, validissimis mœnibus, celsissimis ædificiis, ita ut terrorem quendam gravitate et firmitate incuteret. *Bohadin*, apud *Schultens*, pp. 100-201. *Ibn Alat.* p. 523-525. *Vinisauf*, lib. iv.

"Jerusalem," says the king, "we consider to be the seat of our religion, and every one of us will perish rather than abandon it. Do you restore to us the country on this side Jordan, together with the holy cross, which is of no value to you, being in your eyes a mere piece of wood, but which we Christians prize greatly; we will then make peace, and repose from our incessant toils." "When the sultan," says Bohadin, who was himself a participator in the negotiation, "had read this letter, he took counsel with his emirs, and sent a reply to the following effect:—'The Holy City is held in as great reverence and estimation by the Moslems, as it is by you, ay, and in much greater reverence. From thence did our prophet Mahomet undertake his nocturnal journey to heaven, and upon that holy spot have the angels and the prophets at different periods been gathered together. Think not that we will ever surrender it. Never would we be so unmindful of our duty, and of that which it behoves us to do, as good Mussulmen. As to the country you speak of, it hath belonged to us of old, and if you took it from the Moslems when they were weak, they have taken it from you now that they are strong, as they have a right to do. You may continue the war, but God will not give you a stone of the land as a possession, for he hath given the country to the Moslems, to be by them plentifully and bountifully enjoyed. As to the cross, the reverence you pay to that bit of wood is a scandalous idolatry, disrespectful to the Most High, and hateful in the sight of God. We will, therefore, not give it to you, unless by so doing we can secure some great and manifest advantage for Islam.'"

On the 15th of November, the Templars marched out of Jaffa with king Richard and his army, and proceeded through the plain towards Jerusalem. As they advanced, Saladin slowly retired before them, laying waste the surrounding country, destroying all the towns and villages, and removing the inhabitants. Between noon and evening prayers, the sultan rode over to the city of Lidda, where St. Peter cured Æneas of the palsy, and employed his army, and a number of Christian slaves, in the destruction of the noble cathedral church erected by Justinian, and in the demolition of the town. He then fell back with his army to Beitnubah, a small village seated upon an eminence at the extremity of the plain of Ramleh, at the commencement of the hill country of Judea, and there encamped. "On Friday morning, at an early hour," says Bohadin, "the sultan mounted on horseback, and ordered me to accompany him. The rain fell in torrents. We marched towards Jerusalem. We dismounted at the monastery near the church of the Resurrection, and Saladin remained there to pass the night." The next morning at dawn the sultan again mounted on horseback, and rode round the walls of the Holy City. The whole population, together with two thousand Christian captives, had for weeks past been diligently employed in the reparation and reconstruction of the fortifications. Forty expert masons had arrived from Mossul, together with engineers and artificers from all the Mussulman countries of Asia. Two enormous towers were constructed, new walls were built, ditches were hollowed out of the rocks, and countless sums, says Bohadin, were spent upon the undertaking. Saladin's sons, his emirs, and his brother Adel, were charged with the inspection of the works; and the sultan himself was on horseback every morning from sunrise to sunset, stimulating the exertions of the workmen.

Whilst Saladin was making these vigorous preparations for the defense of Jerusalem, the Templars halted at Ramleh, the ancient Arimathea, situate in the middle of the plain, about nine miles from Jaffa, and lingered with the crusaders amid the ruins of the place for six weeks. In one of their midnight sallies they captured and brought into the camp more than two hundred oxen. On New Year's day, A. D. 1192, they marched to Beitnubah, and encamped at the entrance of the gorges and defiles leading to the Holy City; but these defiles were guarded by a powerful army under the personal command of Saladin, and the warriors of the cross ventured not to penetrate them. The weather became frightful; tempests of rain and hail, thunder and lightning, succeeded one another without cessation; the tents were torn to pieces by furious whirlwinds, and all the provisions of the army were destroyed by the wet. Many of the camels, horses, and beasts of burthen, perished from fatigue and the inclemency of the weather, and orders were given for a retrograde movement to the Mediterranean.

The Templars faithfully adhered to the standard of Cœur de Lion, and marched with him from Jaffa along the sea-coast to the ruins of Ascalon; but the other warriors, who owned no allegiance to the sovereign of England, abandoned him. The duke of Burgundy and the French proceeded to enjoy themselves in the luxurious city of Acre: some of the crusaders remained at Jaffa, and others went to Tyre and joined the rebellious party of Conrad, marquis of Montferrat. During the march from Jaffa to Ascalon, a distance of twenty-eight miles, the Templars suffered great hardships from hail-storms and terrific showers of rain and sleet; and on their arrival amid the ruins of the once flourishing city, they were nearly starved, by reason of the shipwreck of their vessels freighted with the necessary supplies. They pitched their tents among the ruins on the 20th of January, A. D. 1192, and for eight days were compelled to subsist on the scanty supply of food they had brought with them from Jaffa. During the winter they assisted king Richard in the reconstruction of the fortifications, and took an active part in the capture of several convoys and caravans which were traversing the adjoining desert from Egypt.

Whilst the Templars and the kings of England and Jerusalem thus remained under tents or in the open fields planning the overthrow and destruction of the infidels, Conrad, marquis of Montferrat, the pretender to the throne of the Latin kingdom, was traitorously intriguing with Saladin for the advancement of his own schemes of private ambition. He was supported by the duke of Burgundy and the French, and was at the head of a strong party who hated king Richard, and envied him the fame of his military exploits. The marquis of Montferrat went to Saladin's camp. He offered, Bohadin tells us, to make war upon king Richard, to attack the city of Acre, and join his forces to those of the sultan, provided the latter would cede to him the maritime towns of Tyre, Sidon, and Beirout, and all the sea-coast between them; but before these traitorous designs could be carried into execution, the marquis of Montferrat was assassinated. Six days after his death, the fickle princess Isabella, his wife, the younger sister of the late queen Isabella, married Henry, count of Champagne, nephew of king Richard. This nobleman possessed great influence in the councils of the Christian chieftains, and a general desire was manifested for his recognition as *king* of Jerusalem. The Templars accordingly induced Guy de Lusignan to abdicate in favor of Isabella and the count of Champagne, offering him as a recompense the wealthy and important island of Cyprus, which had been ceded to them, as before mentioned, by king Richard.

Cœur de Lion and the Templars remained encamped amid the ruins of Ascalon, and employed themselves in intercepting the caravans and convoys which were crossing the neighboring desert, from Egypt to Palestine, and succeeded in setting at liberty many Christian captives. The second Sunday after Trinity, the tents were struck, and they once more resumed their march, with the avowed intention of laying siege to the Holy City. They again proceeded, by easy stages, across the plain of Ramleh, and on the 11th of June, five days after they had left Ascalon, they reached Beitnubah where they again halted for the space of an entire month, under the pretence of waiting for Henry, the new king of Jerusalem, and the forces which were marching under his command from Tyre and Acre. But the rugged mountains between Beitnubah and Jerusalem were the real cause of delay, and again presented a barrier to their further progress. Saladin had fixed his station in the Holy City, leaving the main body of his army encamped among the mountains near Beitnubah. His Mamlooks appear to have been somewhat daunted by the long continuance of the war, and the persevering obstinacy of the Christians. They remembered the bloody fate of their brethren at Acre, and pressed the sultan to reserve *his* person and *their* courage for the future defense of their religion and empire. Bohadin gives a curious account of their misgivings and disinclination to stand a siege within the walls of Jerusalem. He made an address to them at the request of the sultan, and when he had ceased to speak, Saladin himself arose. A profound silence reigned throughout the assembly,—"they were as still as if BIRDS *were sitting on their* HEADS." "Praise be to God," said Saladin, "and may his blessing rest upon our Master, Mahomet, his prophet. Know ye not, O men, that ye are the only army of Islam, and its only defense. The lives and fortunes and children of the Moslems are committed to your protection. If ye now quail from the fight, (which God avert,) the foe will roll up these countries as the angel of the Lord rolls up the book in which the actions of men are written down." After an eloquent harangue from the sultan, Saifeddin Meshtoob, and the Mamlooks exclaimed with one voice, "My Lord, we are thy servants and slaves; we swear, by God, that none of us will quit thee so long as we shall live."* But the anxiety of Saladin and the Mamlooks was speedily calmed by the retreat of the Christian soldiers who fell back upon the sea-coast and their shipping. The health of king Richard and of Saladin was in a declining state, they were mutually weary of the war, and a treaty of peace was at last entered into between the sultan, the king of England, Henry, king of Jerusalem, and the Templars and Hospitallers, whereby it was stipulated that the Christian pilgrims should enjoy the privilege of visiting the Holy City and the Holy Sepulcher without tribute or molestation; that the cities of Tyre, Acre, and Jaffa, with all the sea-coast between them, should belong to the Latins, but that the fortifications recently erected at Ascalon should be demolished. Immediately after the conclusion of peace, king Richard, being anxious to take the shortest and speediest route to his dominions, induced Robert de Sablè, the Grand Master of the Temple, to place a galley of the order at his disposal, and it was determined that, whilst the royal fleet pursued its course with queen Berengaria through the Straits of Gibraltar to Britain, Cœur de Lion himself, disguised in the habit of a Knight Templar, should secretly embark and make for one of the ports of the Adriatic. The plan was carried into effect on the night of the 25th of October, and king Richard set sail, accompanied by some attendants, and four trusty Templars. The habit he had assumed, however, protected him not, as is well known, from the cowardly vengeance of the base duke of Austria.[*]

In the year 1194, Robert de Sablè, the Grand Master of the Temple, was succeeded by Brother Gilbert Horal or Erail, who had previously filled the high office of Grand Preceptor of France.[†] The Templars, to retain and strengthen their dominion in Palestine, commenced the erection of several strong fortresses, the stupendous ruins of many of which remain to this day. The most famous of these was the Pilgrim's Castle, which commanded the coast-road from Acre to Jerusalem. It derived its name from a solitary tower erected by the early Templars to protect the passage of the pilgrims through a dangerous pass in the mountains bordering the sea-coast, and was commenced shortly after the removal of the chief house of the order from Jerusalem to Acre. A small promontory which juts out into the sea a few miles below Mount Carmel, was converted into a fortified camp. Two gigantic towers, a hundred feet in height and seventy-four feet in width, were erected, together with enormous bastions connected together by strong walls furnished with all kinds of military engines. The vast inclosure contained a palace for the use of the Grand Master and knights, a magnificent church, houses and offices for the serving brethren and hired soldiers, together with pasturages, vineyards, gardens, orchards, and fishponds. On one side of the walls was the salt sea, and on the other, within the camp, were delicious springs of fresh water. The garrison amounted to four thousand men in time of war.[‡] Considerable

---

[*] *Bohadin*, apud *Schultens*, cap. 156, p. 235, 236.
[*] *Vinisauf*, lib. vi. *Bohadin*, p. 238. *Abulfeda*, p. 51. Contin. Hist. col. 638, 641.
[†] *Cotton* MS. Nero E. VI. 23, i.

remains of this famous fortress are still visible on the coast, a few miles to the south of Acre. It is still called by the Levantines, *Castel Pellegrino.* Pocock describes it as "very magnificent, and so finely built, that it may be reckoned one of the things that are best worth seeing in these parts." "It is encompassed," says he, "with two walls fifteen feet thick, the inner wall on the east side cannot be less than forty feet high, and within it there appear to have been some very grand apartments. The offices of the fortress seem to have been at the west end, where I saw an oven fifteen feet in diameter. In the castle there are remains of a fine lofty church of ten sides, built in a light gothic taste: three chapels are built to the three eastern sides, each of which consists of five sides, excepting the opening to the church; in these it is probable the three chief altars stood." Irby and Mangles, referring at a subsequent period to the ruins of the church, describe it as a double hexagon, and state that the half then standing had six sides. Below the cornice are human heads and heads of animals in alto relievo, and the walls are adorned with a double line of arches in the gothic style, the architecture light and elegant.

On the death of Saladin, (13th of March, A. D. 1193,) the vast and powerful empire that he had consolidated fell to pieces, the title to the thrones of Syria and Egypt was disputed between the brother and the sons of the deceased sultan; and the pope, thinking that these dissensions presented a favorable opportunity for the recovery of the Holy City, caused another (the fourth) crusade to be preached. Two expeditions organized in Germany proceeded to Palestine and insisted on the immediate commencement of hostilities, in defiance of the truce. The Templars and Hospitallers, and the Latin Christians, who were in the enjoyment of profound peace under the faith of treaties, insisted upon the impolicy and dishonesty of such a proceeding, but were reproached with treachery and lukewarmness in the Christian cause; and the headstrong Germans sallying out of Acre, committed some frightful ravages and atrocities upon the Moslem territories. The infidels immediately rushed to arms; their intestine dissensions were at once healed, their chiefs extended to one another the hand of friendship, and from the distant banks of the Nile, from the deserts of Arabia, and the remote confines of Syria, the followers of Mahomet rallied again around the same banner, and hastened once more to fight in defense of *Islam.* Al-Ma-lek, Al-a-del, Abou-becr Mohammed, the renowned brother of Saladin, surnamed *Saif-ed-din,* "Sword of the Faith," took the command of the Moslem force, and speedily proved himself a worthy successor to the great "Conqueror of Jerusalem." He concentrated a vast army, and by his rapid movements speedily compelled the Germans to quit all the open country, and throw themselves into the fortified city of Jaffa. By a well-executed manœuvre, he then induced them to make a rash sortie from the town, and falling suddenly upon the main body of their forces, he defeated them with terrific slaughter. He entered the city, pell-

---

‡ *Jac. de Vitry*, Gest. Dei, tom i. pars. 9, p. 1113.

mell, with the fugitives, and annihilated the entire German force. The small garrison of the Templars maintained in the Temple of Jaffa was massacred, the fortifications were razed to the ground, and the city was left without a single Christian inhabitant.[*] Such were the first results of this memorable crusade.

The Templars on the receipt of this disastrous intelligence, assembled their forces, and marched out of the city of Acre, in the cool of the evening, to encamp at Caiphas, four miles distant from the town. The king placed himself at the castle window to see them pass, and was leaning forward watching their progress across the neighboring plain, when he unfortunately overbalanced himself, and fell headlong into the moat. He was killed on the spot, and queen Isabella was a second time a widow, her divorced husband, Humphry de Thoron being, however, still alive. She had three daughters by king Henry, Mary, who died young, Alix, and Philippine. Radolph of Tiberias became an aspirant for the hand of the widowed queen, but the Templars rejected his suit because he was too poor, declaring that they would not give the queen and the kingdom to a man who had nothing. They sent the chancellor of the emperor of Germany, who was staying at Acre, to Amauri, king of Cyprus, offering him the hand of Isabella and the crown of the Latin kingdom. Amauri had succeeded to the sovereignty of the island on the death of his brother Guy de Lusignan, (A. D. 1194,) and he eagerly embraced the offer. He immediately embarked in his galleys at Nicosia, landed at Acre, and was married to queen Isabella and solemnly crowned a few weeks after the death of the late king.

On the arrival of a second division of the crusaders, under the command of the dukes of Saxony and Brabant, the Templars again took the field and overthrew the Arab cavalry in a bloody battle, fought in the plain between Tyre and Sidon. The entire Mussulman army was defeated, and Saif-ed-din, desperately wounded, fell back upon Damascus. Beirout was then besieged and taken, and the fall of this important city was followed by the reduction of Gabala and Laodicea, and all the maritime towns between Tripoli and Jaffa.[†] Intelligence now reached Palestine of the death of the emperor Henry VI., whereupon all the German chieftains hurried home, to pursue upon another theatre their own schemes of private ambition. After having provoked a terrific and sanguinary war they retired from the contest, leaving their brethren in the East to fight it out as they best could. These last, on viewing their desolated lands, their defenseless cities, and their dwellings destroyed by fire, exclaimed with bitterness and truth, "Our fellow Christians and self-styled allies found us at *peace*, they have left us at WAR. They are like those ominous birds of passage whose appearance portends the coming tempest." To add to the difficulties and misfortunes of the Latin Christians, a quarrel sprung up between the Templars and Hospitallers touching their respective rights to certain property in

---

[*] *Michaud*, Hist. des Croisades, tom. iii. p. 39.
[†] *Othonis de S. Blazio*, apud *Martene*, tom. vi. p. 886. Contin. Hist. ib. tom. v.

Palestine. The matter was referred to the pope, who gravely admonished them, representing that the infidels would not fail to take advantage of their dissensions, to the great injury of the Holy Land, and to the prejudice of all Christendom. He exhorts them to maintain unity and peace with one another, and appoints certain arbitrators to decide the differences between them. The quarrel was of no great importance, nor of any long duration, for the same year pope Innocent wrote to both orders, praising them for their exertions in the cause of the cross, and exhorting them strenuously and faithfully to support with all their might the new king of Jerusalem.[*]

In the year 1201 the Grand Master of the Temple, Gilbert Horal, was succeeded by brother Philip Duplessies, or De Plesseis,[†] who found himself, shortly after his accession to power, engaged in active hostilities with Leon I., king of Armenia, who had taken possession of the castle of Gaston, which belonged to the Knights Templars. The Templars drove King Leon out of Antioch, compelled him to give up the castle of Gaston and sue for peace. A suspension of arms was agreed upon; the matters in dispute between them were referred to the pope, and were eventually decided in favor of the Templars. The Templars appear at this period to have recovered possession of most of their castles and strongholds in the principalities of Tripoli and Antioch. Taking advantage of the dissensions between the neighboring Moslem chieftains, they gradually drove the infidels across the Orontes, and restored the strong mountain districts to the Christian arms. Some European vessels having been plundered by Egyptian pirates, the Templars unfolded their war-banner, and at midnight they marched out of Acre, with the king of Jerusalem, to make reprisals on the Moslems; they extended their ravages to the banks of the Jordan, and collected together a vast booty, informing their brethren in Acre of their movements by letters tied to the necks of pigeons. Coradin, sultan of Damascus, assembled a large body of forces at Sepphoris, and then marched against the hill fort Doc, which belonged to the Templars. The place was only three miles distant from Acre, and the population of the town was thrown into the utmost consternation. But the military friars, assembling their forces from all quarters, soon repulsed the invaders, and restored tranquillity to the Latin kingdom.

At this period king Amauri, having partaken somewhat too plentifully of a favorite dish of fish, was seized with an alarming illness, and died at Acre on the 1st of April, A. D. 1205. He had issue by Isabella one daughter; but before the close of the year both the mother and the child died. The crowns of Jerusalem and Cyprus, which were united on the heads of Amauri and Isabella, were now after their decease again divided. Mary, the eldest daughter of the queen, by the famous Conrad, marquis of Montferrat, was acknowledged heiress to the crown of the Latin kingdom, and Hugh de Lusignan, the eldest son of Amauri by his first wife, succeeded to the sovereignty of the island of Cyprus. This young prince

---

[*] Lib. i. ii. epistolarum. *Inn. III.*, epist. 138, 567.
[†] *Cotton* MS. Nero E. VI., p. 60, fol. 466. *Ducange*, Gloss. tom. vi. p. 1036.

married the princess Alice, daughter of Isabella by king Henry, count of Champagne, and half sister to the young queen Mary by the mother's side. The young and tender princess who had just now succeeded to the throne of the Latin kingdom, was fourteen years of age, and the Templars and Hospitallers became her natural guardians and protectors. They directed the military force of the Latin empire in the field, and the government of the country in the cabinet: and defended the kingdom during her minority with zeal and success against all the attacks of the infidels. As soon as the young queen arrived at marriageable years, the Templars and Hospitallers sent over the bishop of Acre and Aimar, lord of Cæsarea, to Philip Augustus, king of France, requesting that monarch to select a suitable husband for her from among his princes and nobles. The king's choice fell upon the count of Brienne, who left France with a large cortége of knights and foot soldiers, and arrived in Palestine on the 13th of September. The day after his arrival he was married to the young queen, who had just then attained her seventeenth year, and on the succeeding Michaelmas-day, he was crowned king of Jerusalem.

At this period the truce with the infidels had expired, the Grand Master of the Temple having previously refused to renew it. Hostilities consequently recommenced, and the Templars again took the field with the new king of Jerusalem and his French knights. Some important successes were gained over the Moslems, but the Latin kingdom was thrown into mourning by the untimely death of the young queen Mary. She died at Acre, in the twentieth year of her age, leaving by the king her husband, an infant daughter, named Violante. The count de Brienne continued, after the example of Guy de Lusignan, to wear the crown, and exercise all the functions of royalty, notwithstanding the death of the queen. Pope Innocent III. had long been endeavoring to throw an additional lustre around his pontificate by achieving the re-conquest of Jerusalem. By his bulls and apostolical letters he sought to awaken the ancient enthusiasm of Christendom in favor of the holy war; and following the example of pope Urban, he at last called together a general council of the church to aid in the arming of Europe for the recovery of the Holy City. This council assembled at Rome in the summer of the year 1215, and decreed the immediate preaching of another crusade. The emperor Frederick, John, king of England, the king of Hungary, the dukes of Austria and Bavaria, and many prelates, nobles, and knights, besides crowds of persons of inferior degree, assumed the cross. Some prepared to fulfill their vow, and embark for the far East, but the far greater portion of them paid sums of money to the clergy to be exempt from the painful privations, dangers, and difficulties consequent upon the long voyage. The king of Hungary, and the dukes of Austria and Bavaria, were the first to set out upon the pious enterprise. They placed themselves at the head of an army composed of many different nations, embarked from Venice, and landed at the port of St. Jean d'Acre at the commencement of the year 1217. The day after the feast of All Saints they marched out of Acre, and pitched their tents upon the banks of the brook Kishon; and the next day the patriarch of Jerusalem, and the Templars and Hospitallers, came with great pomp and solemnity into the camp, bearing with them "a piece of the true cross!" It was pretended that this piece of the cross had been cut off before the battle of Tiberias, and carefully preserved by the oriental clergy. The kings and princes went out bare-foot and uncovered to receive the holy relic; they placed it at the head of their array, and immediately commenced a bold and spirited march to the Jordan.

Under the guidance of the Templars they followed the course of the brook Kishon, by the ruins of Endor, to the valley of Jezreel, and traversing the pass through the mountains of Gilboa to Bisan or Scythopolis, they descended into the valley of the Jordan, and pitched their tents on the banks of that sacred river. From Bisan they proceeded up the valley of the Jordan to the lake of Tiberias, skirted its beautiful shores to Bethsaida, passing in front of the strong citadel of Tiberias, and then proceeded across the country to Acre, without meeting an enemy to oppose their progress. The Templars then pressed the Christian chieftains to undertake without further loss of time the siege of the important fortress of Mount Thabor, and at the commencement of the autumn the place was regularly invested, but the height and steepness of the mountain rendered the transportation of heavy battering machines and military engines to the summit a tedious and laborious undertaking. The troops suffered from the want of water, their patience was exhausted, and the four kings and their followers, being anxious to return home, speedily found excuses for the abandonment of the siege. The customary scene of disorder and confusion then ensued; a large body of Arab horsemen, which had crossed the Jordan, infested the rear of the retiring crusaders. The disordered pilgrims and foot soldiers were panic-stricken, and fled to the hills; and the retreat would have been disastrous, but for the gallant conduct of the Templars and Hospitallers, who covered the rear and sustained the repeated charges of the Arab cavalry. The two orders sustained immense loss in men and horses, and returned in sorrow and disgust to their quarters at Acre.[*]

The Grand Master Philip Duplessies had been unable to take part in the expedition; he was confined to the Temple at Acre by a dangerous illness, of which he died a few days after the return of the Templars from Mount Thabor. Immediately after his decease a general chapter of knights was assembled, and Brother William de Chartres was elevated (A. D. 1217) to the vacant dignity of Grand Master.[†] Shortly after his election he was called upon to take the command of a large fleet fitted out by the order of the Temple against the Egyptians. He set sail from Acre in the month of May, cast anchor in the mouth of the Nile, and proceeded, in conjunction with the crusaders, to lay siege to the wealthy and populous city of Damietta. The Templars pitched their tents in the plain on the left bank of the Nile, opposite the town, and surrounded their position with a ditch and

---

[*] *Bernardus* Thesaurarius, Script, rer. Italicar. tom. vii. cap. 187. p. 823.
[†] *Cotton*, MS. Nero E. VI. fol. 23 i.—p. 60, fol. 466. *Ducange*, Gloss. tom. vi. col. 1036.

a wall. They covered the river with their galleys, and with floating rafts furnished with military engines, and directed their first attacks against a castle in the midst of the stream, called the castle of Taphnis.

Large towers were erected upon floating rafts to protect their operations, but they were constantly destroyed by the terrible Greek fire, which was blown out of long copper tubes, and could be extinguished with nothing but vinegar and sand. At last a number of flat-bottomed boats were lashed together, and a tower, higher than the castle of the enemy, was erected upon them. It was ninety feet in height, thirteen cubits in length, and was divided into platforms or stages, filled with archers; numerous loop-holes were pierced in the walls, and the ponderous structure was thickly covered in every part with raw hides, to preserve it from the liquid fire of the enemy. Upon the top of the tower was a drawbridge, which could be raised and lowered with chains, and on each platform were grappling irons, to be made fast to the battlements and parapets of the castle. On the 24th of August, the vast floating tower was towed to the point of attack, and the left bank of the Nile was covered with a long procession of priests and monks, who traversed the winding shore, with naked feet and uplifted hands, praying to the God of battles for victory. Whilst the infidels were hurrying to the summit of the castle of Taphnis, to direct the Greek fire upon the wooden tower, and to pour boiling oil and red-hot sand upon the heads of the assailants, some Templars, who were stationed in the lowest platform of the structure near the water, threw out their grapling-irons, and made a lodgment upon the causeway in front of the castle. Without a moment's delay, they handed out a battering-ram, and with one blow knocked in the door of the fortress. Combustibles were immediately thrown into the interior of the building, the place was enveloped in smoke and flames, and the garrison surrendered at discretion. The vast chain between the castle and the river was then rent asunder, and the large ships of the crusaders ascended the Nile, and took up a position in front of the town.

Toward the close of autumn, when the inundation of the Nile was at its height, a strong north wind arose, and impeded the descent of the waters to the Mediterranean. The Christian camp was overflowed, the Templars lost all their provisions, arms, and baggage; and when the waters receded, several large fish were found in their tents. This catastrophe was followed by an epidemic fever, which carried off the Grand Master, William de Chartres, and many of the brethren. The Grand Master was succeeded (A. D. 1218) by the veteran warrior, Brother Peter de Montaigu, Grand Preceptor of Spain. At this period the renowned Saif-ed-din, "sword of the faith," the brother and successor of Saladin, died, having appointed his *fifteen* sons to separate and independent commands in his vast dominions. After his decease they quarrelled with one another for the supremacy, and the Templars crossed the Nile to take advantage of the dispute. The infidels fiercely opposed their landing, and one of the Temple vessels being boarded by an overpowering force, the military friars cut a hole in the bottom of it with their hatchets, and all on board met with a watery grave in the deep bosom of the Nile. When the landing was effected, the Templars were the first to charge the enemy; the Moslems fled and abandoned their tents, provisions, and arms, and their camp was given up to plunder. A trench was then drawn around the city of Damietta, and the army took up a position which enabled them to deprive the town of all succor. Two bridges of boats were thrown across the Nile to communicate between the new camp of the crusaders and the one they had just quitted; and one of these bridges was placed under the protection of the Templars. After many brilliant exploits and sanguinary encounters, Damietta was reduced to great straits; terms of surrender were offered and refused; and on the 5th of November a wooden bridge was thrown over the ditch; scaling ladders were reared against the battlements, and the town was taken by assault. When the Templars entered the place, they found the plague in every house, and the streets strewed with the dead.

Immediately after the capture of Damietta, the Grand Master of the Temple returned with the king of Jerusalem to Palestine, to oppose a fresh army of Moslems who, under the command of Coradin, a famous chieftain, had invaded the country, blockaded the city of Acre, and laid siege to the Pilgrim's Castle. In their intrenched camp at this castle, the Templars mustered a force of upwards of four thousand men, who valiantly and successfully defended the important position against the obstinate and persevering attacks of the infidels. During the different assaults upon the place, Coradin lost six emirs, two hundred Mamlooks, and a number of archers; and on one day alone he had a hundred and twenty valuable horses slain, one of which cost fourteen thousand marks.[*] The Templars sent urgent letters to the pope for succor. They exhorted his holiness to compel the emperor Frederick to perform his vow, and no longer to permit the crusaders to compound with money for the non-fulfilment of their engagements, declaring that such compositions had been most injurious to the cause of the cross. The Grand Master also wrote to the pope, complaining to his holiness of the misapplication by the clergy of the money collected from their flocks, towards the expenses of the holy war, declaring that not a twentieth part of it ever reached the empty treasury of the Latin kingdom. The holy pontiff, in his reply, protests that he has not himself fingered a farthing of the money. "If you have not received it," says he, "it is not our fault, it is because we have not been obeyed."

In a mournful letter to the bishop of Ely, the Grand Master gives the following gloomy picture of the state of affairs. "Brother Peter de Montaigu, Master of the Knights of the Temple, to the reverend brother in Christ, N, by the grace of God, bishop of Ely, salvation. We proceed by these our letters to inform your paternity how we have managed the affairs of our Lord Jesus Christ since the capture of Damietta and the castle of

---

[*] *Bern* Thesaur. cap. 190-200, Script. Ital. tom. viii. *Jac. de Vitr.* p. 1135-1143. *Martene.* Thesaur. anec. tom. iii. col. 294, &c. *Ibn Ferat* p. 770. *Ibn Alat.* p. 538. *Oliverii*, Hist. Damiatana, tom. ii. cap. 31.

Taphnis. Be it known to you, that during the spring passage to Europe, immediately subsequent to the capture of Damietta, so many of the pilgrims returned home, that the residue of them scarce sufficed to garrison the town, and the two intrenched camps. Our lord the legate, and the clergy, earnestly desiring the advancement of the army of Jesus Christ, constantly and diligently exhorted our people forthwith to take the field against the infidels; but the chieftains from these parts, and from beyond the sea, perceiving that the army was totally insufficient in point of numbers to guard the city and the camps, and undertake further offensive operations for the advancement of the faith of Jesus Christ, would on no account give their consent. The sultan of Egypt, at the head of a vast number of the perfidious infidels, lies encamped a short distance from Damietta, and he has recently constructed bridges across both branches of the Nile, to impede the further progress of our Christian soldiers. He there remains, quietly awaiting their approach; and the forces under his command are so numerous, that the faithful cannot quit their intrenchments around Damietta, without incurring imminent risk. In the mean time, we have surrounded the town, and the two camps, with deep trenches, and have strongly fortified both banks of the river as far as the sea-coast, expecting that the Lord will console and comfort us with speedy succor. But the Saracens, perceiving our weakness, have already armed numerous galleys, and have inflicted vast injury upon us by intercepting all the succors from Europe; and such has been our extreme want of money, that we have been unable for a considerable period to man and equip our galleys and send them to sea for our protection. Finding, however, that the losses go on increasing to the great detriment of the cause of the cross, we have now managed to arm some galleys, galliots, and other craft, to oppose the ships of the infidels.

"Also be it known to you that Coradin, sultan of Damascus, having collected together a vast army of Saracens, hath attacked the cities of Tyre and Acre; and as the garrisons of these places have been weakened to strengthen our forces in Egypt, they can with difficulty sustain themselves against his attacks. Coradin hath also pitched his tents before our fortress, called the Pilgrim's Castle, and hath put us to immense expense in the defense of the place. He hath also besieged and subjugated the castle of Cæsarea of Palestine. We have now for a long time been expecting the arrival of the emperor, and the other noble personages who have assumed the cross, by whose aid we hope to be relieved from our dangers and difficulties, and to bring all our exertions to a happy issue. But if we are disappointed of the succor we expect in the ensuing summer (which God forbid) all our newly-acquired conquests, as well as the places that we have held for ages past, will be left in a very doubtful condition. We ourselves, and others in these parts, are so impoverished by the heavy expenses we have incurred in prosecuting the affairs of Jesus Christ, that we shall be unable to contribute the necessary funds, unless we speedily receive succor and subsidies from the faithful. Given at Acre, xii. kal. Octob., A. D. 1220."[*]

The urgent solicitations of the Templars for money created loud murmurs in England, and excited the wrath of the great historian, Matthew Paris, the monk of St. Albans, who hated the order on account of its vast privileges, and the sums it constantly drew away from the hands of other religious bodies. The clergy, who had probably misapplied the money collected by them for the relief of the Holy Land, joined eagerly in an outcry against the Templars, accusing them of squandering their funds upon magnificent churches and expensive buildings in Europe, or of spending them at home in luxurious ease at their different preceptories, instead of faithfully employing them in the prosecution of the holy war. The pope instituted an inquiry into the truth of the charges, and wrote to his legate at Damietta, to the patriarch of Jerusalem, and the principal chieftains of the army of the crusaders, for information. In their reply, the legate and the patriarch state that the charges were untrue, and that the Templars had expended their money in the prosecution of the siege of Damietta, and had impoverished themselves by their heavy expenses in Egypt. During the summer of the year 1221, considerable succors arrived in Palestine and Egypt from Europe; the troops of the sultan of Damascus were repulsed and driven beyond the frontier of the Latin kingdom, and the Grand Master of the Temple returned to Damietta to superintend the military operations in Egypt. Cardinal Pelagius, the papal legate, though altogether ignorant of the art of war, had unfortunately assumed the inconsistent character of commander-in-chief of the army of the cross. Contrary to the advice of the Templars, he urged the crusaders, during the autumnal season, when the waters of the Nile were rising, to march out of Damietta to undertake an expedition against Grand Cairo. The disastrous results of that memorable campaign are narrated in the following letter from Peter de Montaigu to the Master of the English province of the order.

"Brother Peter de Montaigu, humble Master of the soldiers of Christ, to our vicegerent and beloved brother in Christ, Alan Marcell, Preceptor of England. Hitherto we have had favorable information to communicate unto you touching our exertions in the cause of Christ; now, alas! such have been the reverses and disasters which our sins have brought upon us in the land of Egypt, that we have nothing but ill news to announce. After the capture of Damietta, our army remained for some time in a state of inaction, which brought upon us frequent complaints and reproaches from the eastern and the western Christians. At length, after the feast of the holy apostles, the legate of the holy pontiff, and all our soldiers of the cross, put themselves in march by land and by the Nile, and arrived in good order at the spot where the sultan was encamped, at the head of an immense number of the enemies of the cross. The river Taphneos, an arm of the great Nile, flowed between the camp of the sultan and our forces, and

[*] Epist. apud *Matt. Par.* p. 312, 313. *Martene*, tom. v. col. 1480.

being unable to ford this river, we pitched our tents on its banks, and prepared bridges to enable us to force the passage. In the mean time, the annual inundation rapidly increased, and the sultan, passing his galleys and armed boats through an ancient canal, floated them into the Nile below our positions, and intercepted our communications with Damietta.".... "Nothing now was to be done but to retrace our steps. The sultans of Aleppo, Damascus, Hems, and Coilanbar, the two brothers of the sultan, and many chieftains and kings of the pagans, with an immense multitude of infidels who had come to their assistance, attempted to cut off our retreat. At night we commenced our march, but the infidels cut through the embankments of the Nile, the water rushed along several unknown passages and ancient canals, and encompassed us on all sides. We lost all our provisions, many of our men were swept into the stream, and the further progress of our Christian warriors was forthwith arrested. The waters continued to increase upon us, and in this terrible inundation we lost all our horses and saddles, our carriages, baggage, furniture, and moveables, and everything that we had. We ourselves could neither advance nor retreat, and knew not whither to turn. We could not attack the Egyptians on account of the great lake which extended itself between them and us; we were without food, and being caught and pent up like fish in a net, there was nothing left for us but to treat with the sultan.

"We agreed to surrender Damietta, with all the prisoners which we had in Tyre and at Acre, on condition that the sultan restored to us the wood of the true cross and the prisoners that he detained at Cairo and Damascus. We, with some others, were deputed by the whole army to announce to the people of Damietta the terms that had been imposed upon us. These were very displeasing to the bishop of Acre, (James de Vitry, the historian,) to the chancellor, and some others, who wished to defend the town, a measure which we should indeed have greatly approved of, had there been any reasonable chance of success; for we would rather have been thrust into perpetual imprisonment than have surrendered, to the shame of Christendom, this conquest to the infidels. But after having made a strict investigation into the means of defense, and finding neither men nor money wherewith to protect the place, we were obliged to submit to the conditions of the sultan, who, after having extracted from us an oath and hostages, accorded to us a truce of eight years. During the negotiations the sultan faithfully kept his word, and for the space of fifteen days furnished our soldiers with the bread and corn necessary for their subsistence. Do you, therefore, pitying our misfortunes, hasten to relieve them to the utmost of your ability. Farewell."[*]

Shortly after the disasters in Egypt, and the conclusion of the eight years' truce with the infidels, John de Brienne, the titular king of Jerusalem, prepared to bid adieu for ever to Palestine. Since the death of the young queen, his wife, he had regarded his kingdom as a place of exile,

---

[*] *Matt. Par.* p. 314. See also another letter, p. 313.

and was anxious to escape from the toil and turmoil and incessant warfare in which his feeble dominions were continually involved. His daughter Violante, the young queen of Jerusalem, had just attained her thirteenth year, and the king was anxious to seek a suitable husband for her from among the European princes. Accompanied by the fair Violante, he landed in Italy, and attended a council of the clergy and the laity assembled at Ferentino, in the Campagna di Roma, in the summer of the year 1223. Pope Honorius the Third, the emperor Frederick, the patriarch of the Holy City, the bishop of Bethlehem, the Grand Master of the Hospital, and one of the Grand Preceptors of the Temple, were present at this council, and the pope urged the emperor to fulfill the vow which he had made eight years before to lead an army to the succor of the Holy Land; offering him the hand of the lovely Violante, and with her the crown of the Latin kingdom. This offer was accepted, the nuptials were shortly afterwards celebrated, and the emperor solemnly took his oath upon the Holy Gospel to lead in person a great expedition for the recovery of Jerusalem.

Violante had been accompanied from Palestine by a female cousin, possessed of powerful charms and many graceful accomplishments. The emperor became captivated with her beauty, he dis honored her, and treated his young wife, who was a mere child in years, with coldness and neglect. He then, in the middle of August, A. D. 1227, set sail for Acre with a powerful army, and was at sea three days, when he became sea-sick, and returned to land on a plea of ill health. He was consequently publicly excommunicated by the pope in the great church of Anagni. Without troubling himself to obtain a reconciliation with the holy see, he again embarked with his forces, and arrived in the port of St. Jean d'Acre on the 8th of September, A. D. 1228. The pope then sent letters to Palestine denouncing him as publicly excommunicated, and commanded the Templars not to join his standard. They accordingly refused to take the field, and as the forces under the command of the emperor did not amount to ten thousand men, he was obliged to remain inactive during the winter. He, however, carried on friendly negotiations with the infidels, and a treaty was entered into whereby Jerusalem was nominally surrendered to him. It was stipulated that the Christian and Mussulman religion should meet with equal toleration in the Holy City; that the followers of Mahomet should possess the Mosque of Omar, and the Christians the great church of the Resurrection; that the Moslems should be governed by their own laws, and that the court of judicature in the forum of Al Rostak should be under the direction of a Moslem governor.[*]

Immediately after the conclusion of this curious treaty, the emperor made a peaceful march to the Holy City with a few attendants, and performed the solemn farce of crowning himself in the church of the Resurrection. After a stay of a few days in Jerusalem, he hurried back to Acre to prepare for his departure for Europe. No Christian garrison was

---

[*] *Ibn Schunah*, ad ann. Hejir 626. *Tyr.* Contin. Hist. col. 695-699. *Marin Sanut.* p. 213.

C. G. Addison

established in the city, nor did the Templars and Hospitallers venture to
return to their ancient abodes. His conduct, immediately preceding his
departure, is thus described in a letter from the patriarch of Jerusalem to
the pope. "The emperor placed archers at the gates of the city of Acre, to
prevent the Templars from entering into or proceeding out of the town. He
moreover placed soldiers in all the streets leading to our quarter and the
Temple, keeping us in a state of siege; and it is evident that he has never
treated the Saracens half so badly as he has treated the Christians. For a
long time he refused to permit any provisions to be brought to us, and
instructed his soldiers to insult the priests and the Templars whenever they
met them. He moreover got possession of the magazines, and removed all
the military machines and arms, preserved for the defense of the city, with
a view of rendering good service to his kind friend the sultan of Egypt; and
afterwards, without saying adieu to anybody, he embarked secretly on the
1st of May, (A. D. 1229,) leaving us worse off than he found us."[*]

The Grand Master of the Temple, Peter de Montaigu, died at Acre at
an advanced age, and was succeeded (A. D. 1233) by Brother Hermann de
Perigord, Grand Preceptor of Calabria and Sicily.[†] Shortly after his
accession to power, the truce with the sultan of Aleppo expired, and
Brother William de Montferrat, Preceptor of Antioch, having besieged a
fortress of the infidels, refused to retreat before a superior force, and was
surrounded and overwhelmed; a hundred knights of the Temple, and three
hundred cross-bowmen were slain, together with many secular warriors,
and a large number of foot soldiers. The *Balcanifer*, or standard-bearer, on
this occasion, was an English Knight Templar, named Reginald
d'Argenton, who performed prodigies of valor. He was disabled and
covered with wounds, yet he unflinchingly bore the Beauseant aloft with
his bleeding arms into the thickest of the fight, until he at last fell dead
upon a heap of his slaughtered comrades. The Preceptor of Antioch, before
he was slain, "sent sixteen infidels to hell." As soon as the Templars in
England heard of this disaster, they sent, (A. D. 1236,) in conjunction with
the Hospitallers, instant succor to their brethren. "Having made their
arrangements," says Matthew Paris, "they started from the house of the
Hospitallers at Clerkenwell in London, and passed through the city with
spears held aloft, shields displayed, and banners advanced. They marched
in splendid pomp to the bridge, and sought a blessing from all who
crowded to see them pass. The brothers indeed, uncovered, bowed their
heads from side to side, and recommended themselves to the prayers of
all."

A new crusade had already been preached in Europe by Pope
Gregory IX., and the Templars, expecting the arrival of speedy succor, and
being desirous of taking advantage of the dissensions that had arisen
amongst the Saracens, had recommenced hostilities with the sultans of
Egypt and Damascus. Thibaut I., king of Navarre, and count of

[*] *Od Rainald*, ad ann. 1229.
[†] *Cotton* MS. Nero E. VI. 23 i. p. 60, fol. 466. L'Art de Verif. tom. v. p. 351.

Champagne, the duke of Burgundy, and the counts of Brittany and Bar, who had arrived in Palestine with several other nobles and knights, and a considerable force of armed pilgrims, marched with a party of Templars to attack the sultan of Egypt, whilst the Grand Master prepared to invade the territory of the sultan of Damascus. In a bloody battle fought with the Mamlooks, near Gaza, the count de Bar and many knights and persons of quality, and all the foot soldiers, were slain; the count de Montfort was taken prisoner, and all the equipage and baggage of the army was lost. The king of Navarre and the survivors then retreated to Jaffa, and set sail from that port for St. Jean d'Acre. On their arrival at this place, they joined the Grand Master of the Temple, who was encamped at the palm-grove of Caiphas. Thence they marched towards Tiberias, and on their arrival at Sepphoris, they met some messengers who were proceeding from Saleh Ismael, the sultan of Damascus, to the Grand Master of the Temple, with overtures of peace, and offers to surrender Jerusalem upon the following terms:—The Moslem and Christian prisoners of war were immediately to be set at liberty; all Palestine, between the sea-coast and the Jordan, excepting the cities of St. Abraham, Naplous, and Bisan, was to be surrendered to the Christians; the Christians were to assist the sultan of Damascus in a war which had broken out between him and Nojmoddin Ayoub sultan of Egypt; they were to march with all their forces to the south to occupy Jaffa and Ascalon, and prevent the latter potentate from marching through Palestine to attack the sultan of Damascus; and lastly, no truce was to be entered into with the sultan of Egypt by the Christians, unless the sultan of Damascus was included therein. The Grand Master of the Temple acceded to these terms, and induced the chiefs of the crusaders to assent to the compact; but the Grand Master of the Hospital refused to be a party to it. It is said that he entered into a separate and independent treaty with Nojmoddin Ayoub, who had just mounted the throne of Egypt, so that one of the great military orders remained at war with the sultan of Damascus, and the other with the sultan of Egypt. Immediately after the conclusion of this treaty, the Templars assembled all their disposable forces and proceeded to Jaffa with the count de Nevers, and a body of newly arrived crusaders, and co-operated with an army which the sultan of Damascus had sent into that neighborhood to act against the Egyptians. In the mean time, Richard, earl of Cornwall, the brother of Henry III., king of England, having assumed the cross, arrived in Palestine, and proceeded with a small force of English pilgrims, knights, and foot soldiers, to the camp of the Templars at Jaffa. With this welcome reinforcement the Grand Master of the Temple marched at once upon Ascalon, re-constructed the castle and restored the fortifications to the state in which they were left by Richard Cœur de Lion. The Templars then endeavored to obtain possession of their ancient fortress of Gaza, a place of very great importance. An invading army from the south could approach Jerusalem only by way of Gaza, or by taking a long and tedious route through the desert of Arabia Petræa, to Karac, and from thence to Hebron, by the southern extremity of the Dead Sea. The want of water and forage presented an insuperable obstacle to the march of a large body of forces in any other direction. Towards the close of autumn, the Templars marched against Gaza in conjunction with Saleh Ismael, sultan of Damascus; they drove out the Egyptians, and obtained possession of the dismantled fortifications. Large sums of money were expended in the re-construction of the walls of the castle, a strong garrison was established in the important post, and the Templars then marched upon Jerusalem.

The fortifications of the Holy City had been dismantled by Malek Kamel, at the period of the siege of Damietta, when alarmed at the military success of the Franks in Egypt, he was anxious to purchase the safety of the country by the cession of Jerusalem. The Templars, consequently, entered the Holy City without difficulty or resistance; the Mussulman population abandoned their dwellings on their approach, and the military friars once more entered the city of David, bare-footed and bare-headed, singing loud hymns and songs of triumph. They rushed to the church of the Resurrection, and fell prostrate on their knees before the shrine of the Holy Sepulcher; they ascended Mount Calvary, and visited the reputed scene of the crucifixion, and then hastened in martial array, and with sound of trumpet, through the forlorn and deserted streets of the city of Zion, to take possession of their ancient quarters on Mount Moriah.

The golden crescent was once more removed from the lofty pinnacle of the Temple of the Lord, or Mosque of Omar, and this Holy Mussulman house of prayer was once again surmounted by the glittering cross. The Temple of the Knights Templars or Mosque at Acsa, was again purified and re-consecrated, and its sombre halls and spacious areas were once more graced with the white, religious, and military habit of the knights of the Temple. The greater part of the old convent, adjoining the Temple, had been destroyed, as before mentioned, by the great Saladin, and the military friars were consequently obliged to pitch numerous tents in the spacious area for the accommodation of the brethren. The sound of the bell once more superseded the voice of the muezzin, "the exiled faith returned to its ancient sanctuary," and the name of Jesus was again invoked in the high places and sanctuaries of *Mahomet*. The great court of the Mussulmen around the revered Mosque of Omar, called by them *El Scham Schereef*, "the noble retirement," again rung with the tramp of the war-steed, and its solitudes were once more awakened with the voice of the trumpet.

Nothing could exceed the joy with which the intelligence of the re-occupation of Jerusalem was received throughout Palestine, and through all Christendom. The Hospitallers, now that the policy of the Templars had been crowned with success, and that Jerusalem had been regained, no longer opposed the treaty with the sultan of Damascus, but hastened to co-operate with them for the preservation of the Holy City, which had been so happily recovered. The patriarch returned to Jerusalem, (A. D. 1241,) with all his clergy; the churches were re-consecrated, and the Templars and Hospitallers emptied their treasuries in rebuilding the walls. The following account of these gratifying events was transmitted by brother Hermann de Perigord to the Master of the Temple at London. "Brother Hermann de Perigord, humble minister of the poor knights of the Temple, to his beloved brother in Christ Robert de Sandford, Preceptor in England, salvation through the Lord.

"Since it is our duty, whenever an opportunity offers, to make known to the brotherhood, by letters or by messengers, the state and prospects of the Holy Land, we hasten to inform you, that after our great successes against the sultan of Egypt, and Nasser, his supporter and abettor, the great persecutor of the Christians, whom we have unceasingly endeavored with all our might to subdue, they were unwillingly compelled to treat with us concerning the establishment of a truce, promising us to restore to the followers of Jesus Christ all the territory on this side Jordan. We despatched certain of our brethren, noble and discreet personages, to Cairo, to have an interview with the sultan upon these matters. But the latter broke the promise which he had made to us, retaining in his own hands Gaza, St. Abraham, Naplous, Varan, and other places; he detained our messengers in custody for more than half a year, and endeavored to amuse us with deceitful words and unmeaning propositions. But we, with the Divine assistance, were enabled to penetrate his craft and perfidy, and plainly saw that he had procured the truce with us that he might be enabled the more readily to subjugate to his cruel dominion the sultan of Damascus, and Nasser lord of Carac, and their territories; and then, when he had got possession of all the country surrounding our Christian provinces, we plainly foresaw that he would break faith with us, after the custom of his unbelieving generation, and attack our poor Christianity on this side the sea, which in its present weak and feeble state would have been unable effectually to resist him.

"Having therefore deliberated, long and earnestly, upon these matters, we determined, with the advice of the bishops and some of the barons of the land, to break off at once with the sultan of Egypt, and enter into a treaty with the sultan of Damascus, and with Nasser lord of Carac, whereby all the country on this side Jordan, excepting St. Abraham, Naplous, and Bisan, has been surrendered to the Christian worship; and, to the joy of angels and of men, the holy city of Jerusalem is now inhabited by Christians alone, all the Saracens being driven out. The holy places have been re-consecrated and purified by the prelates of the churches, and in those spots where the name of the Lord has not been invoked for fifty-six years, now, blessed be God, the divine mysteries are daily celebrated. To all the sacred places there is again free access to the faithful in Christ, nor is it to be doubted but that in this happy and prosperous condition we might long remain, if our Eastern Christians would from henceforth live in greater concord and unanimity. But, alas! opposition and contradiction, arising from envy and hatred, have impeded our efforts in the promotion of these and other advantages for the Holy Land. With the exception of the prelates of the churches, and a few of the barons, who afford us all the assistance in their power, the entire burthen of its defense rests upon our house alone. With the assistance of the sultan of Damascus, and the lord of Carac, we have obtained possession of the city of Gaza, situate on the confines of the territory of Jerusalem and the territory of Egypt. And as this important place commands the entrance from the latter country into the Holy Land, we have, by vast exertions, and at an enormous expense, and after having incurred great risk and danger, put it into a state of defense. But we are afraid that God will take heavy vengeance for past ingratitude, by punishing those who have been careless, and indifferent, and rebellious in the prosecution of these matters.

"For the safeguard and preservation of the holy territory, we propose to erect a fortified castle near Jerusalem, which will enable us the more easily to retain possession of the country, and to protect it against all enemies. But indeed we can in nowise defend for any great length of time the places that we hold, against the powerful and crafty sultan of Egypt, unless Christ and his faithful followers extend to us an efficacious support."[*]

We must now refer to a few events connected with the English province of the order of the Temple.

Brother Geoffrey, who was Master of the Temple at London, at the period of the consecration of the Temple Church by Heraclius, patriarch of Jerusalem, died shortly after the capture of the Holy City by Saladin, and was succeeded by Brother Amaric de St. Maur, who is an attesting witness to the deed executed by king John, (A. D. 1203,) granting a dowry to his young queen, the beautiful Isabella of Angouleme. King John frequently resided in the Temple for weeks together, the writs to his lieutenants, sheriffs, and bailiffs, being dated therefrom. The orders for the concentration of the English fleet at Portsmouth, to resist the formidable French invasion instigated by the pope, are dated from the Temple at London, and the convention between the king and the count of Holland, whereby the latter agreed to assist King John with a body of knights and men-at-arms, in case of the landing of the French, was published at the same place. In all the conferences and negotiations between king John and the Roman pontiff, the Knights Templars took an active and distinguished part. Two brethren of the order were sent to him by Pandulph, the papal legate, to arrange that famous conference between them which ended in the complete submission of the king to all the demands of the holy see. By the advice and persuasion of the Templars, John repaired to the preceptory of Temple Ewell, near Dover, where he was met by the legate Pandulph, who crossed over from France to confer with him, and the mean-hearted king was there frightened into that celebrated resignation of the kingdoms of England and Ireland, "to God, to the holy apostles Peter and Paul, to the holy Roman church his mother, and to his lord, Pope Innocent the Third, and his catholic successors, for the remission of all his sins and the sins of

---

[*] *Matt. Par.* p. 615. *Tyr.* Contin. Hist. col. 722-725. *Marin Sanut.* cap. 15. *Michaud*, Extr. p. 549. *Ibn Schunah*, Hejir. 638.

all his people as well the living as the dead." The following year, the commands of king John for the extirpation of the heretics in Gascony, addressed to the seneschal of that province, were issued from the Temple at London, and about the same period, the Templars were made the depositaries of various private and confidential matters pending between king John and his illustrious sister-in-law, "the royal, eloquent, and beauteous" Berengaria of Navarre, the youthful widowed queen of Richard *Cœur de Lion*. The Templars in England managed the money transactions of that fair princess. She directed her dower to be paid in the house of the New Temple at London, together with the arrears due to her from the king, amounting to several thousand pounds.

John was resident at the Temple when he was compelled by the barons of England to sign Magna Charta. Matthew Paris tells us that the barons came to him whilst he was residing in the New Temple at London, "in a very resolute manner, clothed in their military dresses, and demanded the liberties and laws of king Edward, with others for themselves, the kingdom, and the church of England."[*]

Brother Amaric de St. Maur, the Master of the English province of the order, was succeeded by brother Alan Marcell, the friend and correspondent of the Grand Master Peter de Montaigu. He was at the head of the order in England for the space of sixteen years, and was employed by king Henry the Third in various important negotiations. He was Master of the Temple at London, when Reginald, king of the island of Man, by the advice and persuasion of the legate Pandulph, made a solemn surrender at that place of his island to the pope and his catholic successors, and consented to hold the same from thenceforth as the feudatory of the church of Rome. On the 28th of April, A. D. 1224, the Master, Brother Alan Marcell, was employed by king Henry to negotiate a truce between himself and the king of France. The king of England appears at that time to have been resident at the Temple, the letters of credence being made out at that place, in the presence of the archbishop of Canterbury, several bishops, and Hubert, the chief justiciary. The year after, Alan Marcell was sent into Germany, to negotiate a treaty of marriage between king Henry and the daughter of the duke of Austria.[†] Brother Alan Marcell was succeeded by Brother Amberaldus. The next Master of the English province was Robert Mounford, and he was followed by Robert Sanford.

During the Mastership of Robert Sanford, on Ascension Day, A. D. 1240, the oblong portion of the Temple Church, which extendeth eastward from "THE ROUND," was consecrated in the presence of king Henry the Third and all his court, and much of the nobility of the kingdom. This portion of the sacred edifice was of a lighter and more florid style of architecture than the earlier Round Church consecrated by the patriarch Heraclius. The walls were pierced with numerous triple lancet windows

---

[*] Acta *Rymeri*, tom. i. p. 134, 165, 170, 194, 195, 208, 209. *Matt. Par.* p. 234-237, 253. *Matt. West.* p. 271.
[†] Acta *Rymeri*, tom. i. p. 234, 258, 270, 275, 311, 373, 380.

filled with stained glass, and the floor was covered with tesselated pavement. The roof was supported by dark grey Purbeck marble columns, and the vaulted ceiling was decorated with the star of Bethlehem, and with ornaments of frosted silver placed on a blue ground. The extensive area of the church was open and unencumbered by pews, and the beauty of the columns and windows, the lively colors of the tiled floor, and the elegant proportions of the fabric were seen at a glance. After the consecration, the king made provision for the maintenance in the Temple of three chaplains, who were to say three masses daily for ever, one for the king himself, another for all Christian people, and the third for the faithful departed.*

INTERIOR OF THE TEMPLE CHURCH

King Henry III. was one of the greatest of the benefactors of the order. He granted to the Templars the manors of Lilleston, Hechewayton, and Saunford, the wood of Carletone, Kingswood near Chippenhan, a messuage, and six bovates of land with their appurtenances in Great Lymburgh; a fair at Walnesford, in the county of Essex, every three years

---

* *Addison's* Temple Church.

for three days, to commence on the anniversary of the beheading of St. John the Baptist; also annual fairs and weekly markets at Newburgh, Walnesford, Balsall, Kirkeby, and a variety of other places; he granted them free warren in all their demesne lands; and by his famous charter, dated the 9th day of February, in the eleventh year of his reign, he confirmed to them all the donations of his predecessors, and of their other benefactors, and conferred upon them vast privileges and immunities in the following pious and reverential terms.

"The king, &c., to all the archbishops, bishops, barons, &c. &c., to whom these presents shall come, salvation through the Lord. Be it known to you that we have granted and confirmed to God and the blessed Mary, and the brethren of the chivalry of the Temple of Solomon, all reasonable donations of lands, men, and eleemosynary gifts, bestowed on them by our predecessors, or by others in times past, or by ourselves at this present period, or which may be hereafter conferred on them by kings or by the liberality of subjects, or may be acquired, or be about to be acquired in any other manner, as well churches as worldly goods and possessions; wherefore we will and firmly command that the aforesaid brethren and their men may have and hold all their possessions and eleemosynary donations with all liberties and free customs and immunities, in wood and plain, in meadow and pasture, in water and water-mills, on highways and byeways, in ponds and running streams, in marshes and fisheries, in granges and broad acres, within burgh and without the burgh, with soc and sac, tol and theam, infangenethef and unfangenethef, and hamsoc and grithbrich, and blodwit and fictwit, and flictwit and ferdwite, and hengewite and lierwite, and flemenefrith, murder, robbery, forstall, ordel, oreste, in season and out of season, at all times and in all places, &c.

"We ordain, likewise, that the aforesaid brethren shall for ever hereafter be freed from royal aids, and sheriff's aids, and officer's aids, and from hidage and carucage, and danegeld and hornegeld, and from military and wapentake services, and scutages and lastages and stallages, shires and hundreds, pleas and quarrels, ward and wardpeny, and averpeni and hundredspeni, and borethalpeni and thethingepeni, and from the works of castles, parks, bridges, and inclosures; and from the duty of providing carriages and beasts of burthen, boats, and vessels, and from the building of royal houses, and all other works. And we prohibit all persons from taking timber from their woods and forests for such works, or for any other purposes whatever: neither shall their corn, nor the corn of their men, nor any of their goods, nor the goods of any belonging to them, be taken to fortify castles. We will also that they shall have free and full liberty to cut and fell timber whenever they please, in all their woods, for the use of their fraternity, without any let or hindrance whatever; and for doing so they shall not incur forfeiture or waste, or in any way be punishable by law. And all their lands, and the ground which they or their men have cleared of wood, and recovered from the forest, or which they may clear in time to come, with the assent of the king, we make quit and free for ever hereafter from waste regard, and view of foresters, and from all other customs. And we concede also to the aforesaid brethren the privilege of cutting down trees in all the woods they possess at present within the forest boundaries, and of clearing and bringing the land into cultivation without any license from our bailiffs, so that they may never at any time hereafter be in any way called to account by ourselves, or our heirs, or any of our bailiffs.

"We ordain, moreover, that the aforesaid brethren and their men shall be quit and free from every kind of toll in all markets and fairs, and upon crossing bridges, roads, and ferries, throughout the whole of our kingdom, and throughout all lands in which we are able to grant liberties; and all their markets, and the markets of their men, shall in like manner be quit and free from all toll. We grant and confirm also to the aforesaid brethren, that if any of their men be condemned to lose life or limb for crime, or shall have fled from justice, or have committed any offence for which he hath incurred forfeiture of his goods and chattels, the goods and chattels so forfeited shall belong to the aforesaid brethren, whether the cognizance of the offence belongeth to our court or to any other inferior court; and it shall be lawful for the aforesaid brethren, under such circumstances and in such cases, to put themselves in possession of the aforesaid goods and chattels at such time as our bailiffs would or ought to have seized them into our hands, had such goods and chattels belonged to ourselves, without the molestation or hindrance of the sheriffs or bailiffs, or any other persons whatever.

"We concede also to the aforesaid brethren, that animals called *waif*, lost by their owners, and found within the feud of the Templars, shall belong to the aforesaid brethren, unless they are followed by some one able and willing to prove that they are his own, and unless they shall be sought after and taken possession of by the owner within a moderate period of time, according to the custom of the country. And if any of the tenants of the aforesaid brethren shall happen to have incurred a forfeiture of his feud, it shall be lawful for the said brethren to take possession of the said feud, and hold the same, notwithstanding the law which concedes to ourselves the possession of the feud of fugitives and criminals, for the space of a year and a day. In like manner, if any of the men of the aforesaid brethren shall have incurred a fine to be paid to ourselves or to any of our bailiffs, under any process, or for any crime, or any other matter, the amercements of money shall be collected and brought in a purse to our exchequer, and there handed over to the aforesaid brethren; judgment of death and limb being always reserved to the royal authority.

"We moreover ordain, that if any of the liberties and privileges contained in this our charter shall happen to have been disused for a length of time, such disuse shall in no respect prejudice the right, but such liberty or privilege may be again exercised without contradiction, notwithstanding that it may have been discontinued and disused as aforesaid. And all the aforesaid things, and all other secular services and customs which are not included in this present writing, we, through love of God, and for the good of the soul of the lord king John, our father, and for the good of the souls of all our predecessors and successors, grant and confirm to them, as a perpetual alms-gift, with all liberties and free customs, as fully, freely, and effectually as the royal power can confer them upon any religious house. And we prohibit all persons, on pain of forfeiture, from proceeding against them or their men contrary to this our charter, for we have taken the aforesaid brethren, and all their goods, and possessions, and all their men, under our especial guardianship and protection. As witness the king, at Westminster, the 9th day of February, in the eleventh year of our reign."[*]

By the royal grant of *soc* and *sac*, *tol* and *theam*, &c. &c., the Templars were clothed with the power of holding courts to impose and levy fines and amerciaments upon their tenants, to judge and punish their villeins and vassals—to take cognizance of quarrels and controversies that arose amongst them—to try thieves and malefactors belonging to their manors, and all foreign thieves taken within the precincts thereof—to try and punish trespasses and breaches of the peace, and all unlawful entries into the houses of their tenants—to impose and levy amerciaments for cutting and maiming, and for bloodshed—to judge and punish by fine or imprisonment the seducers of their bond women, and all persons who committed adultery and fornication within their manors. They had the power of trying criminals by ordeal, or the terrible test of fire and water; and they had, lastly, the tremendous privilege of pit or gallows, i. e. the power of putting convicted thieves to death, by hanging them if they were men, and drowning them if they were women! By the royal charter, the Templars were, in the next place, freed from the fine of right payable to the king for the hanging of thieves without a formal trial and judgment according to law; they were exempted from the taxes on pasture-lands, and plough-lands, and horned cattle; from the Danish tribute, and from all military services, and from all the ordinary feudal burthens.[†]

---

[*] Cart. 11, *Hen.* 3, m. 33. *Dugd.* Monast. Angl. vol. vi. part 2. p. 844.
[†] *Plac. de Quo Warranto* temp. Edw. 1, rot. 4, d. p. 191. *Spelman*, Gloss p. 251.

Chapter VI.

"The Knights of the Temple ever maintained their fearless and fanatic character; if they neglected to *live*, they were prepared to *die* in the service of Christ."—*Gibbon.*

Shortly after the recovery of the holy city, (A. D. 1242,) Djemal'eddeen, the Mussulman, paid a visit to Jerusalem. "I saw," says he, "the monks and the priests masters of the Temple of the Lord. I saw the vials of wine prepared for the sacrifice. I entered into the Mosque Al Acsa, and I saw a bell suspended from the dome. The rites and ceremonies of the Mussulmen were abolished; the call to prayer was no longer heard. The infidels publicly exercised their idolatrous practices in the sanctuaries of the Mussulmen."[*] By the advice of Benedict, bishop of Marseilles, who came to the holy city on a pilgrimage, the Templars rebuilt their ancient and once formidable castle of Saphet, the dilapidated ruins of which had been ceded to them by their recent treaty with Saleh Ismael. During a pilgrimage to the lake of Tiberias and the banks of the Jordan, the bishop of Marseilles had halted at Saphet, and spent a night amid the ruins of the ancient castle, where he found a solitary Knight Templar keeping watch in a miserable hovel. Struck with the position of the place, and its importance in a military point of view, he sought on his return to Acre an interview with the Grand Master of the Temple, and urged him to restore the castle of Saphet to its pristine condition. The bishop was invited to attend a general chapter of the order of the Temple, when the matter was discussed, and it was unanimously determined that the mountain of Saphet should immediately be refortified. The bishop himself laid the first stone, and animated the workmen by a spirited oration. Eight hundred and fifty masons and artificers, and four hundred slaves, were employed in the task. During the first thirty months after the commencement of operations, the Templars expended eleven thousand golden bezants upon the works, and in succeeding years they spent upwards of forty thousand. The walls, when finished, were sixty French feet in width, one hundred and seventy in height, and the circuit of them was two thousand two hundred and fifty feet. They were flanked by seven large round towers, sixty feet in diameter, and seventy-two feet higher than the walls. The fosse surrounding the fortress was thirty-six feet wide, and was pierced in the solid rock to a depth of forty-three feet. The garrison in time of peace amounted to one

---

[*] *Djemal'eddeen*, ad ann. Hejir. 841. *Michaud*, Extraits Arabes, p. 549.

thousand seven hundred men, and to two thousand two hundred in time of war. Twelve thousand mule loads of corn and barley were consumed annually within the walls of the fortress; and in addition to all the ordinary expenses and requirements of the establishment, the Templars maintained a well-furnished table and excellent accommodation for all way-worn pilgrims and travelers. "The generous expenditure of the Templars at this place," says a cotemporary historian, "renders them truly worthy of the liberality and largesses of the faithful."[*]

The ruins of this famous castle, crowning the summit of a lofty mountain, torn and shattered by earthquakes, still present a stupendous appearance. In Pocock's time "two particularly fine large round towers" were entire: and Van Egmont and Heyman give the following account of the condition of the fortress at the period of their visit. "The next place that engaged our attention was the citadel, which is the greatest object of curiosity in Saphet, and is generally considered one of the most ancient structures remaining in the country. In order to form some idea of this fortification in its present state, imagine a lofty mountain, and on its summit a round castle, with walls of incredible thickness, and with a *corridor* or covered passage extending round the walls, and ascended by a winding staircase. The thickness of the walls and corridor together was twenty paces. The whole was of hewn stone, and some of the stones are eight or nine spans in length.... This castle was anciently surrounded with stupendous works, as appears from the remains of two moats lined with free-stone, several fragments of walls, bulwarks, towers, &c., all very solid and strongly built; and below these moats other massive works, having corridors round them in the same manner as the castle; so that any person, on surveying these fortifications, may wonder how so strong a fortress could ever be taken." Amongst the various interesting remains of this castle, these intelligent travelers describe "a large structure of free-stone in the form of a cupola or dome. The stones, which are almost white, are of astonishing magnitude, some being twelve spans in length and five in thickness. The inside is full of niches for placing statues, and near each niche is a small cell. An open colonnade extends quite round the building, and, like the rest of the structure, is very massive and compact."[†]

When the sultan of Egypt had been informed of the march of the Templars to Jerusalem, and the re-possession by the military friars of the holy places and sanctuaries of the Mussulmen, he sent an army of several thousand men across the desert, to drive them out of the Holy City before they had time to repair the fortifications and re-construct the walls. The Templars assembled all their forces and advanced to meet the Egyptians. They occupied the passes and defiles of the hill country leading to Jerusalem, and gained a glorious victory over the Moslems, driving the greater part of them into the desert. Ayoub, sultan of Egypt, finding himself unable to resist the formidable alliance of the Templars with Saleh

---

[*] *Steph. Baluz*, Miscell. lib. vi. p. 357, de constructione Castri Saphet.
[†] *Conder's* Modern traveler.—Palestine, p. 335, 337-339.

Ismael, called in to his assistance the fierce pastoral tribes of the Carizmians. These were a warlike race of people, who had been driven from their abodes, in the neighborhood of the Caspian, by the successful arms of the Moguls, and had rushed headlong upon the weak and effeminate nations of the south. They had devastated and laid waste Armenia and the north-western parts of Persia, cutting off by the sword, or dragging away into captivity, all who had ventured to oppose their progress. For years past they had been leading a migratory, wandering life, exhausting the resources of one district, and then passing onwards into another, without making any fixed settlement, or having any regular places of abode, and their destructive progress has been compared by the Arabian writers to the wasting tempest or the terrible inundation. The rude hardships of their roving life had endowed them with a passive endurance which enabled them to surmount all obstacles, and to overcome every difficulty. Their clothing consisted of a solitary sheep's skin, or a wolf's skin, tied around their loins; boiled herbs and some water, or a little milk, sufficed them for food and beverage; their arms were the bow and the lance; and they shed the blood of their fellow-creatures with the same indifference as they would that of the beasts of the field. Their wives and their children accompanied their march, braving all dangers and fatigues; their tents were their homes, and the site of their encampment their only country. Nothing could exceed the terror inspired in Armenia and Persia by the military expeditions of these rude and ferocious shepherds of the Caspian, who were the foes of all races and of all people, and manifested a profound indifference for every religion.

The Carizmians were encamped on the left bank of the Euphrates, pasturing their cavalry in the neighboring plains, when their chief, Barbeh Khan, received a deputation from the sultan of Egypt, inviting their co-operation and assistance in the reduction of Palestine. Their cupidity was awakened by an exaggerated account of the fertility and the wealth of the land, and they were offered a settlement in the country as soon as it was rescued from the hands of the Franks. The messengers displayed the written letters of the sultan of Egypt; they presented to the Carizmian chief some rich shawls and magnificent presents, and returned to their master at Grand Cairo with promises of speedy support. The Carizmians assembled together in a body; they crossed the Euphrates (A. D. 1244) in small leathern boats, ravaged the territories of the sultan of Aleppo, and marched up the plain of the Orontes to Hems, wasting all the country around them with fire and the sword. The intelligence of these events reached the Grand Master of the Temple when he was busily engaged in rebuilding the vast and extensive fortifications of the Holy City. A council of war was called together, and it was determined that Jerusalem was untenable, and that the Holy City must once again be abandoned to the infidels. The Hospitallers in their black mantles, and the Templars in their white habits, were drawn up in martial array in the streets of Jerusalem, and the weeping Christians were exhorted once again to leave their homes and avail themselves of the escort and protection of the military friars to Jaffa. Many gathered together their little property and quitted the devoted city, and many lingered behind amid the scenes they loved and cherished. Soon, however, frightful reports reached Jerusalem of the horrors of the Carizmian invasion, and the fugitives, who had fled with terror and astonishment from their destructive progress, spread alarm and consternation throughout the whole land. Several thousand Christians, who had remained behind, then attempted to make their escape, with their wives and children, through the mountains to the plain of Ramleh and the sea-coast, relying on the truce and treaty of alliance which had been established with Nasser Daoud, lord of Carac, and the mountaineers. But the inhabitants of the mountain region, being a set of lawless robbers and plunderers, attacked and pillaged them. Some were slain, and others were dragged away into captivity. A few fled back to Jerusalem, and the residue, after having been hunted through the mountains, descended into the plain of Ramleh, where they were attacked by the Carizmians, and only three hundred out of the whole number succeeded in reaching Jaffa in safety. All the women and children had been taken captive in the mountains, and amongst them were several holy nuns, who were sent to Egypt and sold in the common slave-markets.

The Carizmians had advanced into the plain of Ramleh by way of Baalbec, Tiberias, and Naplous, and they now directed their footsteps towards Jerusalem. They entered the Holy City sword in hand, massacred the few remaining Christians in the church of the Holy Sepulcher, pillaged the town, and rifled the tombs of the kings for treasure. They then marched upon Gaza, stormed the city, and put the garrison to the sword, after which they sent messengers across the desert to the sultan of Egypt to announce their arrival. Ayoub immediately sent a robe of honor and sumptuous gifts to their chief, and despatched his army from Cairo in all haste, under the command of Rokmeddin Bibars, one of his principal Mamlooks, to join them before Gaza. The Grand Masters of the Temple and the Hospital, on the other hand, collected their forces together, and made a junction with the troops of the sultan of Damascus and the lord of Carac. They marched upon Gaza, attacked the united armies of the Egyptians and Carizmians, and were exterminated in a bloody battle of two days' continuance. The Grand Master of the Temple and the flower of his chivalry perished in that bloody encounter, and the Grand Master of the Hospital was taken prisoner, and led away into captivity.*

The government of the order of the Temple, in consequence of the death of the Grand Master, temporarily devolved upon the Knight Templar, Brother William de Rochefort, who immediately despatched a melancholy letter addressed to the pope and the archbishop of Canterbury, detailing the horrors and atrocities of the Carizmian invasion. "These perfidious savages," says he, "having penetrated within the gates of the holy city of Israel, the small remnant of the faithful left therein, consisting of children,

---

* *Marin. Sanut.* p. 217. *Tyr.* Contin. Hist. col. 731, 732. *Michaud,* Extraits, p. 551, 718. *Matt. Par.* 631, 632.

women, and old men, took refuge in the church of the Sepulcher of our Lord. The Carizmians rushed to that holy sanctuary; they butchered them all before the very Sepulcher itself, and cutting off the heads of the priests who were kneeling with uplifted hands before the altars, they said one to another, 'Let us here shed the blood of the Christians *on the very place where they offer up wine to their God, who they say was hanged here.*' Moreover, in sorrow be it spoken, and with sighs we inform you, that laying their sacrilegious hands on the very Sepulcher itself, they sadly knocked it about, utterly battering to pieces the marble shrine which was built around that holy sanctuary. They have defiled, with every abomination of which they were capable, Mount Calvary, where Christ was crucified, and the whole church of the resurrection. They have taken away, indeed, the sculptured columns which were placed as a decoration before the Sepulcher of the Lord; and, as a mark of victory, and as a taunt to the Christians, they have sent them to the Sepulcher of the wicked Mahomet. They have violated the tombs of the happy kings of Jerusalem in the same church, and they have scattered, to the hurt of Christendom, the ashes of those holy men to the winds, irreverently profaning the revered Mount Sion. The Temple of the Lord, the church of the Valley of Jehoshaphat, where the Virgin lies buried, the church of Bethlehem, and the place of the nativity of our Lord, they have polluted with enormities too horrible to be related, far exceeding the iniquity of all the Saracens, who, though they frequently occupied the land of the Christians, yet always reverenced and preserved the holy places...." The subsequent military operations are then described; the march of the Templars and Hospitallers, on the 4th of October, A. D. 1244, from Acre to Cæsarea; the junction of their forces with those of the Moslem sultans; the retreat of the Carizmians to Gaza, where they received succor from the sultan of Egypt; and the preparation of the Hospitallers and Templars for the attack before that place. "Those holy warriors," say they, "boldly rushed in upon the enemy, but the Saracens who had joined us, having lost many of their men, fled, and the warriors of the cross were left alone to withstand the united attack of the Egyptians and Carizmians. Like stout champions of the Lord, and true defenders of catholicity, whom the same faith and the same cross and passion make true brothers, they bravely resisted; but as they were few in number in comparison with the enemy, they at last succumbed, so that of the convents of the house of the chivalry of the Temple, and of the house of the hospital of St. John at Jerusalem, only thirty-three Templars and twenty-six Hospitallers escaped; the archbishop of Tyre, the bishop of St. George, the abbot of St. Mary of Jehoshaphat, and the Master of the Temple, with many other clerks and holy men, being slain in that sanguinary fight. We ourselves, having by our sins provoked this dire calamity, fled half dead to Ascalon; from thence we proceeded by sea to Acre, and found that city and the adjoining province filled with sorrow and mourning, misery and death. There was not a house or a family that had not lost an inmate or a relation...."

The Knights Templars

"The Carizmians have now pitched their tents in the plain of Acre, about two miles from the city. They have spread themselves over the whole face of the country as far as Nazareth and Saphet. They have slaughtered or driven away the house-holders, occupied their houses, and divided their property amongst them. They have appointed bailiffs and tax-gatherers in the towns and villages, and they compel the countrymen and the villeins of the soil to pay to themselves the rents and tribute which they have heretofore been wont to pay to the Christians, so that the church of Jerusalem and the Christian kingdom have now no territory, except a few fortifications, which are defended with great difficulty and labor by the Templars and Hospitallers.... To you, dear Father, upon whom the burthen of the defense of the cause of Christ justly resteth, we have caused these sad tidings to be communicated, earnestly beseeching you to address your prayers to the throne of grace, imploring mercy from the Most High; that he who consecrated the Holy Land with his own blood in redemption of all mankind, may compassionately turn towards it and defend it, and send it succor. But know, assuredly, that unless, through the interposition of the Most High, or by the aid of the faithful, the Holy Land is succored in the next spring passage from Europe, its doom is sealed, and utter ruin is inevitable. Given at Acre, this fifth day of November, in the year of our Lord one thousand two hundred and forty-four."[*]

The above letter was read before a general council of the church, which had been assembled at Lyons by pope Innocent IV., and it was resolved that a new crusade should be preached. It was provided that those who assumed the cross should assemble at particular places to receive the pope's blessing; that there should be a truce for four years between all Christian princes; that during all that time there should be no tournaments, feasts, nor public rejoicings; that all the faithful in Christ should be exhorted to contribute, out of their fortunes and estates, to the defense of the Holy Land; and that ecclesiastics should pay towards it the tenth, and cardinals the twentieth, of all their revenues, for the term of three years successively. The ancient enthusiasm, however, in favor of distant expeditions to the East had died away; the addresses and exhortations of the clergy now fell on unwilling ears, and the Templars and Hospitallers, for several years, received only some small assistance in men and money. The emperor Frederick, who still bore the empty title of king of Jerusalem, made no attempt to save the wreck of his feeble kingdom. His bride, the fair and youthful Violante, queen of the Latin kingdom, had been dead several years, killed by his coldness and neglect; and the emperor bestowed no thought upon his eastern subjects and the Holy Land, except to abuse those by whom that land had been so gallantly defended. In a letter to Richard earl of Cornwall, the brother of Henry the Third, king of England, Frederick accuses the Templars of making war upon the sultan of Egypt, in defiance of a treaty entered into with that monarch, of compelling him to

---

[*] *Matt. Par.* p. 631 to 633. *Abulpharag,* p. 486. *D'Herbelot,* Bib. Orient. p. 357, 628.

call in the Carizmians to his assistance; and he compares the union of the Templars with the infidel sultan, for purposes of defense, to an attempt to extinguish a fire by pouring upon it a quantity of oil. "The proud religion of the Temple," says he, in continuation, "nurtured amid the luxuries of the barons of the land, waxeth wanton. It hath been made manifest to us, by certain religious persons lately arrived from parts beyond sea, that the aforesaid sultans and their trains were received with pompous alacrity within the gates of the houses of the Temple, and that the Templars suffered them to perform within them their superstitious rites and ceremonies, with invocation of Mahomet, and to indulge in secular delights."[*] In the midst of all these terrible disasters, a general chapter of Knights Templars was assembled in the Pilgrim's Castle, and the veteran warrior, Brother William de Sonnac, was chosen (A. D. 1247) Grand Master of the Order.[†] Circular mandates were, at the same time, sent to the western preceptories, summoning all the brethren to Palestine, and directing the immediate transmission of all the money in the different treasuries to the head-quarters of the Order at Acre. These calls were promptly attended to, and the pope praises both the Templars and Hospitallers for the zeal and energy displayed by them in sending out the newly admitted knights and novices with armed bands and a large amount of treasure to the succor of the holy territory.

Whilst the proposed crusade was slowly progressing, the holy pontiff wrote to the sultan of Egypt, the ally of the Carizmians, proposing a peace or a truce, and received the following grand and magnificent reply to his communication:—"To the pope, the noble, the great, the spiritual, the affectionate, the holy, the thirteenth of the apostles, the leader of the sons of baptism, the high priest of the Christians, (may God strengthen him and establish him, and give him happiness!) from the most powerful sultan ruling over the necks of nations; wielding the two great weapons, the sword and the pen; possessing two pre-eminent excellencies—that is to say, learning and judgment; king of two seas; ruler of the South and North; king of the region of Egypt and Syria, Mesopotamia, Media, Idumea, and Ophir; king Saloph Beelpheth, Jacob, son of Sultan Kamel, Hemevafar Mehameth, son of Sultan Hadel, Robethre, son of Jacob, whose kingdom may the Lord God make happy.

"In the name of God the most merciful and compassionate. The letters of the pope, the noble, the great, &c., &c., have been presented to us. May God favor him who earnestly seeketh after righteousness and doeth good, and wisheth peace, and walketh in the ways of the Lord. May God assist him who worshippeth him in truth. We have considered the aforesaid letters, and have understood the matters treated of therein, which have pleased and delighted us; and the messenger sent by the holy pope came to us, and we caused him to be brought before us with honor, and love, and reverence; and we brought him to see us face to face, and

---

[*] *Cotton* MS. Nero E. VI. p. 60, fol. 466. L'Art de Verif. tom. v. 552. *Matt. Par.* p. 618-620.
[†] *Cotton* MS. Nero E. VI. p. 60, fol. 466. L'Art de Verif. tom. v. 552. *Matt. Par.* p. 618-620.

inclining our ears towards him, we listened to his speech, and we have put faith in the words he hath spoken unto us concerning Christ, upon whom be salvation and praise. But we know more concerning that same Christ than ye know, and we magnify him more than ye magnify him. And as to what you say concerning your desire for peace, tranquillity, and quiet, and that you wish to put down war, so also do we; we desire and wish nothing to the contrary. But let the pope know, that between ourselves and the emperor (Frederick) there hath been mutual love, and alliance, and perfect concord, from the time of the sultan, my father, (whom may God preserve and place in the glory of his brightness!) and between you and the emperor there is, as ye know, strife and warfare; whence it is not fit that we should enter into any treaty with the Christians until we have previously had his advice and assent. We have therefore written to our envoy at the imperial court upon the propositions made to us by the pope's messenger, &c.... This letter was written on the seventh of the month *Maharan*. Praise be to the one only God, and may his blessing rest upon our master, *Mahomet*."[*]

In the course of a few years the Carizmians were annihilated. The sultan of Egypt having no further need of their services, left them to perish in the lands they had wasted. They were attacked by the sultans of Aleppo and Hems, and were pursued with equal fury by Moslems and by Christians. Several large bodies of them were cut up in detail by the Templars and Hospitallers, and they were at last slain to a man. Their very name perished from the face of the earth, but the traces of their existence were long preserved in the ruin and desolation they had spread around them.[†] The Holy Land, although happily freed from the destructive presence of these barbarians, had yet everything to fear from the powerful sultan of Egypt, with whom hostilities still continued; and Brother William de Sonnac, the Grand Master of the Temple, for the purpose of stimulating the languid energies of the English nation, and reviving their holy zeal and enthusiasm in the cause of the cross, despatched a distinguished Knight Templar to England, charged with the duty of presenting to king Henry the Third a magnificent crystal vase, containing, as it was alleged, a portion of the blood of Jesus Christ!

A solemn attestation of the genuineness of this precious relic, signed by the patriarch of Jerusalem, and the bishops, abbots, and barons of the Holy Land, was forwarded to London, and was deposited, together with the vase and its contents, in the cathedral church of St. Paul. The king ordered the bishops and clergy devoutly and reverently to assemble at St. Paul's, on the anniversary of the translation of St. Edward the Confessor, in full canonicals, with banners, crosses, and lighted wax-candles. On the eve of that day, according to the monk of St. Albans, who personally assisted at the ceremony, "our lord the king, with a devout and contrite spirit, as became that most Christian prince, fasting on bread and water, and watching all night with a great light, and performing many pious exercises,

---

[*] *Matt. Par.* p. 711.
[†] *Matt. Par.* p. 733.

prudently prepared himself for the morrow's solemnity." On the morrow a procession of bishops, monks, and priests, having been duly marshaled and arranged, king Henry made his appearance upon the steps at the south door of St. Paul's cathedral, and receiving with "the greatest honor, and reverence, and fear, the little vase containing the memorable treasure, he bore it publicly through the streets of London, holding it aloft just above his face. Bareheaded, and clothed in a humble habit, he walked afoot without halting, to Westminster Abbey; and although he passed over rough and uneven pavements, yet he invariably kept his eyes stedfastly fixed, either on heaven or on that vase." He made a solemn procession round the Abbey, then round the palace at Westminster, and then round his own bed-chamber, all the while unweariedly bearing aloft the precious relic, after which he presented it to God, and the church of St. Peter, to his dear Edward, and the sacred convent at Westminster.[*]

In the mean time the Comans, another fierce pastoral tribe of wandering Tartars, made their way through the Christian province of Armenia into the principality of Antioch, and ravaged both banks of the Orontes, carrying away the inhabitants into captivity. The king of Armenia and the prince of Antioch despatched messengers to the Templars and Hospitallers for succor; and the Grand Masters, collecting all their disposable forces, hurried to the relief of the distressed provinces. In a long and bloody battle, fought in the neighborhood of the iron bridge over the Orontes, the Comans were overthrown and slaughtered, and the vast and wealthy city of Antioch was saved from pillage. The Hospitallers suffered severe loss in this engagement, and Brother Bertrand de Comps, their Grand Master, died of his wounds four days after the battle.

In the month of June, A. D. 1249, the galleys of the Templars left Acre with all their disposable forces on board, under the command of the Grand Master William de Sonnac, and joined the great French expedition of Louis king of France which had been directed against the infidels in Egypt. After the capture of Damietta, the following letter was forwarded by Brother William de Sonnac to the Master of the Temple at London:—
"Brother William de Sonnac, by the grace of God Master of the poor chivalry of the Temple, to his beloved brother in Christ, Robert de Sanford, Preceptor of England, salvation through the Lord. We hasten to unfold to you by these presents, agreeable and happy intelligence.... (He details the landing of the French, the defeat of the infidels with the loss of one Christian soldier, and the subsequent capture of the city.) Damietta, therefore, has been taken, not by our deserts, nor by the might of our armed bands, but through the divine power and assistance. Moreover, be it known to you that king Louis, with God's favor, proposes to march upon Alexandria or Cairo for the purpose of delivering our brethren there detained in captivity, and of reducing, with God's help, the whole land to the Christian worship. Farewell."[†]

---

[*] *Matt. Par.* p. 736, et in additamentis, p. 161, ad ann. 1247.
[†] *Matt. Par.* in additamentis, p. 168, 169.

The Knights Templars

The Lord de Joinville, the friend of king Louis, and one of the bravest of the French captains, gives a lively and most interesting account of the campaign, and of the exploits of the Templars. During the march towards Cairo, they led the van of the Christian army, and on one occasion, when the king of France had given strict orders that no attack should be made upon the infidels, and that an engagement should be avoided, a body of Turkish cavalry advanced against them. "One of these Turks," says Joinville, "gave a Knight Templar in the first rank so heavy a blow with his battle-axe, that it felled him under the feet of the Lord Reginald de Vichier's horse, who was Marshal of the Temple; the Marshal, seeing his man fall, cried out to his brethren, 'At them in the name of God, for I cannot longer stand this.' He instantly stuck spurs into his horse, followed by all his brethren, and as their horses were fresh, not a Saracen escaped." After marching for some days, the Templars arrived on the banks of the Tanitic branch of the Nile, (the ancient Pelusiac mouth of the river,) and found the sultan encamped with his entire force on the opposite side, to prevent and oppose their passage. King Louis attempted to construct a bridge to enable him to cross the stream, and long and earnestly did the Templars labor at the task, "but," says Joinville, "as fast as we advanced our bridge the Saracens destroyed it; they dug, on their side of the river, wide and deep holes in the earth, and as the water recoiled from our bridge it filled these holes with water, and tore away the bank, so that what we had been employed on for three weeks or a month they ruined in one or two days." To protect the soldiers employed upon the construction of the bridge large wooden towers were erected, and *chas chateils* or covered galleries, and the infidels exerted all their energies to destroy them with the terrible Greek fire. "At night," says Joinville, "they brought forward an engine called by them La Perriere, a dreadful engine to do mischief, and they flung from it such quantities of Greek fire that it was the most horrible sight ever witnessed.... This Greek fire was like a large tun, and its tail was of the length of a long spear; the noise which it made was like to thunder, and it seemed a great dragon of fire flying through the air, giving so great a light with its flame, that we saw in our camp as clearly as in broad day."

The military engines and machines were all burnt, and the Christians were about to yield themselves up to despair, when a Bedouin Arab offered, for a bribe of five hundred golden bezants, to show a safe ford. At dawn of day, on Shrove Tuesday, the French knights mounted on horseback to make trial of the ford of the Bedouin. "Before we set out," says Joinville, "the king had ordered that the Templars should form the van, and the Count d'Artois, his brother, should command the second division after the Templars; but the moment the Count d'Artois had passed the ford, he and all his people fell on the Saracens, and putting them to flight, galloped after them. The Templars sent to call the Count d'Artois back, and to tell him that it was his duty to march behind and not before them; but it happened that the Count d'Artois could not make any answer by reason of my Lord Foucquault du Melle, who held the bridle of his horse, and my Lord Foucquault, who was a right good knight, being deaf, heard nothing the Templars were saying to the Count d'Artois, but kept bawling out, '*Forward! forward!*' ('Or a eulz! or a eulz!') When the Templars perceived this, they thought they should be dis honored if they allowed the Count d'Artois thus to take the lead; so they spurred their horses more and more, and faster and faster, and chased the Turks, who fled before them, through the town of Mansourah, as far as the plains towards Babylon."*

The Arabian writers, in their account of the entry of the Templars into Mansourah, tell us that 2,000 horsemen galloped into the place sword in hand and surprised Fakho'ddin Othman, commonly called Ibn Saif, the Moslem general, and one of the principal Mamlook emirs, in the bath, and barbarously cut him to pieces as he was painting his beard before a glass.† But the impetuous courage of the Count d'Artois and the Templars had led them far away from the support of the main body of the army, and their horsemen became embarrassed in the narrow streets of Mansourah, where there was no room to charge or manœuvre with effect. The infidels rallied; they returned to the attack with vast reinforcements; the inhabitants of the town mounted to their house-tops, and discharged stones and brickbats upon the heads of the Christian knights, and the Templars were defeated and driven out of the city with dreadful carnage. "The Count d'Artois and the Earl of Leicester were there slain, and as many as three hundred other knights. The Templars lost, as their chief informed me, full fourteen score men-at-arms, and all their horsemen." The Grand Master of the Temple also lost an eye, and cut his way through the infidels to the main body of the Christian army, accompanied only by two Knights Templars. There he again mixed in the affray, took the command of a vanguard, and is to be found fighting by the side of the lord de Joinville at sunset.

At the close of the long and bloody day, the Christians regained their camp in safety. King Louis, Joinville, and the Grand Master of the Temple had been fighting side by side during a great part of the afternoon; Joinville had his horse killed under him, and performed prodigies of valor. He was severely wounded, and on retiring to his quarters he found that a magnificent tent had been sent to him by the Grand Master of the Temple, as a testimony of regard and esteem. On the first Friday in Lent, Bendocdar, the great Mamlook general and lieutenant of the sultan of Egypt, advanced at the head of a vast army of horse and foot to attack the Crusaders in their intrenchments. King Louis drew out his army in battle array, and posted them in eight divisions in front of the camp. The Templars, under their venerable Grand Master, formed the fourth division, and the fate of their gallant chieftain is thus described by the lord de Joinville. "The next battalion was under the command of Brother William de Sonnac, Master of the Temple, who had with him the small remnant of the brethren of his order who survived the battle of Shrove Tuesday. The

---

* *Joinville*, p. 47.
† *Ibn Schunah*, ad ann. Hejir, 648.

Master of the Temple made of the engines which he had taken from the Saracens a sort of rampart in his front, but when the Saracens marched up to the assault, they threw Greek fire upon it, and as the Templars had piled up many planks of fir-wood amongst these engines, they caught fire immediately; and the Saracens, perceiving that the brethren of the Temple were few in number, dashed through the burning timbers, and vigorously attacked them. In the preceding battle of Shrove Tuesday, Brother William, the Master of the Temple, lost one of his eyes, and in this battle the said lord lost his other eye, and was slain. God have mercy on his soul! And know that immediately behind the place where the battalion of the Templars stood, there was a good acre of ground, so covered with darts, arrows, and missiles, that you could not see the earth beneath them, such showers of these had been discharged against the Templars by the Saracens."[*]

The command over the surviving brethren of the order now devolved upon the Marshal, Brother Reginald de Vichier, who, collecting together the small surviving remnant of the Templars, retreated to the camp to participate in the subsequent horrors and misfortunes of the campaign. "At the end of eight or ten days," says Joinville, "the bodies of those who had been slain and thrown into the Nile rose to the top of the water. These bodies floated down the river until they came to the small bridge that communicated with each part of our army; the arch was so low that it prevented the bodies from passing underneath, and the river was consequently covered with them from bank to bank, so that the water could not be seen.... God knows how great was the stench. I never heard that any who were exposed to this infectious smell ever recovered their health. The whole army was seized with a shocking disorder, which dried up the flesh on our legs to the bone; and our skins became tanned as the ground, or like an old boot that has long lain behind a coffer.... The barbers were forced to cut away very large pieces of flesh from the gums to enable their patients to eat; it was pitiful to hear the cries and groans, they were like the cries of women in labor."

The army attempted to retreat when retreat was almost impossible; the soldiers became dispersed and scattered; thousands died by the wayside, and thousands fell alive into the hands of the enemy, among which last were the king and Joinville. They were both attacked by the disease, and king Louis laid himself down to die in an Arab hut, where he was found and kindly treated by the Saracens. Reginald de Vichier, the Marshal of the Templars, and a few of his brethren, reached Damietta in safety, and took measures for the defense of the place. All those of the prisoners who were unable to redeem their lives by services as slaves to the conquerors, or by ransom, were inhumanly massacred, and a grim circle of Christian heads decorated the walls and battlements of Cairo. The Egyptians required as the price of the liberty of the French monarch the surrender of all the

[*] *Joinville*, p. 58. *Matt. Par.* Chron. Nan. p. 790.

fortresses of the order of the Temple in Palestine; but the king told them that the Templars were not subject to his command, nor had he any means of compelling them to give effect to such an agreement. Louis and his friend Joinville at last obtained their deliverance from captivity by the surrender of Damietta, and by the payment of two hundred thousand pieces of gold; and the liberation of the king's brother, and of the other captive nobles and knights was to be purchased by the payment of a similar sum. The king immediately went on board the French fleet which was at anchor before Damietta, and exerted himself to raise the residue of the ransom; and all Saturday and Sunday were employed in collecting it together.

"On Sunday evening," says Joinville, "the king's servants, who were occupied in counting out the money, sent to say that there was a deficiency of thirty thousand livres. I observed to the king that we had better ask the commander and Marshal of the Temple, since the Master was dead, to give us the thirty thousand livres. Brother Stephen d'Otricourt, knight commander of the Temple, hearing the advice I gave to the king, said to me, 'Lord de Joinville, the counsel you give the king is not right nor reasonable, for you know that we receive every farthing of our money on our oaths;' and Brother Reginald de Vichier, who was Marshal of the Temple, said to the king, 'Sire, it is as our commander has said, we cannot dispose of any of the money intrusted to us but for the means intended, in accordance with the rules of our institution, without being perjured. Know that the seneschal hath ill advised you to take our money by force, but in this you will act as you please; should you, however, do so, *we will make ourselves amends out of the money you have in Acre.*' I then told the king that if he wished I would go and get the money, and he commanded me so to do. I instantly went on board one of the galleys of the Templars, and demanded of the treasurer the keys of a coffer which I saw before me. They refused, and I was about to break it open with a wedge in the king's name, when the Marshal, observing I was in earnest, ordered the keys to be given to me. I opened the coffer, took out the sum wanting, and carried it to the king, who was much rejoiced at my return." King Louis returned with the Templars to Palestine; and was received with great distinction by the order at Acre, where he remained four years!

In the year 1251 a general chapter of Knights Templars being assembled in the Pilgrim's Castle, the Marshal, Brother Reginald de Vichier, who had commanded with great skill and prudence in Egypt after the death of Brother William de Sonnac, was chosen to fill the vacant dignity of Grand Master. Henry III., king of England, had assumed the cross shortly after intelligence had been conveyed to England of the horrors and atrocities committed by the Carizmians in the Holy City. Year after year, he had promised to fulfill his vow, and the pope issued numerous bulls, kindly providing for the tranquillity and security of his dominions during his absence, and ordered prayers to be offered up to God for the success of his arms, in all the churches of Christendom. King Henry assembled a parliament to obtain the necessary supplies, and fixed the 24th day of June, A. D. 1255, as the period of his departure. His knights and barons, however, refused him the necessary funds, and the needy monarch addressed the military orders of the Temple and the Hospital in the following very curious letter. "As you are said to possess a well-equipped fleet, we beseech you to set apart for our own use some of your strongest vessels, and have them furnished and equipped with provisions, sailors, and all things requisite for a twelvemonth's voyage, so that we may be able, ere the period for our own departure arrives, to freight them with the soldiers, arms, horses, and munitions of war that we intend to send to the succor of the Holy Land. You will also be pleased to provide secure habitations and suitable accommodation for the said soldiers and their equipage, until the period of our own arrival. You will then be good enough to send back the same vessels to England to conduct ourselves and suite to Palestine; and by your prompt obedience to these our commands, we shall judge of your devotion to the interests of the Holy Land, and of your attachment to our person."[*]

King Louis, in the mean time, assisted the Templars in repairing the fortifications of Jaffa and Cæsarea. The lord de Joinville who was with him tells us that the scheik of the assassins, who still continued to pay tribute to the Templars, sent ambassadors to the king to obtain a remission of the tribute. He gave them an audience, and declared that he would consider of their proposal. "When they came again before the king," says Joinville, "it was about vespers, and they found the Master of the Temple on one side of him, and the Master of the Hospital on the other. The ambassadors refused to repeat what they had said in the morning, but the Masters of the Temple and the Hospital commanded them so to do. Then the Masters of the Temple and Hospital told them that their lord had very foolishly and impudently sent such a message to the king of France, and had they not been invested with the character of ambassadors, they would have thrown them into the filthy sea of Acre, and have drowned them in despite of their master. 'And we command you,' continued the Masters, 'to return to your lord, and to come back within fifteen days with such letters from your prince, that the king shall be contented with him and with you.'" The ambassadors accordingly did as they were bid, and brought back from their scheik a shirt, the symbol of friendship, and a great variety of rich presents, "crystal elephants, pieces of amber, with borders of pure gold," &c., &c. "You must know that when the ambassadors opened the case containing all these fine things, the whole apartment was instantly embalmed with the odor of their sweet perfumes."

The treaty entered into between king Louis and the infidels having been violated by the murder of the sick at Damietta, and by the detention, in a state of slavery, of many knights and soldiers, as well as of a large body of Christian children, the Templars recommenced hostilities, and marched with Joinville and the French knights against the strong castle of

---

[*] Acta *Rymeri*, tom. i. p. 473.

Panias, and after an obstinate resistance, carried the place sword in hand. The sultan of Damascus immediately took the field; he stormed the Temple fort Dok, slaughtered the garrison, and razed the fortifications to the ground; the castle of Ricordane shared the same fate, and the city of Sidon was taken by assault, (A. D. 1254,) whilst the workmen and artificers were diligently employed in rebuilding the walls; eight hundred men were put to the sword, and four hundred masons and artificers were taken prisoners and carried off to Damascus. After residing nearly two years at Acre, and spending vast sums of money upon the defenses of the maritime towns of Palestine, king Louis returned to France. He set sail from Acre on the 24th of April, with a fleet of fourteen sail, his ship being steered by Brother Rèmond, the pilot of the Grand Master of the Temple, who was charged to conduct the king across the wide waters in safety to his own dominions. On his arrival in France, Louis manifested his esteem for the Templars by granting them the château and lordship of Bazèes, near Bauvez, in Aquitaine. The deed of gift is expressed to be made in consideration of the charitable works which the king had seen performed amongst the Templars, and in acknowledgment of the services they had rendered to him, and to the intent that he might be made a participator in the good works done by the fraternity, and be remembered in the prayers of the brethren. This deed was delivered on the day of Pentecost to Brother Hugh, Grand Preceptor of Aquitaine, in the cathedral church of Angouleme, in the presence of numerous archbishops, bishops, counts, and barons.[*]

At the period of the return of the king of France to Europe, Henry the Third, king of England, was in Gascony with Brother Robert de Sanford, Master of the Temple at London, who had been previously sent by the English monarch into that province to appease the troubles which had there broken out. King Henry proceeded to the French capital, and was magnificently entertained by the Knights Templars at the Temple in Paris, which Matthew Paris tells us was of such immense extent that it could contain within its precincts a numerous army. The day after his arrival, king Henry ordered an innumerable quantity of poor people to be regaled at the Temple with meat, fish, bread, and wine; and at a later hour the king of France and all his nobles came to dine with the English monarch. "Never," says Matthew Paris, "was there at any period in bygone times so noble and so celebrated an entertainment. They feasted in the great hall of the Temple, where hang the shields on every side, as many as they can place along the four walls, according to the custom of the order beyond sea...." The Knights Templars in this country likewise exercised a magnificent hospitality, and constantly entertained kings, princes, nobles, prelates, and foreign ambassadors at the Temple. Immediately after the return of king Henry to England, some illustrious ambassadors from Castile came on a visit to the Temple at London; and as the king "greatly delighted to honor them," he commanded three pipes of wine to be placed

[*] Gal. Christ. nov. tom. ii. col. 1008. *Tyr.* Contin. col. 735.

in the cellars of the Temple for their use, and ten fat bucks to be brought them at the same place from the royal forest in Essex. He, moreover, commanded the mayor and sheriffs of London, and the commonalty of the same city, to take with them a respectable assemblage of the citizens, and to go forth and meet the said ambassadors without the city, and courteously receive them, and honor them, and conduct them to the Temple.*

During the first and second years of the pontificate of pope Alexander IV. ten bulls were published in favor of the Templars, addressed to the bishops of the church universal, commanding them to respect and maintain the privileges conceded to them by the holy see; to judge and punish all persons who should dare to exact tythe from the fraternity; to institute to the ecclesiastical benefices of the order, all clerks presented to them by the preceptors, without previously requiring them to make a fixed maintenance for such clerks, and severely to punish, all who appropriated to their own use the alms gifts and eleemosynary donations made to the brotherhood. By these bulls the Templars are declared to be exempt from the duty of contributing to the travelling expenses of all nuncios and legates of the holy see, under the dignity of a cardinal, when passing through their territories, unless express orders to the contrary are given by apostolic letters, and all the bishops are required earnestly and vigorously to protect and defend the right of sanctuary accorded the houses of the Temple.†

In the year 1257, Brother Reginald de Vichier, the Grand Master of the Temple, fell sick and died, at an advanced age. He was succeeded by the English Knight Templar Brother Thomas Berard. Shortly after his election the terrible Moguls and Tartars, those fierce vagrant tribes of shepherds and hunters, whose victorious arms had spread terror and desolation over the greater part of Europe and Asia, invaded Palestine, under the command of the famous Holagou, and spread themselves like a cloud of devouring locusts over the whole country. The Templars, under the command of Brother Etienne de Sisi, Grand Preceptor of Apulia, hastened to meet them, and were cut to pieces in a sanguinary fight. The Tartars besieged and took the rich and populous cities of Aleppo, Hamah, Hems, Damascus, Tiberias, and Naplous, and at last entered in triumph the holy city of Jerusalem.‡ The Grand Master Brother Thomas Berard wrote a melancholy letter to king Henry the Third for succor. "With continual letters and many prayers," says he, "has our poor Christianity on this side the sea besought the assistance of the kings and princes of this world, and above all, the aid and succor of your majesty, imploring your royal compassion with sighs and tears, and a loud sounding voice, and crying out with a bitter cry in the hope that it would penetrate the royal ear, and reach the ends of the earth, and arouse the faithful from their slumbers, and draw them to the protection of the Holy Land."§ The king of England, however,

---

* Acta *Rymeri*, tom. i. p. 474, 557, 558. *Matt. Par.* p. 899.
† Reg. et constit. ord. Cisterc. p. 480. Acta *Rymeri*, tom. i. p. 575-582.
‡ *Od. Rainald*, ad ann. 1257. *Tyr.* Contin. col. 732, 735-737.

was in pecuniary embarrassments, and unable to afford the necessary succor. He was reduced, indeed, to the cruel necessity of borrowing money in France upon the security of his regalia and crown jewels, which were deposited in the Temple at Paris, as appears from the letter of the queen of France "to her very dear brother Henry, the illustrious king of England," giving a long list of golden wands, golden combs, diamond buckles, chaplets, and circlets, golden crowns, imperial beavers, rich girdles, golden peacocks, and rings innumerable, adorned with sapphires, rubies, emeralds, topazes, and carbuncles, which she says she had inspected in the presence of the treasurer of the Temple at Paris, and that the same were safely deposited in the coffers of the Templars.*

In the mean time the Mamlooks, "who had breathed in their infancy the keenness of a Scythian air," advanced from the banks of the Nile to contend with the Tartars for the dominion of Palestine. Under the command of Bendocdar, the Mamlook general, they gained a complete victory over them in the neighborhood of Tiberias, and drove back the stream of hostility to the eastward of the Euphrates. Bendocdar returned to Egypt the idol of his soldiers, and clothed with a popularity which rendered him too powerful for a subject. He aspired to the possession of the throne which he had so successfully defended, and slew with his own hand his sovereign and master Kothuz, the third Mamlook sultan of Egypt. The Mamlooks hailed him with acclamations as their sovereign, and on the 24th day of October, A. D. 1260, he was solemnly proclaimed sultan of Egypt, in the town of Salahieh in the Delta. Bendocdar was one of the greatest men of the age, and soon proved the most formidable enemy that the Templars had encountered in the field since the days of Saladin. The first two years of his accession to power were employed in the extension and consolidation of his sway over the adjoining Mussulman countries. The holy cities of Mecca and Medina acknowledged him for their sovereign, as did Damascus, Aleppo, Hems, and Jerusalem. His sway extended over Egypt, Nubia, Arabia, and Syria; and his throne was defended by twenty-five thousand Mamlook cavalry. His power was further strengthened by an army of one hundred and seven thousand foot, and by the occasional aid of sixty-six thousand Arabians.

After receiving the homage and submission of the rulers and people of Aleppo, Bendocdar made a hostile demonstration against the vast and wealthy city of Antioch; but finding the place well defended, he retired with his army, by way of Hems, Damascus, and Tiberias, to Egypt. The next year (A. D. 1264) he crossed the desert at the head of thirty thousand cavalry, and overran all Palestine up to the very gates of Acre. He burned the great churches of Nazareth and Mount Tabor; and sought to awaken the zeal and enthusiasm of his soldiers in behalf of Islam by performing the pilgrimage to Jerusalem, and visiting with great devotion the Mosque of Omar. He then retired to Cairo with his troops, and the Templars and

---

§ Acta *Rymeri*, tom. i. p. 698.
* Ib. p. 730, 878, 879.

Hospitallers became the assailants. They surprised and stormed the castle of Lilion, razed the walls and fortifications to the ground, and brought off three hundred prisoners of both sexes, together with a rich prize of sheep and oxen. On the 15th of June, they marched as far as Ascalon, surprised and slew two Mamlook emirs, and put twenty-eight of their followers to the sword. They then turned their footsteps towards the Jordan, and on the 5th of November, they destroyed Bisan or Scythopolis, and laid waste with fire and sword all the valley of the Jordan, as far as the lake of Tiberias.

In the depth of winter, (A. D. 1265,) Bendocdar collected his forces together, and advanced, by rapid marches, from Egypt. He concealed his real intentions, made a long march during the night, and at morning's dawn presented himself before the city of Cæsarea. His troops descended into the ditch by means of ropes and ladders, and climbed the walls with the aid of iron hooks and spikes; they burst open the gates, massacred the sentinels, and planted the standard of the prophet on the ramparts, ere the inhabitants had time to rouse themselves from their morning slumbers. The citadel, however, still remained to be taken, and the garrison being forewarned, made an obstinate defense. The Arabian writers tell us, that the citadel was a strong and handsome fortification, erected by king Louis, and adorned with pillars and columns. It stood on a small neck of land which jutted out into the sea, and the ditches around the fortress were filled with the blue waters of the Mediterranean. Bendocdar planted huge catapults and cross-bows upon the tower of the cathedral, and shot arrows, darts, and stones, from them upon the battlements of the citadel. He encouraged the exertions of his soldiers by promises of reward, and gave robes of honor to his principal emirs. Weapons of war were distributed in the most lavish manner, every captain of a hundred horse receiving for the use of himself and his men *four thousand arrows*!

During a dark winter's night the garrison succeeded in making their escape, and the next morning the Moslems poured into the citadel by thousands, and abandoned themselves to pillage. The fortifications were leveled with the dust, and Bendocdar assisted with his own hands in the work of demolition. He then detached some Mamlook emirs with a body of cavalry against Caiphas, and proceeded himself to watch the movements of the Templars, and examine into the defenses of the Pilgrim's Castle. Finding the place almost impregnable, and defended by a numerous garrison, he suddenly retraced his steps to the south, and stormed, after a brave and obstinate defense, the strongly fortified city of Arsoof, which belonged to the Knights Hospitallers of St. John. The greater part of the garrison was massacred, but one thousand captives were reserved to grace the triumph of the conqueror. They were compelled to march at the head of his triumphal procession, with their banners reversed, and with their crosses, broken into pieces, hung round their necks. Bendocdar had already despatched his bravest Mamlook generals, at the head of a considerable body of forces, to blockade Beaufort and Saphet, two strong fortresses of the order of the Temple, and he now advanced at the head of a vast army to conduct the siege of the latter place in person. On 21 Ramadan, the separate timbers of his military machines arrived from Damascus at Jacob's bridge on the Jordan; the sultan sent down his emirs and part of his army, with hundreds of oxen, to drag them up the mountains to Saphet, and went with his principal officers to assist in the transport of them. "I worked by the sultan's side, and aided him with all my might," says the cadi Mohieddin; "being fatigued, I sat down. I began again, and was once more tired, and compelled to take rest, but the sultan continued to work without intermission, aiding in the transport of beams, bolts, and huge frames of timber." The Grand Master of the Temple ordered out twelve hundred cavalry from Acre to create a diversion in favor of the besieged; but a treacherous spy conveyed intelligence to Bendocdar, which enabled him to surprise and massacre the whole force, and return to Saphet with their heads stuck on the lances of his soldiers. At last, after an obstinate defense, during which many Moslems, say the Arabian writers, obtained the crown of martyrdom, the huge walls were thrown down, and a breach was presented to the infidels; but that breach was so stoutly guarded that none could be found to mount to the assault. Bendocdar offered a reward of three hundred pieces of gold to the first man who entered the city; he distributed robes of honor and riches to all who were foremost in the fight, and the outer inclosure, or first line of the fortifications was, at last, taken.

The Templars retired into the citadel, but their efforts at defense were embarrassed by the presence of a crowd of two thousand fugitives, who had fled to Saphet for shelter, and they agreed to capitulate on condition that the lives and liberties of the Christians should be respected, and that they should be transported in safety to Acre. Bendocdar acceded to these terms, and solemnly promised to fulfill them; but as soon as he had got the citadel into his power, he offered to all the Templars the severe alternative of the Koran or death, and gave them until the following morning to make their election. The preceptor of Saphet, a holy monk and veteran warrior, assisted by two Franciscan friars, passed the night in pious exhortations to his brethren, conjuring them to prefer the crown of martyrdom to a few short years of miserable existence in this sinful world, and not to disgrace themselves and their order by a shameful apostasy. At sunrise, on the following morning, the Templars were led on to the brow of the hill, in front of the castle of Saphet, and when the first rays of the rising sun gilded the wooded summits of Mount Hermon, and the voice of the muezzin was heard calling the faithful to morning prayer, they were required to join in the Moslem chaunt, *La-i-la i-la Allah, Mahommed re sul Allah,* "There is no God but God, and Mahomet is his apostle;" the executioners drew near with their naked scimitars, but not a man of the noble company of knightly warriors, say the Christian writers, would renounce his faith, and one thousand five hundred heads speedily rolled at the feet of Bendocdar. "The blood," says Sanutus, "flowed down the declivities like a rivulet of water." The preceptor of Saphet, the priests of the order, and brother Jeremiah, were beaten with clubs, flayed alive, and then beheaded! The Arabian writers state that the lives of two of the garrison were spared, one being an Hospitaller whom the besieged had sent to Bendocdar to negotiate the treaty of surrender, and the other a Templar, named *Effreez Lyoub*, who embraced the Mahomedan faith, and was circumcised and entered into the service of the sultan.[*] Immediately after the fall of Saphet, the infidels stormed the castles of Hounin and Tebnin, and took possession of the city of Ramleh.

The Grand Master of the Hospital now sued for peace, and entered into a separate treaty with the infidels. He agreed to renounce the ancient tribute of one hundred pieces of gold paid to the order by the district of Bouktyr; also the annual tribute of four thousand pieces of gold paid to them by the sultans of Hems and Hamah; a tribute of twelve hundred pieces of gold, fifty thousand bushels of wheat, and fifty thousand bushels of barley annually rendered to them by the Assassins or Ismaelians of the mountains of Tripoli: and the several tributes paid by the cities or districts of Schayzar, Apamea, and Aintab, which consisted of five hundred crowns of Tyrian silver, two measures of wheat, and two pieces of silver for every two head of oxen pastured in the district. These terms being arranged, the emir Fakir-eddin, and the cadi Schams-eddin were sent to receive the oath of the Grand Master of the Hospital to fulfill them, and a truce was then accorded him for ten years, ten days, and ten months.

Bendocdar then concentrated his forces together at Aleppo, and marched against the Christian province of Armenia. The prince of Hamah blockaded Darbesak, which was garrisoned by the Knights Templars, and forced the mountain passes leading into the ancient Cilicia. The Moslems then marched with incredible rapidity to Sis, the capital of the country, which fell into their hands after a short siege. Leon, king of Armenia, was led away into captivity, together with his uncle, his son, and his nephew; many others of the royal family were killed, and some made their escape. All the castles of the Templars in Armenia were assaulted and taken, and the garrisons massacred. The most famous of these was the castle of Amoud, which was stormed after an obstinate defense, and every soul found in it was put to the sword. The city of Sis was pillaged, and then delivered up to the flames; the inhabitants of all the towns were either massacred or reduced to slavery; their goods and possessions were divided amongst the soldiers, and the Moslems returned to Aleppo laden with booty and surrounded by captives fastened together with ropes. Great was the joy of Bendocdar. The musicians were ordered to play, and the dancing girls to beat the tambour and dance before him. He made a triumphant entry into Damascus, preceded by his royal captives and many thousand prisoners bound with chains. "Thus did the sultan," says the Arabian historian, "cut the sugar-canes of the Franks!"

---

[*] *Tyr.* Contin. Hist. col. 737, 742. *Sanut.* p. 220-222. *Abulfeda*, apud *Wilkins*, p. 223. *Ibn Ferat* Chron. Arab ad ann. Hejir. 662, 664. *Mohieddin*, by *Schafi Ibn Ali Abbas. Michaud* Extraits, 668, 669, 673, 674.

On the 1st of May, A. D. 1267, Bendocdar collected together a strong body of cavalry, divided them into two bodies, and caused them to mount the banners and emblems of the Hospital and Temple. By this ruse he attempted to penetrate the east gate of Acre, but the cheat was fortunately discovered, and the gates were closed ere the Arab cavalry reached them. The infidels then slaughtered five hundred people outside the walls, cut off their heads and put them into sacks. Amongst them were some poor old women who gained a livelihood by gathering herbs! The ferocious Mamlooks then pulled down all the houses and windmills, plucked up the vines, cut down all the fruit trees and burnt them, and filled up the wells. Some deputies, sent to sue for peace, were introduced to Bendocdar through a grim and ghastly avenue of Christian heads planted on the points of lances, and their petition was rejected with scorn and contempt. "The neighing of our horses," said the ferocious sultan, "shall soon strike you with deafness, and the dust raised by their feet shall penetrate to the inmost chambers of your dwellings."

On the 7th of March, A. D. 1268, the sultan stormed Jaffa, put the garrison to the sword, set fire to the churches, and burnt the crucifixes and crosses and holy relics of the saints. "He took away the head of St. George and burnt the body of St. Christina," and then marched against the strongly fortified city of Beaufort, which belonged to the order of the Temple. Twenty-six enormous military engines were planted around the walls, and the doctors of the law and the *Fakirs*, or teachers of religion, were invited to repair to the Moslem camp, and wield the sword in behalf of Islam. The town was defended by two citadels, the ancient and the new one. The former was garrisoned by the Templars, and the latter by the native militia. These last, after sustaining a short siege, set fire to their post and fled during the night. "As for the other citadel," says the cadi Mohieddin, "it made a long and vigorous defense," and Bendocdar, after losing the flower of his army before the place, was reluctantly compelled to permit the garrison to march out, sword in hand, with all the honors of war. The fortress was then razed to the ground so effectually that not a trace of it was left.

The sultan now separated his army into several divisions, which were all sent in different directions through the principality of Tripoli to waste and destroy. All the churches and houses were set on fire; the trees were cut down, and the inhabitants were led away into captivity. A tower of the Templars, in the environs of Tripoli, was taken by assault, and every soul found in it was put to death. The different divisions of the army were then concentrated at Hems, to collect together and to divide their spoil. They were then again separated into three corps, which were sent by different routes against the vast and wealthy city of Antioch, the ancient "Queen of Syria." The first division was directed to take a circuitous route by way of Darbesak, and approach Antioch from the north; the second was to march upon Suadia, and to secure the mouth of the Orontes, to prevent all succor from reaching the city by sea; and the third and last division, which was led by Bendocdar in person, proceeded to Apamea, and from thence marched down the left bank of the river Orontes along the base of the ancient Mons Casius, so as to approach and hem in Antioch from the south. On the 1st Ramadan, all these different divisions were concentrated together, and the city was immediately surrounded by a vast army of horse and foot, which cut off all communication between the town and the surrounding country, and exposed a population of 160,000 souls to all the horrors of famine. The famous stone bridge of nine arches, which spanned the Orontes, and communicated between the city and the right bank of the river, was immediately attacked; the iron doors which guarded the passage were burst open with the battering-rams, and the standard of the prophet was planted beneath the great western gate. The Templars of the principality, under the command of their Grand Preceptor, made a vain effort to drive back the infidels and relieve the city. They sallied out of the town, with the constable of Antioch, but were defeated by the Mamlook cavalry, after a sharp encounter in the plain, and were compelled to take refuge behind the walls.

For three days successively did the sultan vainly summon the city to surrender, and for three days did he continue his furious assaults. On the fourth day the Moslems scaled the walls where they touch the side of the mountain; they rushed across the ramparts, sword in hand, into the city, and a hundred thousand Christians are computed to have been slain! About eight thousand soldiers, accompanied by a dense throng of women and children, fled from the scene of carnage to the citadel, and there defended themselves with the energy of despair. Bendocdar granted them their lives, and they surrendered. They were bound with cords, and the long string of mournful captives passed in review before the sultan, who caused the scribes and notaries to take down the names of each of them. After several days of pillage, all the booty was brought together in the plain of Antioch, and equally divided amongst the Moslems; the gold and silver were distributed by measure, and merchandize and property of all kinds, piled up in heaps, were drawn for by lot. The captive women and girls were distributed amongst the soldiery, and they were so numerous that each of the slaves of the conquerors was permitted to have a captive at his disposal. The sultan halted for several weeks in the plain, and permitted his soldiers to hold a large market, or fair, for the sale of their booty. This market was attended by Jews and pedlars from all parts of the East, who greedily bought up the rich property and costly valuables of the poor citizens of Antioch.

These last might have borne with fortitude the loss of their worldly possessions, and the luxuries of this life, but when they were themselves put up to auction—when the mother saw her infant child handed over to the avaricious Jew for the paltry sum of five pieces of silver, and sold into irredeemable bondage, the bitter cries that resounded through the plain, touched even the hearts of the Moslems. "It was," says the cadi Mohieddin, "a fearful and a heart-rending sight. Even the hard stones were softened with grief." He tells us, that the captives were so numerous, that a fine hearty boy might be purchased for *twelve* pieces of silver, and a little girl for *five*! When the work of pillage had been completed, when all the ornaments and decorations had been carried away from the churches, and the lead torn from the roofs, Antioch was fired in different places, amid the loud thrilling shouts of Allah Acbar, "God *is* VICTORIOUS!" The great churches of St. Paul and St. Peter burnt with terrific fury for many days, and the vast and venerable city was left without a habitation, and without an inhabitant!

Thus fell Antioch, one hundred and seventy years after its recovery from the dominion of the infidels by the crusaders, under the command of the valiant Godfrey, Boemond, and Tancred. Near six centuries of Moslem domination have now again rolled over the ancient Queen of the East, but the genius of destruction which accompanied the footsteps of the armies of the ferocious Bendocdar has ever since presided over the spot. The once fair and flourishing capital of Syria, the ancient "throne of the successors of Alexander, the seat of Roman government in the east, which had been decorated by Cæsar with the titles of free, and holy, and inviolate," is, at this day, nothing more than a miserable mud village; and the ancient and illustrious church of Antioch, which, in the fourth century of the Christian era, numbered one hundred thousand persons, now consists only of a few Greek families, who still cling to the Christian faith amid the insults and persecutions of the infidels. Immediately after the destruction of the city, Bendocdar caused the following letter to be written to the prince of Antioch, who was at Tripoli: "Since not a soul has escaped to tell you what has happened, we will undertake the pleasing task of informing you.... We have slain all whom you appointed to defend Antioch. We have crushed your knights beneath the feet of our horses, and have given up your provinces to pillage: your gold and silver have been divided amongst us by the quintal, and four of your women have been bought and sold for a crown. There is not a single Christian in the province that does not now march bound before us, nor a single young girl that is not in our possession. Your churches have been made level with the dust, and our chariot wheels have passed over the sites of your dwellings. If you had seen the temples of your God destroyed, the crosses broken, and the leaves of the gospel torn and scattered to the winds of heaven; if you had seen your Mussulman enemy marching into your tabernacles, and immolating upon your shrines and your altars, the priest, the deacon, and the bishop; if you had seen your palaces delivered to the flames, and the bodies of the dead consumed by the fire of this world, whilst their souls were burning in the everlasting *fire of* HELL; doubtless, you would have exclaimed, *Lord, I am become but as dust*; your soul would have been ready to start from its earthly tenement, and your eyes would have rained down tears sufficient to have extinguished the fires that we have kindled around you."[*]

---

[*] *Ibn Ferat.* Hejir. 666. *Michaud*, Extr. 675-785. *Tyr.* Contin. col. 743

The Knights Templars

On the fall of Antioch the Templars abandoned Bagras, a rich and flourishing town, on the road to Armenia and Cilicia, which had belonged to the order for more than a century. This town of the Templars, Mohieddin tells us, had long been a source of intense anxiety and annoyance to the Moslems. "Over and over again," says he, "it had been attacked, but the Templars foiled the utmost efforts of the faithful, until, at last, Providence gave it into our hands." The Templars also abandoned the castles of Gaston and Noche de Rusol, and the territory of Port Bounel, at the entrance of Armenia. The towns of Darbesak, Sabah, Al Hadid, and the sea-port of Gabala, successively fell into the hands of Bendocdar, and the whole country from Tripoli to Mount Taurus was made desolate, the houses were set on fire, the fruit trees were cut down, and the churches were leveled with the dust. The wealthy and populous maritime towns of Laodicea, Tripoli, Tortosa, Beirout, Tyre, and Sidon, however, still remained to the Christians, and as these cities were strongly fortified, and the Christian fleets kept the command of the sea, Bendocdar postponed their destruction for a brief period, and granted separate truces to them in consideration of the payment of large sums of money.

In the year 1269, a terrible famine, consequent upon the ravages of the infidels, afflicted Syria and Palestine, and many of those whom the sword had spared, now died of hunger. Louis IX., king of France, being deeply affected by the intelligence of the misfortunes of the Latin Christians, attended an assembly of Preceptors of the Temple in France, to devise means of forwarding succor to the Holy Land, and caused a quantity of corn to be sent from Languedoc to Palestine. He moreover determined to embark in another crusade, and he induced prince Edward of England to assume the cross, and prepare to join his standard. Bendocdar, on the other hand, returned from Egypt to Palestine; he surprised and cut to pieces several bands of Christians, and made his public entry into Damascus, preceded by many hundred ghastly heads stuck on the points of lances, and by a vast number of weeping captives of both sexes, and of every age. He then proceeded to Hamah and Kafarthab, and attempted to undertake the siege of the strong fortress of Merkab, but the winter rains and the snow on the mountain compelled him to abandon the enterprise. He then made an attack upon the castle of the Kurds, which belonged to the Hospitallers, but receiving intelligence of the sailing of the expedition of king Louis, who had left the ports of France with an army of sixty thousand men, and a fleet of eighteen hundred vessels; he hurried with all his forces to Egypt to protect that country against the French. Instead of proceeding direct to the Holy Land, king Louis was unfortunately induced to steer to Tunis. He fell a victim to the insalubrity of the climate, and his army, decimated by sickness, sailed back to France. Bendocdar immediately returned to Palestine. He halted at Ascalon, and completed the destruction of the fortifications of that place; he stormed Castel Blanc, a fortress of the Templars, and appeared with his Mamlook cavalry before the gates of Tripoli. He ravaged the surrounding country, and then retired into winter quarters, leading away many Christian prisoners of both sexes into captivity. The next year he stormed the fortified town of Safitza, and laid siege to Hassan el Akrad, or the castle of the Kurds. His victorious career was checked by the arrival (A. D. 1271) of prince Edward of England, who joined the Grand Master of the Temple at the head of a welcome reinforcement of knights and foot soldiers. Various successes were then obtained over the infidels, and on the 21st Ramadan, (April 23rd, A. D. 1272,) a truce was agreed upon for the space of ten years and ten months, as far as regarded the town and plain of Acre, and the road to Nazareth.

On the 18th of June, prince Edward was stabbed with a poisoned dagger by an assassin. Though dangerously wounded, he struck the assailant to the ground, and caused him to be immediately despatched by the guards. The same day the prince made his will; it is dated at Acre, June 18, A. D. 1272, and Brother Thomas Berard, Grand Master of the Temple, appears as an attesting witness. The life of the prince, however, was happily preserved, the effects of the poison being obviated by an antidote administered by the Grand Master of the Temple. On the 14th of September, the prince returned to Europe, and thus terminated the last expedition undertaken for the relief of Palestine. Whilst prince Edward was pursuing his voyage to England, his father, king Henry III., died, and the council of the realm, composed of the archbishops of Canterbury and York, and the English bishops and barons, assembled in the Temple at London, and swore allegiance to the prince. They there caused him to be proclaimed king of England, and, with the consent of the queen-mother, they appointed Walter Giffard, archbishop of York, and the earls of Cornwall and Gloucester, guardians of the realm. Letters were written from the Temple to acquaint the young sovereign with the death of his father, and many of the acts of the new government emanated from the same place.[*]

The Grand Master of the Temple, Brother Thomas Berard, died at Acre on the 8th of April, and on the 13th of May, A. D. 1273, the general chapter of the Templars being assembled in the Pilgrim's Castle, chose for his successor Brother William de Beaujeu, Grand Preceptor of Apulia. The late Vice-Master, Brother William de Poucon, was sent to Europe with Brother Bertrand de Fox, to announce to him the tidings of his elevation to the chief dignity of the order. The following year William de Beaujeu, accompanied by the Grand Master of the Hospital, proceeded to Lyons, to attend a general council which had been summoned by the pope to provide succor for the Holy Land. The two Grand Masters took precedence of all the ambassadors and peers present at that famous assembly. It was determined that a new crusade should be preached, that all ecclesiastical dignities and benefices should be taxed to support an armament, and that the sovereigns of Europe should be compelled by ecclesiastical censures to suspend their private quarrels, and afford succor to the desolate land of

---

[*] *Tyr.* Contin. col. 745. *Sanut*, p. 224. *Michaud*, p. 757. *Trivet*, ad ann. 1272. *Walsingham*, p. 43. Acta *Rymeri*, tom. i. p. 885, 889; tom. ii. p. 2.

promise. More than a thousand bishops, archbishops, and ambassadors from the different princes and potentates of Europe, graced the assembly with their presence. From Lyons, the Grand Master William de Beaujeu proceeded to England, and called together a general chapter of the order at London. Whilst resident at the Temple in that city, he received payment of a large sum of money, which the young king Edward had borrowed of the Templars during his stay at Acre.[*]

Pope Gregory X. died in the midst of his exertions for the creation of another crusade. The enthusiasm which had been partially awakened subsided; those who had assumed the cross forgot their engagements, and the Grand Master of the Temple at last returned, in sorrow and disappointment, to the far East. He reached Acre on St. Michael's day, A. D. 1275, attended by a band of Templars, drawn from the preceptories of England and France. Shortly after his arrival Bendocdar was poisoned, and was succeeded by his son, Malek Said. Malek Said only mounted the throne to descend from it. He was deposed by the rebellious Mamlooks, and the scepter was grasped by Malek-Mansour-Kelaoun, the bravest and most distinguished of the emirs. As there was now no hope of recovering the towns, castles, and territories taken by Bendocdar, the Grand Master directed all his energies to the preservation of the few remaining possessions of the Christians in the Holy Land. At the expiration of the ten years' truce, he entered into various treaties with the infidels. One of these, called "the peace of Tortosa," is expressed to be made between sultan Malek-Mansour-Kelaoun, and his son Malek-Saleh-Ali, " honor of the world and of religion," of the one part, and Afryz Dybadjouk, (William de Beaujeu,) Grand Master of the order of the Templars, of the other part. It relates to the territories and possessions of the order of the Temple at Tortosa, and provides for their security and freedom from molestation by the infidels. The truce is prolonged for ten years and ten months from the date of the execution of the treaty, (A. D. 1282,) and the contracting parties strictly bind themselves to make no irruptions into each other's territories during the period. To prevent mistakes, the lands and villages, towers, corn-mills, gardens, brooks, and plantations, belonging to the Templars are specified and defined, together with the contiguous possessions of the Moslems. By this treaty, the Templars engage not to rebuild any of their citadels, towers, or fortresses, nor to cut any new ditch or fosse in their province of Tortosa.

Another treaty entered into between William de Beaujcu and the infidels, is called the peace of Acre. It accords to the Christians Caiphas and seven villages, the province of Mount Carmel the town and citadel of Alelyet, the farms of the Hospitallers in the province of Cæsarea, the half of Alexandretta, the village of Maron, &c., and confirms the Templars in the possessions of Sidon and its citadel, and its fifteen cantons. By this treaty, sultan Malek Mansour conceded to the inhabitants of Acre a truce of

---

[*] *Tyr.* Contin. col. 746, 747. Acta *Rymeri*, tom. ii. p. 34.

ten years, ten months, and ten days; and he swore to observe its provisions and stipulations in the presence of the Grand Master of the Temple and the vizir Fadhad. But all these treaties were mere delusions. Bendocdar had commenced the ruin of the Christians, and sultan Kelaoun now proceeded to complete it.

The separate truces and treaties of peace which Bendocdar had accorded to the maritime towns of Palestine, in return for payments of money, were encumbered with so many minute provisions and stipulations, that it was almost impossible for the Christians to avoid breaking them in some trifling and unimportant particular; and sultan Kelaoun soon found a colorable pretence for recommencing hostilities. He first broke with the Hospitallers and stormed their strong fortress of Merkab, which commanded the coast road from Laodicea to Tripoli. He then sought out a pretext for putting an end to the truce which the count of Tripoli had purchased of Bendocdar by the payment of eleven thousand pieces of gold. He maintained that a watch-tower had been erected on the coast between Merkab and Tortosa, in contravention of the stipulation which forbad the erection of new fortifications; and he accordingly marched with his army to lay siege to the rich and flourishing city of Laodicea. The Arabian writers tell us that Laodicea was one of the most commercial cities of the Levant, and was considered to be the rival of Alexandria. A terrible earthquake, which had thrown down the fortifications, and overturned the castle at the entrance of the port, unfortunately facilitated the conquest of the place, and Laodicea fell almost without a struggle. The town was pillaged and set on fire, and those of the inhabitants who were unable to escape by sea, were either slaughtered or reduced to slavery, or driven out homeless wanderers from their dwellings, to perish with hunger and grief in the surrounding wilderness. Shortly after the fall of Laodicea, the castle of Krak, which belonged to the Hospitallers, was besieged and stormed; the garrison was put to the sword, and some other small places on the sea-coast met with a similar fate.

On the 13th Moharran (9th of February,) A. D. 1287, the sultan marched against Tripoli at the head of ten thousand horse, and thirty-three thousand foot. The separate timbers of nineteen enormous military engines were transported in many hundred wagons drawn by oxen; and fifteen hundred engineers and firework manufacturers were employed to throw the terrible Greek fire and combustible materials, contained in brass pots, into the city. After thirty-four days of incessant labor, the walls were undermined and thrown into the ditch, and the engineers poured an incessant stream of Greek fire upon the breach, whilst the Moslems below prepared a path for the cavalry. Brother John de Breband, Preceptor of the Temple at Tripoli, fought upon the ramparts with a few knights and serving brethren of the order; but they were speedily overthrown, and the Arab cavalry dashed through the breach into the town. Upwards of one thousand Christians fell by the sword, and the number of captives was incalculable. Twelve hundred trembling women and children were crowded together for safety in a single magazine of arms, and the conquerors were embarrassed with the quantity of spoil and booty. More than four thousand bales of the richest silks were distributed amongst the soldiers, together with ornaments and articles of luxury and refinement, which astonished the rude simplicity of the Arabs. When the city had been thoroughly ransacked, orders were issued for its destruction. Then the Moslem soldiers were to be seen rushing with torches and pots of burning naphtha to set fire to the churches, and the shops, and the warehouses of the merchants; and Tripoli was speedily enveloped in one vast, fearful, wide-spreading conflagration. The command for the destruction of the fortifications was likewise issued, and thousands of soldiers, stonemasons, and laborers, were employed in throwing down the walls and towers. The Arabian writers tell us that the ramparts were so wide that three horsemen could ride abreast upon them round the town. Many of the inhabitants had escaped by sea during the siege, and crowds of fugitives fled before the swords of the Moslems, to take refuge on the little island of Saint Nicholas at the entrance of the port. They were there starved to death; and when Abulfeda visited the island a few days after the fall of Tripoli, he found it covered with the dead bodies of the unburied Christians. Thus fell Tripoli, with its commerce, its silk manufactories, churches, and public and private buildings. Everything that could contribute to prosperity in peace, or defense in war, perished beneath the sword, the hammer, and the pick-axe of the Moslems. In the time of the crusaders, the port was crowded with the fleets of the Italian republics, and carried on a lucrative trade with Marseilles, Amalfi, Genoa, Pisa, Venice, and the cities of the Grecian islands; but the rich stream of commerce hath never since revisited the inhospitable shore.

Shortly after the fall of Tripoli, Gabala, Beirout, and all the maritime towns and villages between Sidon and Laodicea, fell into the hands of the infidels; and sultan Kelaoun was preparing to attack the vast and populous city of Acre, when death terminated his victorious career. He was succeeded, A. D. 1291, by his eldest son, Aschraf Khalil, who hastened to execute the warlike projects of his father. He assembled the ulemas and cadis around his father's tomb, and occupied himself in reading the Koran, in prayer, and invocation of Mahomet. He then made abundant alms-giving, collected his troops together, and marched across the desert to Damascus, where he was joined by Hosam-eddin Ladjin, viceroy of Syria, Modaffer, prince of Hems, and Saifeddin, lord of Baalbec, with the respective forces under their command. Ninety-two enormous military engines had been constructed at Damascus, which were transported across the country by means of oxen; and in the spring of the year, after the winter rains had subsided, sultan Khalil marched against Acre at the head of sixty thousand horse, and a hundred and forty thousand foot.

After the loss of Jerusalem, the city of Acre became the metropolis of the Latin Christians, and was adorned with a vast cathedral, with numerous stately churches, and elegant buildings, and with acqueducts, and an artificial port. The houses of the rich merchants were decorated with pictures and choice pieces of sculpture, and boasted of the rare advantage of glass windows. An astonishing, and probably an exaggerated, account has been given of the wealth and luxury of the inhabitants. We read of silken canopies and curtains stretched on cords to protect the lounger from the scorching sunbeams, of variegated marble fountains, and of rich gardens and shady groves, scented with the delicious orange blossom, and adorned with the delicate almond flower; and we are told that the markets of the city could offer the produce of every clime, and the interpreters of every tongue. The vast and stupendous fortifications consisted of a double wall, strengthened at proper intervals with lofty towers, and defended by the castle called the King's Tower, and by the convent or fortress of the Temple. Between the ramparts extended a large space of ground, covered with the chateaus, villas, and gardens of the nobility of Galilee, the counts of Tripoli and Jaffa, the lords of Tyre and Sidon, the papal legate, the duke of Athens, and the princes of Antioch. The most magnificent edifices within the town were, the cathedral church of St. Andrew, the churches of St. Saba, St. Thomas, St. Nicholas, and St. John, the tutelar saint of the city; the abbey of St. Clare, the convents of the Knights Hospitallers and the Knights Templars, and various monasteries and religious houses.

William de Beaujeu, the Grand Master of the Temple, a veteran warrior of a hundred fights, took the command of the garrison, which amounted to about twelve thousand men, exclusive of the forces of the Temple and the Hospital, and a body of five hundred foot and two hundred horse, under the command of the king of Cyprus. These forces were distributed along the walls in four divisions, the first of which was commanded by Hugh de Grandison, an English knight. The siege lasted six weeks, during the whole of which period the sallies and the attacks were incessant. Neither by night nor by day did the shouts of the assailants and the noise of the military engines cease; huge stones and beams of timber and pots of burning tar and naphtha were continually hurled into the city; the walls were battered from without, and the foundations were sapped by miners, who were incessantly laboring to advance their works. More than six hundred catapults, balistæ, and other instruments of destruction, were directed against the fortifications; and the battering machines were of such immense size and weight, that a hundred wagons were required to transport the separate timbers of one of them. Moveable towers were erected by the Moslems, so as to overtop the walls; their workmen and advanced parties were protected by hurdles covered with raw hides, and all the military contrivances which the art and the skill of the age could produce, were used to facilitate the assault. For a long time their utmost efforts were foiled by the valor of the besieged, who made constant sallies upon their works, burnt their towers and machines, and destroyed their miners. Day by day, however, the numbers of the garrison were thinned by the sword, whilst in the enemy's camp the places of the dead were constantly supplied by fresh warriors from the deserts of Arabia, animated with the same wild fanaticism in the cause of *their* religion as that which so eminently distinguished the military monks of the Temple.

On the 4th of May, after thirty-three days of constant fighting, the great tower considered the key of the fortifications, and called by the Moslems "the cursed tower," was thrown down by the military engines. To increase the terror and distraction of the besieged, sultan Khalil mounted three hundred drummers, with their drums, upon as many dromedaries, and commanded them to make as much noise as possible whenever a general assault was ordered. From the 4th to the 14th of May the attacks were incessant. On the 15th, the double wall was forced, and the king of Cyprus, panic-stricken, fled in the night to his ships, and made sail for the island of Cyprus, with all his followers, and with near three thousand of the best men of the garrison. On the morrow the Saracens attacked the post he had deserted; they filled up the ditch with the bodies of dead men and horses, piles of wood, stones, and earth, and their trumpets then sounded to the assault. Ranged under the yellow banner of Mahomet, the Mamlooks forced the breach, and penetrated sword in hand to the very centre of the city; but their victorious career and insulting shouts were there stopped by the mail-clad Knights of the Temple and the Hospital, who charged on horseback through the narrow streets, drove them back with immense carnage, and precipitated them headlong from the walls.

At sunrise on the following morning the air resounded with the deafening noise of drums and trumpets, and the breach was carried and recovered several times, the military friars at last closing up the passage with their bodies, and presenting a wall of steel to the advance of the enemy. Loud appeals to God, and to Mahomet, to Jesus Christ, to the Virgin Mary, to heaven and the saints, were to be heard on all sides; and after an obstinate engagement from sunrise to sunset, darkness put an end to the slaughter. The miners continued incessantly to advance their operations; another wide breach was opened in the walls, and on the third day (the 18th) the infidels made the final assault on the side next the gate of St. Anthony. The army of the Mamlooks was accompanied by a troop of sectaries called *Chagis*, a set of religious fanatics, whose devotion consisted in suffering all sorts of privations, and in sacrificing themselves in behalf of Islam. The advance of the Mamlook cavalry to the assault was impeded by the deep ditch, which had been imperfectly filled by the fallen ruins and by the efforts of the soldiers, and these religious madmen precipitated themselves headlong into the abyss and formed a bridge with their bodies, over which the Mamlooks passed to reach the foot of the wall. Nothing could withstand the fierce onslaught of the Moslems. In vain were the first ranks of their cavalry laid prostrate with the dust, and both horses and riders hurled headlong over the ruined walls and battlements into the moat below; their fall only facilitated the progress of those behind them, who pressed on sword in hand over the lifeless bodies of men and horses, to attack the faint and weary warriors guarding the breach.

The Grand Masters of the Temple and Hospital fought side by side at the head of their knights, and for a time successfully resisted all the efforts of the enemy. But as each knight fell beneath the keen scimitars of the Moslems, there were none in reserve to supply his place, whilst the vast hordes of the infidels pressed on with untiring energy and perseverance. Brother Matthew de Clermont, Marshal of the Hospital, after performing prodigies of valor, fell covered with wounds, and William de Beaujeu, as a last resort, requested the Grand Master of that order to sally out of an adjoining gateway at the head of five hundred horse, and attack the enemy's rear. Immediately after the Grand Master of the Temple had given these orders, he was himself struck down by the darts and the arrows of the enemy; the panic-stricken garrison fled to the port, and the infidels rushed on with tremendous shouts of *Allah acbar! Allah acbar!* "God is victorious!" Thousands of panic-stricken Christians now rushed to the seaside, and sought with frantic violence to gain possession of the ships and boats that rode at anchor in the port, but a frightful storm of wind, and rain, and lightning, hung over the dark and agitated waters of the sea; the elements themselves warred against the poor Christians, and the loud-pealing thunder became mingled with the din and uproar of the assault and the clash of arms. The boats and vessels were swamped by the surging waves; and the bitter cries of the perishing fugitives ascended alike from the sea and shore. Thousands fled to the churches for refuge, but found none; they prostrated themselves before the altars, and embraced the images of the saints, but these evidences of idolatry only stimulated the merciless fanaticism of the Moslems, and the Christians and their temples, their images and their saints, were all consumed in the raging flames kindled by the inexorable sons of Islam. The churches were set on fire, and the timid virgin and the hardened voluptuary, the nun and the monk, the priest and the bishop, all perished miserably before the altars and the shrines which they had approached in the hour of need, but which many of them had neglected in days of prosperity and peace. The holy nuns of St. Clare, following the example and exhortations of their abbess, mangled and disfigured their faces and persons in a most dreadful manner, to preserve their chastity from violation by the barbarous conquerors, and were gloriously rewarded with the crown of martyrdom, by the astonished and disgusted infidels, who slaughtered without mercy the whole sisterhood!

Three hundred Templars, the sole survivors of their order in Acre, had kept together and successfully withstood the victorious Mamlooks. In a close and compact column they fought their way, accompanied by several hundred Christian fugitives, to the convent of the Temple at Acre, and shut the gates. They then assembled together in solemn chapter, and appointed the Knight Templar, Brother Gaudini, Grand Master. The Temple at Acre was surrounded by walls and towers, and was a place of great strength, and of immense extent. It was divided into three quarters, the first and principal of which contained the palace of the Grand Master, the church, and the habitation of the knights; the second, called the Bourg of the Temple, contained the cells of the serving brethren; and the third, called the Cattle Market, was devoted to the officers charged with the duty of procuring the necessary supplies for the order and its forces. The following morning very favorable terms were offered to the Templars by the victorious sultan, and they agreed to evacuate the Temple on condition that a galley should be placed at their disposal, and that they should be allowed to retire in safety with the Christian fugitives under their protection, and to carry away as much of their effects as each person could load himself with. The Mussulman conqueror pledged himself to the fulfilment of these conditions, and sent a standard to the Templars, which was mounted on one of the towers of the Temple. A guard of three hundred Moslem soldiers, charged to see the articles of capitulation properly carried into effect, was afterwards admitted within the walls of the convent. Some Christian ladies and women of Acre were amongst the fugitives, and the Moslem soldiers, attracted by their beauty, broke through all restraint, and violated the terms of the surrender. The enraged Templars closed and barricaded the gates of the Temple; they set upon the treacherous infidels, and put every one of them, "from the greatest to the smallest," to death. Immediately after this massacre, the Moslem trumpets sounded to the assault, but the Templars successfully defended themselves until the next day (the 20th). The Marshal of the order and several of the brethren were then deputed by Gaudini with a flag of truce to the sultan, to explain the cause of the massacre of his guard. The enraged monarch, however, had no sooner got them into his power, than he ordered every one of them to be decapitated, and pressed the siege with renewed vigour.

In the night, Gaudini, with a chosen band of his companions, collected together the treasure of the order, and the ornaments of the church, and sallying out of a secret postern of the Temple which communicated with the harbor, they got on board a small vessel, and escaped in safety to the island of Cyprus. The residue of the Templars retired into the large tower of the Temple, called "The Tower of the Master," which they defended with desperate energy. The bravest of the Mamlooks were driven back in repeated assaults, and the little fortress was everywhere surrounded with heaps of the slain. The sultan, at last, despairing of taking the place by assault, ordered it to be undermined. As the workmen advanced, they propped the foundations with beams of wood, and when the excavation was completed, these wooden supports were consumed by fire; the huge tower then fell with a tremendous crash, and buried the brave Templars in its ruins. The sultan set fire to the town in four places; the walls, the towers, and the ramparts were demolished, and the last stronghold of the Christian power in Palestine was speedily reduced to a smoking solitude.[*]

---

[*] De excidio urbis Acconis apud *Martene*, tom. v. col. 757, 782. *De Guignes*, Hist. des Huns, tom. iv. p. 162. *Abulfarag*. Chron. Syr. p. 595. *Wilkens*, Comment. Abulfed. Hist. p. 231-234. *Marin. Sanut. Torsell*, lib. iii. pars 12, cap. 21, 22. *Makrisi*, ad ann. Hejir. 689, 690. *Hermann*

C. G. Addison

A few years back, the ruins of the Christian city of Acre were well worthy of the attention of the curious. You might still trace the remains of thirty churches; and the quarter occupied by the Knights Templars continued to present many interesting memorials of that proud and powerful order. "The carcass," says Sandys, "shows that the body hath been strong, doubly immured; fortified with bulwarks and towers, to each wall a ditch lined with stone, and under those, divers secret posterns. You would think, by the ruins, that the city consisted of divers conjoining castles, which witness a notable defense, and an unequal assault; and that the rage of the conquerors extended beyond conquest; the huge walls and arches turned topsy-turvy, and lying like rocks upon the foundation." At the period of Dr. Clarke's visit to Acre, the ruins, with the exception of the cathedral, the arsenal, the convent of the knights, and the palace of the Grand Master, were so intermingled with modern buildings, and in such a state of utter subversion, that it was difficult to afford any satisfactory description of them. "Many superb remains were observed by us," says he, "in the pasha's palace, in the khan, the mosque, the public bath, the fountains, and other parts of the town, consisting of fragments of antique marble, the shafts and capitals of granite and marble pillars, masses of the verd antique breccia, of the ancient serpentine, and of the syenite and trap of Egypt. In the garden of Djezzar's palace, leading to his summer apartment, we saw some pillars of variegated marble of extraordinary beauty."

After the fall of Acre, the head-quarters of the Templars were established at Limisso in the island of Cyprus, and urgent letters were sent to Europe for succor. The armies of sultan Kelaoun in the mean time assaulted and carried Tyre, Sidon, Tortosa, Caiphas, and the Pilgrim's Castle. The last three places belonged to the Templars, and were stoutly defended, but they were attacked by the Egyptian fleet by sea, and by countless armies of infidels by land, and were at last involved in the common destruction. The Grand Master, Gaudini, overwhelmed with sorrow and vexation at the loss of the Holy Land, and the miserable situation of his order, stripped of all its possessions on the Asiatic continent, died at Limisso, after a short illness, and was succeeded (A. D. 1295) by Brother James de Molay, of the family of the lords of Longvic and Raon in Burgundy. This illustrious nobleman was at the head of the English province of the order at the period of his election to the dignity of Grand Master. He was first appointed Visitor-General, then Grand Preceptor of England, and was afterwards placed at the head of the entire fraternity. During his residence in Britain he held several chapters or assemblies of the brethren at the Temple at London, and at the different preceptories, where he framed and enforced various rules and regulations for the government of the fraternity in England.[*] Shortly after his

---

Cornarius, Collect. *d'Ekard Michaud*, Bib. des Croisades, tom. ii.
[*] Concil. Mag. Brit. tom. ii. p. 350-352, 387, 388. *Cotton* MS. Nero E. VI. 23 i. p. 60, fol. 466. L'Art de Verif. tom. i. p. 523, ed. 1783. *Rainald*, tom. xiv. ad ann. 1294.

appointment to the office of Grand Master, he crossed the sea to France, and had the honor of holding the infant son of Philip le Bel at the baptismal font. He then proceeded to Cyprus, carrying out with him a numerous body of English and French Knights Templars, and a considerable amount of treasure. Soon after his arrival he entered into an alliance with the famous Casan Cham, emperor of the Mogul Tartars, king of Persia, and the descendant or successor of Genghis Khan, and landed in Syria with his knights and a body of forces, to join the standard of that powerful monarch. Casan had married the daughter of Leon, king of Armenia, a Christian princess of extraordinary beauty, to whom he was greatly attached, and who was permitted the enjoyment and public exercise of the Christian worship. The Tartar emperor naturally became favorably disposed towards the Christians, and he invited the Grand Master of the Temple to join him in an expedition against the sultan of Egypt.

In the spring of the year 1299, the Templars landed at Suadia, and made a junction with the Tartar forces which were encamped amid the ruins of Antioch. An army of thirty thousand men was placed by the Mogul emperor under the command of the Grand Master, and the combined forces moved up the valley of the Orontes towards Damascus. In a great battle fought at Hems, the troops of the sultans of Damascus and Egypt were entirely defeated, and pursued with great slaughter until nightfall. Aleppo, Hems, Damascus, and all the principal cities, surrendered to the victorious arms of the Moguls, and the Templars once again entered Jerusalem in triumph, visited the Holy Sepulcher, and celebrated Easter on Mount Zion. Casan sent ambassadors to the pope, and to the sovereigns of Europe, announcing the victorious progress of his arms, soliciting their alliance, and offering them in return the possession of Palestine. But the Christian nations heeded not the call, and none thought seriously of an expedition to the east excepting the ladies of Genoa, who, frightened by an interdict which had been laid upon their town, assumed the cross as the best means of averting the divine indignation. The Grand Master of the Temple advanced as far as Gaza, and drove the Saracens into the sandy deserts of Egypt; but a Saracen chief, who had been appointed by the Tartars governor of Damascus, instigated the Mussulman population of Syria to revolt, and the Grand Master was obliged to retreat to Jerusalem. He was there joined by the Tartar general, Cotulosse, who had been sent across the Euphrates by Casan to support him. The combined armies were once more preparing to march upon Damascus, when the sudden illness of Casan, who was given over by his physicians, disconcerted all their arrangements, and deprived the Grand Master of his Tartar forces. The Templars were then compelled to retreat to the sea-coast and embark their forces on board their galleys. The Grand Master sailed to Limisso, stationing a strong detachment of his soldiers on the island of Aradus, near Tortosa, which they fortified; but they were speedily attacked in that position by a fleet of twenty vessels, and an army of ten thousand men, and after a gallant defense they were compelled to abandon their fortifications, and were all killed or taken prisoners.[*]

Thus ended the dominion of the Templars in Palestine, and thus closed the long and furious struggle between the CRESCENT and the CROSS! The few remaining Christians in the Holy Land were chased from ruin to ruin, and exterminated. The churches, the houses, and the fortifications along the sea-coast, were demolished, and everything that could afford shelter and security, or invite the approach of the crusaders from the west, was carefully destroyed. The houses were all set on fire, the trees were cut down and burnt, the land was everywhere laid waste, and all the maritime country, from Laodicea to Ascalon, was made desert. "Every trace of the Franks," says the Arabian chronicler, Ibn Ferat, "was removed, and thus it shall remain, please God, till the day of judgment!"[†]

Near six centuries have swept over Palestine since the termination of the wars of the cross, and the land still continues *desolate*. The proud memorials of past magnificence are painfully contrasted with present ruin and decay, and the remains of the rich and populous cities of antiquity are surrounded by uncultivated deserts. God hath said, "I will smite the land with a *curse*. I will bring the worst of the heathen and they shall possess it." "Thorns shall come up in her palaces, nettles and brambles in the fortresses thereof, and the defensed city shall be left desolate, and the habitation forsaken, and left like a wilderness."

"The fig-tree shall not blossom, neither shall fruit be on the vine; the labor of the olive shall fail, and the fields shall yield no meat; the flock shall be cut off from the fold, and there shall be no herd in the stall." But brighter and happier times are yet to come, for the Lord God hath also said, "To the mountains of Israel, to the hills, and to the rivers, to the valleys, and the desolate wastes, and the cities that are forsaken, which became a prey and a derision to the heathen. Behold I am for you, I will turn unto you, and ye shall be tilled and sown, and I will multiply men upon you, and they shall build up the old waste cities, the desolation of many generations!"

"In the land of Benjamin, and in the places about Jerusalem, and in the cities of Judah, *shall the flocks pass again under the hand of him that telleth them, saith* the Lord!"

---

[*] *Haiton*, Hist. Tartar. cap. 43. Chron. de *Nangis Rainald*, ad ann. 1299, 1300, n. 34. *Marin. Sanut.* p. 242. *De Guignes*, tom iv. p. 184.
[†] *Ibn Ferat*, ad ann. Hejir. 690. *Sanut.* p. 232.

Chapter VII.

En cel an qu'ai dist or endroit, Et ne sait a tort ou a droit, Furent li Templiers, sans doutance, Tous pris par le royaume de France. Au mois d'Octobre, au point du jor, Et un vendredi fu le jor.

Chron. MS.

It now only remains for us to relate the miserable and cruel fate of the surviving brethren of the order of the Temple, and to tell of the ingratitude they encountered at the hands of their fellow-Christians in the West. After the loss of all the Christian territory in Palestine, and the destruction of every serious hope of recovering and retaining the Holy City, the services of the Templars ceased to be required, and men began to regard with an eye of covetousness their vast wealth and immense possessions. The clergy regarded with jealousy and indignation their removal from the ordinary ecclesiastical jurisdiction, their exemption from tithe, and the privilege they possessed of celebrating divine service during interdict; and their hostility to the order was manifested in repeated acts of injustice, which drew forth many severe bulls from the Roman pontiffs.[*] The Templars, moreover, became unpopular with the European sovereigns and their nobles. The revenues of the former were somewhat diminished through the immunities conceded to the order by their predecessors, and the paternal estates of the latter had been diminished by the grant of many thousand manors, lordships, and fair estates to the fraternity by their pious and enthusiastic ancestors. Considerable dislike also began to be manifested to the annual transmission of large sums of money, the revenues of the Templars, from the European states, to be expended in a distant warfare in which Christendom now took comparatively no interest.

Shortly after the fall of Acre, and the total loss of Palestine, Edward I., king of England, seized and sequestered to his own use the monies which had been accumulated by the Templars, to forward to their brethren in Cyprus, alleging that the property of the order had been granted to it by the kings of England, his predecessors, and their subjects, for the defense of the Holy Land, and that since the loss thereof, no better use could, be made of the money than by appropriating it to the maintenance of the poor. At the earnest request of the pope, however, the king afterwards permitted their revenues to be transmitted to them in the island of Cyprus in the usual manner. King Edward had previously manifested a strong desire to lay

---

[*] Acta *Rymeri*, tom. i. p. 575-579, 582, tom. ii. p. 529. *Martene*, tom. vii. col. 156.

hands on the property of the Templars. On his return from his victorious campaign in Wales, finding himself unable to disburse the arrears of pay due to his soldiers, he went with Sir Robert Waleran and some armed followers to the Temple, and calling for the treasurer, he pretended that he wanted to see his mother's jewels, which were there kept. Having been admitted to the house, he deliberately broke open the coffers of the Templars, and carried away ten thousand pounds with him to Windsor Castle. His son, Edward II, on his accession to the throne, committed a similar act of injustice. He went with his favorite, Piers Gaveston, to the Temple, and took away with him fifty thousand pounds of silver, with a quantity of gold, jewels, and precious stones, belonging to the bishop of Chester. The impunity with which these acts of violence were committed, manifests that the Templars then no longer enjoyed the power and respect which they possessed in ancient times.

As the enthusiasm, too, in favor of the holy war diminished, large numbers of the fraternity remained at home in their western preceptories, and took an active part in the politics of Europe. They interfered in the quarrels of Christian princes, and even drew their swords against their fellow-Christians. Thus we find the members of the order taking part in the war between the houses of Anjou and Aragon, and aiding the king of England in his warfare against the king of Scotland. In the battle of Falkirk, fought on the 22nd of July, A. D. 1298, seven years after the fall of Acre, perished both the Master of the Temple at London, and his vicegerent the Preceptor of Scotland. All these circumstances, together with the loss of the Holy Land, and the extinction of the enthusiasm of the crusades, diminished the popularity of the Templars. The rolls of the English parliament about this time begin to teem with complaints and petitions from the fraternity, of the infringement of their charters, franchises, liberties, and privileges, in all parts of the realm.[*]

At the period of the fall of Acre, Philip the Fair, son of St. Louis, occupied the throne of France. He was a needy and avaricious monarch, and had at different periods resorted to the most violent expedients to replenish his exhausted exchequer. On the death of pope Benedict XI., (A. D. 1304,) he succeeded, through the intrigues of the French Cardinal Dupré, in raising the archbishop of Bordeaux, a creature of his own, to the pontifical chair. The new pope removed the holy see from Rome to France; he summoned all the cardinals to Lyons, and was there consecrated, (A. D. 1305,) by the name of Clement V., in the presence of king Philip and his nobles. Of the ten new cardinals then created, *nine* were Frenchmen, and in all his acts the new pope manifested himself the obedient slave of the French monarch. The character of this pontiff has been painted by the Romish ecclesiastical historians in the darkest colors.

On the 6th of June, A. D. 1306, a few months after his coronation, he addressed letters from Bordeaux to the Grand Masters of the Temple and

---

[*] Acta *Rymeri*, tom. ii. p. 683. *Hemingford*, vol. i. p. 159, 244. Rolls of Parliament, vol. i. p. 2. Ib. No. 7.

Hospital at Limisso, in the island of Cyprus, expressing his earnest desire to consult them with regard to the measures necessary to be taken for the recovery of the Holy Land. He tells them that they are the persons best qualified to give advice upon the subject, and to conduct and manage the enterprise, both from their great military experience and the interest they had in the success of the expedition. "We order you," says he, "to come hither without delay, with as much secrecy as possible, and with a very little retinue, since you will find on this side the sea a sufficient number of your knights to attend upon you." The Grand Master of the Hospital declined obeying this summons; but the Grand Master of the Temple forthwith accepted it, and unhesitatingly placed himself in the power of the pope and the king of France. He landed in France, attended by sixty of his knights, at the commencement of the year 1307, and deposited the treasure of the order, which he had brought with him from Cyprus, in the Temple at Paris. He was received with distinction by the king, and then took his departure for Poictiers to have an interview with the pope.

The secret agents of the French king immediately circulated various dark rumors and odious reports concerning the Templars. According to some writers, Squin de Florian, a citizen of Bezieres, who had been condemned to death or perpetual imprisonment in one of the royal castles for his iniquities, was brought before king Philip, and received a free pardon, and was well rewarded, in return for an accusation on oath, charging the Templars with heresy, and with the commission of the most horrible crimes. According to others, Nosso de Florentin, an apostate Templar, who had been condemned by the Grand Preceptor and chapter of France to perpetual imprisonment for impiety and crime, made in his dungeon a voluntary confession of the sins and abominations charged against the order. Be this as it may, upon the strength of an information sworn to by a condemned criminal, king Philip, on the 14th of September, despatched secret letters to all the baillis of the different provinces in France, accusing the Templars of infidelity; of mocking the sacred image of the Saviour; of sacrificing to idols; and of abandoning themselves to impure practices and unnatural crimes! "We being charged," says he, "with the maintenance of the faith; after having conferred with the pope, the prelates, and the barons of the kingdom, at the instance of the inquisitor, from the informations already laid, from violent suspicions, from probable conjectures, from legitimate presumptions, conceived against the enemies of heaven and earth! and because the matter is important, and it is expedient to prove the just like gold in the furnace, by a rigorous examination, have decreed that the members of the order who are our subjects shall be arrested and detained to be judged by the church, and that all their real and personal property shall be seized into our hands!" &c. The baillis and seneschals were required accurately to inform themselves, with great secrecy, and without exciting suspicion, of the number of the houses of the Temple within their respective jurisdictions; to provide an armed force sufficient to overcome all resistance, and on the 13th of October to surprise the Templars in their preceptories, and make them prisoners. The inquisition is then directed to assemble to examine the guilty, and to employ TORTURE if it be necessary. "Before proceeding with the inquiry," says Philip, "you are to inform them (the Templars) that the pope and ourselves have been convinced, by irreproachable testimony, of the errors and abominations which accompany their vows and profession; you are to promise them *pardon* and favor if they CONFESS the truth, but if not, you are to acquaint them that they will be condemned to death."

As soon as Philip had issued these orders, he wrote to the principal sovereigns of Europe, urging them to follow his example, and sent a confidential agent, named Bernard Peletin, with a letter to the young king, Edward the Second, who had just then ascended the throne of England, representing in frightful colors the pretended sins of the Templars. On the 22nd of September, (A. D. 1306,) king Edward replied to this letter, observing that he had considered of the matters mentioned therein, and had listened to the statements of that discreet man, Master Bernard Peletin; that he had caused the latter to unfold the charges before himself, and many prelates, earls, and barons of his kingdom, and others of his council; but that they appeared so astonishing as to be beyond belief; that such abominable and execrable deeds had never before been heard of by the king, and the aforesaid prelates, earls, and barons, and it was therefore hardly to be expected that an easy credence could be given to them. The English monarch, however, informs king Philip, that by the advice of his council he had ordered the seneschal of Agen, from whose lips the rumors were said to have proceeded, to be summoned to his presence, that through him he might be further informed concerning the premises; and he states that, at the fitting time, after due inquiry, he will take such steps as will redound to the praise of God, and the honor and preservation of the catholic faith.*

On the night of the 13th of October, all the Templars in the French dominions were simultaneously arrested. Monks were appointed to preach against them in the public places of Paris, and in the gardens of the Palais Royal; and advantage was taken of the folly, the superstition, and the credulity of the age, to propagate the most horrible and extravagant charges against them. They were accused of worshipping an idol covered with an old skin, embalmed, having the appearance of a piece of polished oil-cloth. "In this idol," we are assured, "there were two carbuncles for eyes, bright as the brightness of heaven, and it is certain that all the hope of the Templars was placed in it; it was their sovereign god, and they trusted in it with all their heart." They are accused of burning the bodies of the deceased brethren, and making the ashes into a powder, which they administered to the younger brethren in their food and drink, to make them hold fast their faith and idolatry; of cooking and roasting infants, and anointing their idols with the fat; of celebrating hidden rites and mysteries,

---

* *Dupuy*, tom. ii. p. 309. Chron. St. Denis. Acta *Rymeri*, tom. iii. p. 18.

to which young and tender virgins were introduced, and of a variety of abominations too absurd and horrible to be named. Guillaume Paradin, in his history of Savoy, seriously repeats these monstrous accusations, and declares that the Templars had "un lieu creux ou cave en terre, fort obscur, en laquelle ils avoient un image en forme d'un homme, sur lequel ils avoient appliqué la peau d'un corps humain, et mis deux clairs et luisans escarboucles au lieu des deux yeux. A cette horrible statue etoient contraints de sacrifier ceux qui vouloient etre de leur damnable religion, lesquels avant toutes ceremonies ils contragnoient de renier Jesus Christ, et fouler la croix avec les pieds, et apres ce maudit sacre auquel assistoient femmes et filles (seduites pour etre de ce secte) ils estegnoient les lampes et lumieres qu'ils avoient en cett cave.... Et s'il advenoit que d'un Templier et d'un pucelle nasquit un fils, ils se rangoient tous en un rond, et se jettoient cet enfant de main en main, et ne cessoient de le jetter jusqu'a ce qu'il fu mort entre leurs mains; etant mort ils se rotissoient (chose execrable) et de la graisse ils en ognoient leur grand statue!" The character of the charges preferred against the Templars proves that their enemies had no serious crimes to allege against the order. Their very virtues, indeed, were turned against them, for we are told that, "to conceal the iniquity of their lives, they made much almsgiving, constantly frequented church, comported themselves with edification, frequently partook of the holy sacrament, and manifested always much modesty and gentleness of deportment in the house, as well as in public."

During twelve days of severe imprisonment, the Templars remained constant in the denial of the horrible crimes imputed to the fraternity. The king's promises of pardon extracted from them no confession of guilt, and they were therefore handed over to the tender mercies of the brethren of St. Dominic, who were the most refined and expert torturers of the day. On the 19th of October, the grand inquisitor proceeded with his myrmidons to the Temple at Paris, and a hundred and forty Templars were one after another put to the torture. Days and weeks were consumed in the examination, and thirty-six Templars perished in the hands of their tormentors, maintaining, with unshaken constancy to the very last, the entire innocence of their order! Many of them lost the use of their feet from the application of the torture of fire, which was inflicted in the following manner:—their legs were fastened in an iron frame, and the soles of their feet were greased over with fat or butter; they were then placed before the fire, and a screen was drawn backwards and forwards, so as to moderate and regulate the heat. Such was the agony produced by this roasting operation, that the victim often went raving mad. Brother Bernarde de Vado, on subsequently revoking a confession of guilt, wrung from him by this description of torment, says to the commissary of police, before whom he was brought to be examined, "They held me so long before a fierce fire that the flesh was burnt off my heels, two pieces of bone came away, which I present to you."[*]

---

[*] Ostendens duo ossa quod dicebat illa esse quæ ceciderunt de talis suis. *Processus contra Templarios. Raynouard*, Monumens Historiques, p. 73, ed. 1813.

Another Templar, on publicly revoking his confession, declared that four of his teeth were drawn out, and that he confessed himself guilty to save the remainder. Others of the fraternity deposed to the infliction on them of the most revolting and indecent torments;[*] and, in addition to all this, it appears that forged letters from the Grand Master were shown to the prisoners, exhorting them to confess themselves guilty! Many of the Templars were accordingly compelled to acknowledge whatever was required of them, and to plead guilty to the commission of crimes which, in the previous interrogatories, they had positively denied.

These violent proceedings excited the astonishment of Europe. On the 20th of November, the king of England summoned the seneschal of Agen to his presence, and examined him concerning the truth of the horrible charges preferred against the Templars; and on the 4th of December, the English monarch wrote letters to the kings of Portugal, Castile, Aragon, and Sicily, to the following effect:—"To the magnificent prince the Lord Dionysius, by the grace of God the illustrious king of Portugal, his very dear friend, Edward, by the same grace king of England, &c. Health and prosperity. It is fit and proper, inasmuch as it conduceth to the honor of God and the exaltation of the faith, that we should prosecute with benevolence those who come recommended to us by strenuous labors and incessant exertions in defense of the Catholic faith, and for the destruction of the enemies of the cross of Christ. Verily, a certain clerk (Bernard Peletin,) drawing nigh unto our presence, applied himself, with all his might, to the destruction of the order of the brethren of the Temple of Jerusalem. He dared to publish before us and our council certain horrible and detestable enormities repugnant to the Catholic faith, to the prejudice of the aforesaid brothers, endeavoring to persuade us, through his own allegations, as well as through certain letters which he had caused to be addressed to us for that purpose, that by reason of the premises, and without a due examination of the matter, we ought to imprison all the brethren of the aforesaid order abiding in our dominions. But, considering that the order, which hath been renowned for its religion and its honor, and in times long since passed away was instituted, as we have learned, by the Catholic Fathers, exhibits, and hath from the period of its first foundation exhibited, a becoming devotion to God and his holy church, and also, up to this time, hath afforded succor and protection to the Catholic faith in parts beyond sea, it appeared to us that a ready belief in an accusation of this kind, hitherto altogether unheard of against the fraternity, was scarcely to be expected. We affectionately ask, and require of your royal majesty, that ye, with due diligence, consider of the premises, and turn a deaf ear to the slanders of ill-natured men, who are animated, as we believe, not with a zeal of rectitude, but with a spirit of *cupidity* and envy, permitting no injury unadvisedly to be done to the persons or property of the brethren of the aforesaid order, dwelling within your kingdom, until they have been

---

[*] Ponderibus appensis in genitalibus, usque ad exanimationem. Ib. p. 35.

legally convicted of the crimes laid to their charge, or it shall happen to be otherwise ordered concerning them in these parts."

A few days after the transmission of this letter, king Edward wrote to the pope, expressing his disbelief of the horrible and detestable rumors spread abroad concerning the Templars. He represents them to his holiness as universally respected by all men in his dominions for the purity of their faith and morals. He expresses great sympathy for the affliction and distress suffered by the Master and brethren, by reason of the scandal circulated concerning them; and he strongly urges the holy pontiff to clear, by some fair course of inquiry, the character of the order from the unjust and infamous aspersions cast against it.* On the 22nd of November, however, a fortnight previously, the pope had issued the following bull to king Edward. "Clement, bishop, servant of the servants of God, to his very dear son in Christ, Edward, the illustrious king of England, health and apostolical blessing.

"Presiding, though unworthy, on the throne of pastoral pre-eminence, by the disposition of him who disposeth all things, we fervently seek after this one thing above all others; we with ardent wishes aspire to this, that shaking off the sleep of negligence, whilst watching over the Lord's flock, by removing that which is hurtful, and taking care of such things as are profitable, we may be able, by the divine assistance, to bring souls to God. In truth, a long time ago, about the period of our first promotion to the summit of the apostolical dignity, there came to our ears a light rumor to the effect that the Templars, though fighting ostensibly under the guise of religion, have hitherto been secretly living in perfidious apostasy, and in detestable heretical depravity. But, considering that their order, in times long since passed away, shone forth with the grace of much nobility and honor, and that they were for a length of time held in vast reverence by the faithful, and that we had then heard of no suspicion concerning the premises, or of evil report against them; and also, that from the beginning of their religion, they have publicly borne the cross of Christ, exposing their bodies and goods against the enemies of the faith, for the acquisition, retention, and defense of the Holy Land, consecrated by the precious blood of our Lord and Savior Jesus Christ, we were unwilling to yield a ready belief to the accusation...."

The holy pontiff then states, that afterwards, however, the same dreadful intelligence was conveyed to the king of France, who, animated by a lively zeal in the cause of religion, took immediate steps to ascertain its truth. He describes the various confessions of the guilt of idolatry and heresy made by the Templars in France, and requires the king forthwith to cause all the Templars in his dominions to be taken into custody on the same day. He directs him to hold them, in the name of the pope, at the disposition of the Holy See, and to commit all their real and personal property to the hands of certain trustworthy persons, to be faithfully

---

* Acta *Rymeri*, tom. iii. p. 35, 37.

preserved until the holy pontiff shall give further directions concerning it. King Edward received this bull immediately after he had despatched his letter to the pope, exhorting his holiness not to give ear to the accusations against the order. The young king was now either convinced of the guilt of the Templars, on the high authority of the sovereign pontiff, or hoped to turn the proceedings against them to a profitable account, as he yielded a ready and prompt compliance with the pontifical commands. An order in council was made for the arrest of the Templars, and the seizure of their property. Inventories were directed to be taken of their goods and chattels, and provision was made for the sowing and tilling of their lands during the period of their imprisonment.

On the 26th of December the king wrote to the pope, informing his holiness that he would carry his commands into execution in the best and speediest way that he could; and on the 8th of January, A. D. 1308, the Templars were suddenly arrested in all parts of England, and their property was seized into the king's hands. Brother William de la More was at this period Master of the Temple, or Preceptor of England. He succeeded the Master Brian le Jay, who was slain, as before mentioned, in the battle of Falkirk, and was taken prisoner, together with all his brethren of the Temple at London, and committed to close custody in Canterbury Castle. He was afterwards liberated on bail at the instance of the bishop of Durham.*

On the 12th of August, the pope addressed the bull *faciens misericordiam* to the English bishops as follows:—"Clement, bishop, servant of the servants of God, to the venerable brethren the archbishop of Canterbury, and his suffragans, health and apostolical benediction. The Son of God, the Lord Jesus Christ, using mercy with his servant, would have us taken up into the eminent mirror of the apostleship, to this end, that being, though unworthy, his vicar upon earth, we may, as far as human frailty will permit in all our actions and proceedings, follow his footsteps." He describes the rumors which had been spread abroad in France against the Templars, and his unwillingness to believe them, "because it was not likely, nor did seem credible, that such religious men, who continually shed their blood for the name of Christ, and were thought to expose their persons to danger of death for his sake; and who often showed many and great signs of devotion, as well in the divine offices as in fasting and other observances, should be so unmindful of their salvation as to perpetrate such things; we were unwilling to give ear to the insinuations and impeachments against them, being taught so to do by the example of the same Lord of ours, and the writings of canonical doctrine. But afterwards, our most dear son in Christ, Philip, the illustrious king of the French, to whom the same crimes had been made known, *not from motives of avarice*, (since he does not design to apply or to appropriate to himself any portion of the estates of the Templars, nay, has washed his hands of them!) but

---

* *Knyghton*, apud X. script. col. 2494, 2531. Acta *Rymeri*, tom. iii. p. 30-32, 34, 35, 45.

inflamed with zeal for the orthodox faith, following the renowned footsteps of his ancestors, getting what information he properly could upon the premises, gave us much instruction in the matter by his messengers and letters." The holy pontiff then gives a long account of the various confessions made in France, and of the absolution granted to such of the Templars as were truly contrite and penitent; he expresses his conviction of the guilt of the order, and makes provision for the trial of the fraternity in England. King Edward in the mean time, had begun to make free with their property, and the pope, on the 4th of October, wrote to him to the following effect:

"Your conduct begins again to afford us no slight cause of affliction, inasmuch as it hath been brought to our knowledge from the report of several barons, that in contempt of the Holy See, and without fear of offending the divine Majesty, you have, of your own sole authority, distributed to different persons the property which belonged formerly to the order of the Temple in your dominions, which you had got into your hands at our command, and which ought to have remained at our disposition.... We have therefore ordained that certain fit and proper persons shall be sent into your kingdom, and to all parts of the world where the Templars are known to have had property, to take possession of the same conjointly with certain prelates specially deputed to that end, and to make an inquisition concerning the execrable excesses which the members of the order are said to have committed."* To this letter of the supreme pontiff, king Edward sent the following short and pithy reply:—"As to the goods of the Templars, we have done nothing with them up to the present time, nor do we intend to do with them aught but what we have a right to do, and what we know will be acceptable to the Most High."

On the 13th of September, A. D. 1309, the king granted letters of safe conduct "to those discreet men, the abbot of Lagny, in the diocese of Paris, and Master Sicard de Vaur, canon of Narbonne," the inquisitors appointed by the pope to examine the Grand Preceptor and brethren of the Temple in England; and the same day he wrote to the archbishop of Canterbury, and the bishops of London and Lincoln, enjoining them to be personally present with the papal inquisitors, at their respective sees, as often as such inquisitors, or any one of them, should proceed with their inquiries against the Templars.†

Among the prisoners confined in the Tower were Brother William de la More, Knight, Grand Preceptor of England, otherwise Master of the Temple; Brother Himbert Blanke, Knight, Grand Preceptor of Auvergne, one of the veteran warriors who had fought to the last in defense of Palestine, had escaped the slaughter at Acre, and had accompanied the Grand Master from Cyprus to France, whence he crossed over to England, and was rewarded for his meritorious and memorable services, in defense of the Christian faith, with a dungeon in the Tower. Brother *Radulph de*

---

* Acta *Rymeri*, tom. iii. p. 100-103, 111, 121, 122.
† Acta *Rymeri*, p. 168, 169.

Barton, priest of the order of the Temple, custos or guardian of the Temple church, and prior of London; Brother *Michael de Baskeville*, Knight, Preceptor of London; Brother *John de Stoke*, Knight, Treasurer of the Temple at London; together with many other knights and serving brethren of the same house. There were also in custody in the Tower the Knights Preceptors of the preceptories of Ewell in Kent, of Daney and Dokesworth in Cambridgeshire, of Getinges in Gloucestershire, of Cumbe in Somersetshire, of Schepeley in Surrey, of Samford and Bistelesham in Oxfordshire, of Garwy in Herefordshire, of Cressing in Essex, of Pafflet, Huppleden, and other preceptories, together with several priests and chaplains of the order. A general scramble appears to have taken place for possession of the goods and chattels of the imprisoned Templars; and the king, to check the robberies that were committed, appointed Alan de Goldyngham and John de Medefeld to inquire into the value of the property that had been carried off, and to inform him of the names of the parties who had obtained possession of it. The sheriffs of the different counties were also directed to summon juries, through whom the truth might he better obtained.[*]

On the 22nd of September, the archbishop of Canterbury, acting in obedience to the papal commands, before a single witness had been examined in England, caused to be published in all churches and chapels a papal bull, wherein the pope declares himself perfectly convinced of the guilt of the order, and solemnly denounces the penalty of excommunication against all persons, of whatever rank, station, or condition in life, whether clergy or laity, who should knowingly afford, either publicly or privately, assistance, counsel, or kindness to the Templars, or should dare to shelter them, or give them countenance or protection, and also laying under interdict all cities, castles, lands and places, which should harbor any of the members of the proscribed order! At the commencement of the month of October, the inquisitors arrived in England, and immediately published the bull appointing the commission, enjoining the citation of criminals, and of witnesses, and denouncing the heaviest ecclesiastical censures against the disobedient, and against every person who should dare to impede the inquisitors in the exercise of their functions. Citations were made in St. Paul's Cathedral, and in all the churches of the ecclesiastical province of Canterbury, at the end of high mass, requiring the Templars to appear before the inquisitors at a certain time and place, and the articles of accusation were transmitted to the constable of the Tower, in Latin, French, and English, to be read to all the Templars imprisoned in that fortress.

On Monday, the 20th of October, after the Templars had been languishing in the English prisons for more than a year and eight months, the tribunal constituted by the pope to take the inquisition in the province of Canterbury assembled in the episcopal hall of London. It was composed

---

[*] Concil. Mag. Brit. tom. ii. p. 346, 347. Acta *Rymeri*, tom. iii. p. 174, 175, 178, 179.

of the bishop of London Dieudonné, abbot of the monastery of Lagny, in the diocese of Paris, and Sicard de Vaur, canon of Narbonne, the pope's chaplain, and hearer of causes in the pontifical palace. They were assisted by several foreign notaries. After the reading of the papal bulls, and some preliminary proceedings, the articles of accusation, a monument of human folly, superstition, and credulity, were solemnly exhibited. It was urged against the Templars:

"1. That at their first reception into the order, or at some time afterwards, or as soon as an opportunity occurred, they were induced or admonished by those who had received them within the bosom of the fraternity, to deny Christ or Jesus, or the crucifixion, or at one time God, and at another time the blessed Virgin, and sometimes all the saints. 5. That the receivers told and instructed those that were received, that Christ was not the true God, or sometimes Jesus, or sometimes the person crucified. 7. That they said he had not suffered for the redemption of mankind, nor been crucified but for his own sins. 9. That they made those they received into the order spit upon the cross, or upon the sign or figure of the cross, or the image of Christ. 10. That they caused the cross itself to be trampled under foot. 11. That the brethren themselves did sometimes trample on the same cross. 12. Item quod mingebant interdum, et alios mingere faciebant, super ipsam crucem. 14. That they worshipped a cat, which was placed in the midst of the congregation. 16. That they did not believe the sacrament of the altar nor the other sacraments of the church. 24. That they believed, and so it was told them, that the Grand Master of the order could absolve them from their sins. 25. That the visitor could do so. 26. That the preceptors, of whom many were laymen, could do it. 36. That the receptions of the brethren were made clandestinely. 37. That none were present but the brothers of the said order. 38. That for this reason there has for a long time been a vehement suspicion against them."

The succeeding articles charge the Templars with crimes and abominations too horrible and disgusting to be named.

"46. That the brothers themselves had idols in every province, viz. heads; some of which had three faces, and some one, and some a man's skull. 47. That they adored that idol, or those idols, especially in their great chapters and assemblies 48. That they worshipped them. 49. As their God. 50. As their Saviour. 51. That some of them did so. 52. That the greater part did. 53. They said that those heads could save them. 54. That they could produce riches. 55. That they had given to the order all its wealth. 56. That they caused the earth to bring forth seed. 57. That they made the trees to nourish. 58. That they bound or touched the heads of the said idols with cords, wherewith they bound themselves about their shirts, or next their skins. 59. That at their reception the aforesaid little cords, or others of the same length, were delivered to each of the brothers. 60. That they did this in worship of their idols. 61. That it was enjoined them to gird themselves with the said little cords, as before mentioned, and continually to wear them. 62. That the brethren of the order were generally received in that manner. 63. That they did these things out of devotion. 64. That they did them everywhere. 65. That the greater part did. 66. That those who refused the things above mentioned at their reception, or to observe them afterwards, were killed or cast into prison."* The remaining articles, twenty-one in number, are directed principally to the mode of confession practiced amongst the fraternity, and to matters of heretical depravity. Such an accusation as this, justly remarks Voltaire, *destroys itself.*

Brother William de la More, and thirty more of his brethren, being interrogated before the inquisitors, positively denied the guilt of the order, and affirmed that the Templars who had made the confession alluded to in France *had lied.* They were ordered to be brought up separately to be examined. On the 23rd of October, Brother William Raven, being interrogated as to the mode of his reception into the order, states that he was admitted by Brother William de la More, the Master of the Temple at Temple Coumbe, in the diocese of Bath; that he petitioned the brethren of the Temple that they would be pleased to receive him into the order to serve God and the blessed Virgin Mary, and to end his life in their service; that he was asked if he had a firm wish so to do; and replied that he had; that two brothers then expounded to him the strictness and severity of the order, and told him that he would not be allowed to act after his own will, but must follow the will of the preceptor; that if he wished to do one thing, he would be ordered to do another; and that if he wished to be at one place, he would be sent to another; that having promised so to act, he swore upon the holy gospels of God to obey the Master, to hold no property, to preserve chastity, never to consent that any man should be unjustly despoiled of his heritage, and never to lay violent hands on any man, except in self-defense, or upon the Saracens. He states that the oath was administered to him in the chapel of the preceptory of Temple Coumbe, in the presence only of the brethren of the order; that the rule was read over to him by one of the brothers, and that a learned serving brother, named John de Walpole, instructed him, for the space of one month, upon the matters contained in it. The prisoner was then taken back to the Tower, and was directed to be strictly separated from his brethren, and not to be suffered to speak to any one of them.

The next two days (October 24th and 25th) were taken up with a similar examination of Brothers Hugh de Tadecastre and Thomas le Chamberleyn, who gave precisely the same account of their reception as the previous witness. Brother Hugh de Tadecastre added, that he swore to succor the Holy Land with all his might, and defend it against the enemies of the Christian faith; and that after he had taken the customary oaths and

---

* The original draft of these articles of accusation, with the corrections and alterations, is preserved in the Tresor des Chartres. *Raynouard*, Monumens Historiques, p. 50, 51. The proceedings against the Templars in England are preserved in MS. in the British Museum, Harl. No. 252, 62, f. p. 113; No. 247, 68, f. p. 144. Bib. Cotton. Julius, b. xii. p. 70; and in the Bodleian Library and Ashmolean Museum. The principal part of them has been published by *Wilkins* in the Concilia Magnæ Britanniæ, tom ii. p. 329-401, and by *Dugdale*, in the Monast. Angl. vol. vi. part ii. p. 844-848.

the three vows of chastity, poverty, and obedience, the mantle of the order with the cross and the coif were delivered to him in the church, in the presence of the Master, the knights, and the brothers, all seculars being excluded. Brother Thomas le Chamberleyn added, that there was the same mode of reception in England as beyond sea, and the same mode of taking the vows; that all seculars were excluded, and that when he himself entered the Temple church to be professed, the door by which he entered was closed after him; that there was another door looking into the cemetery, but that no stranger could enter that way. On being asked why none but the brethren of the order were permitted to be present at the reception and profession of brothers, he said he knew of no reason, but that it was so written in their book of rules.

Between the 25th of October and the 17th of November, thirty-three knights, chaplains, and serving brothers, were examined, all of whom positively denied every article imputing crime or infidelity to their order. When Brother Himbert Blanke was asked why they had made the reception and profession of brethren secret, he replied, "through our own unaccountable folly." They avowed that they wore little cords round their shirts, but for no bad end; they declared that they never touched idols with them, but that they were worn by way of penance, or according to a knight of forty-three years standing, by the instruction of the holy father St. Bernard. Brother Richard de Goldyngham says that he knows nothing further about them than that they were called girdles of chastity. They state that the receivers and the party received kissed one another on the face, but everything else regarding the kissing was false, abominable, and had never been done.

Radulph de Barton, priest of the order of the Temple, and custos or guardian of the Temple church at London, stated, with regard to Article 24, that the Grand Master in chapter could absolve the brothers from offences committed against the rules and observances of the order, but not from private sin, as he was not a priest; that it was perfectly true that those who were received into the order swore not to reveal the secrets of the chapter, and that when any one was punished in the chapter, those who were present at it durst not reveal it to such as were absent; but if any brother revealed the mode of his reception, he would be deprived of his chamber, or else stripped of his habit. He declares that the brethren were not prohibited from confessing to priests not belonging to the order of the Temple; and that he had never heard of the crimes and iniquities mentioned in the articles of inquiry previous to his arrest, except as regarded the charges made against the order by Bernard Peletin, when he came to England from king Philip of France. He states that he had been custos of the Temple church at London for ten years, and for the last two years had enjoyed the dignity of preceptor at the same place. He was asked about the death of Brother Walter le Bachelor, knight, formerly Preceptor of Ireland, who died in the Temple at London, but he declares that he knows nothing about it, except that the said Walter was fettered and placed in prison, and there died; that he certainly had heard that great severity had been practiced towards him, but that he had not meddled with the affair on account of the danger of so doing; he admitted also that the aforesaid Walter was not buried in the cemetery of the Temple, as he was considered excommunicated on account of his disobedience of his superior, and of the rule of the order.

Many of the brethren thus examined had been from twenty to thirty, forty, forty-two, and forty-three years in the order, and some were old veteran warriors who had fought for many a long year in the thirsty plains of Palestine. Brother Himbert Blanke, Knight, Preceptor of Auvergne, had been in the order thirty-eight years. He was received at the city of Tyre, had been engaged in constant warfare against the infidels, and had fought to the last in defense of Acre. Brother Robert le Scott, Knight, a brother of twenty-six years' standing, had been received at the Pilgrim's Castle, the famous fortress of the Knights Templars in Palestine, by the Grand Master, Brother William de Beaujeu, the hero who died so gloriously at the head of his knights at the last siege and storming of Acre. He states that from levity of disposition he quitted the order after it had been driven out of Palestine, and absented himself for two years, during which period he came to Rome, and confessed to the pope's penitentiary, who imposed on him a heavy penance, and enjoined him to return to his brethren in the East, and that he went back and resumed his habit at Nicosia in the island of Cyprus, and was re-admitted to the order by command of the Grand Master, James de Molay. He adds, also, that Brother Himbert Blanke (the previous witness) was present at his first reception at the Pilgrim's Castle.

On the 22nd day of the inquiry, the following entry was made on the record of the proceedings:—"Memorandum. Brothers Philip de Mewes, Thomas de Burton, and Thomas de Staundon, were advised and earnestly exhorted to abandon their religious profession, who severally replied that they would rather die than do so." On the 19th and 20th of November, seven lay witnesses, unconnected with the order, were examined before the inquisitors in the chapel of the monastery of the Holy Trinity. Master William le Dorturer, notary public, declared that the Templars rose at midnight, and held their chapters before dawn, and he *thought* that the mystery and secrecy of the receptions were owing to a bad rather than a good motive, but declared that he had never observed that they had acquired, or had attempted to acquire, anything unjustly. Master Gilbert de Bruere, clerk, said that he had never suspected them of anything worse than an excessive correction of the brethren. William Lambert, formerly a "messenger of the Temple," knew nothing bad of the Templars, and thought them perfectly innocent of all the matters alluded to. And Richard de Barton, priest, and Radulph de Rayndon, an old man, both declared that they knew nothing of the order, or of the members of it, but what was good and honorable.

On the 25th of November, a provincial council of the church, composed of the bishops, abbots, priors, heads of colleges, and all the principal clergy, assembled in St. Paul's Cathedral, and a papal bull was read, in which the holy pontiff dwells most pathetically upon the awful sins of the Templars, and their great and tremendous fall from their previous high estate. Hitherto, says he, they have been renowned throughout the world as the special champions of the faith, and the chief defenders of the Holy Land, whose affairs have been mainly regulated by those brothers. The church, following them and their order with the plenitude of its especial favor and regard, armed them with the emblem of the cross against the enemies of Christ, exalted them with much honor, enriched them with wealth, and fortified them with various liberties and privileges. The holy pontiff displays the sad report of their sins and iniquities which reached his ears, filled him with bitterness and grief, disturbed his repose, smote him with horror, injured his health, and caused his body to waste away! He gives a long account of the crimes imputed to the order, of the confessions and depositions that had been made in France, and then bursts out into a paroxysm of grief, declares that the melancholy affair deeply moved all the faithful, that all Christianity was shedding bitter tears, was overwhelmed with grief, and clothed with mourning. He concludes by decreeing the assembly of a general council of the church at Vienne to pronounce the abolition of the order, and to determine on the disposal of its property, to which council the English clergy are required to send representatives.

In Scotland, in the mean time, similar proceedings had been instituted against the order. On the 17th of November, Brother Walter de Clifton being examined in the parish church of the Holy Cross at Edinburgh, before the bishop of St. Andrews and John de Solerio, the pope's chaplain, states that the brethren of the order of the Temple in the kingdom of Scotland received their orders, rules, and observances from the Master of the Temple in England, and that the Master in England received the rules and observances of the order from the Grand Master and the chief convent in the East; that the Grand Master or his deputy was in the habit of visiting the order in England and elsewhere; of summoning chapters and making regulations for the conduct of the brethren, and the administration of their property. Being asked as to the mode of his reception, he states that when William de la More, the Master, held his chapter at the preceptory of Temple Bruere in the county of Lincoln, he sought of the assembled brethren the habit and the fellowship of the order; that they told him that he little knew what it was he asked, in seeking to be admitted to their fellowship; that it would be a very hard matter for him, who was then his own master, to become the servant of another, and to have no will of his own; but notwithstanding their representations of the rigour of their rules and observances, he still continued earnestly to seek their habit and fellowship. He states that they then led him to the chamber of the Master, where they held their chapter, and that there, on his bended knees, and with his hands clasped, he again prayed for the habit and the fellowship of the Temple; that the Master and the brethren then required him to answer questions to the following effect:—Whether he had a dispute with any man, or owed any debts? whether he was betrothed to any woman? and whether he had any secret infirmity of body? or knew of anything to prevent him from remaining within the bosom of the fraternity? And having answered all these questions satisfactorily, the Master then asked of the surrounding brethren, "Do ye give your consent to the reception of Brother Walter?" who unanimously answered that they did; and the Master and the brethren then standing up, received him the said Walter in this manner. On his bended knees, and with his hands joined, he solemnly promised that he would be the perpetual servant of the Master, and of the order, and of the brethren, for the purpose of defending the Holy Land. Having done this, the Master took out of the hands of a brother chaplain of the order the book of the holy gospels, upon which was depicted a cross, and laying his hand upon the book, and upon the cross, he swore to God and the blessed Virgin Mary to be for ever thereafter chaste, obedient, and to live without property. And then the Master gave to him the white mantle, and placed the coif on his head and admitted him to the kiss on the mouth, after which he made him sit down on the ground, and admonished him to the following effect: that from thenceforth he was to sleep in his shirt, drawers, and stockings, girded with a small cord over his shirt; that he was never to tarry in a house where there was a woman in the family way; never to be present at a marriage or at the purification of women; and likewise instructed and informed him upon several other particulars. Being asked where he had passed his time since his reception, he replied that he had dwelt three years at the preceptory of Blancradok in Scotland; three years at Temple Newsom in England; one year at the Temple at London, and three years at Aslakeby. Being asked concerning the other brothers in Scotland, he stated that John de Hueflete was Preceptor of Blancradok, the chief house of the order in that country, and that he and the other brethren, having heard of the arrest of the Templars, threw off their habits, and fled, and that he had not since heard aught concerning them.

Forty-one witnesses, chiefly abbots, priors, monks, priests, and serving men, and retainers of the order in Scotland, were examined upon various interrogatories, but nothing of a criminatory nature was elicited. The monks observed that the receptions of other orders were public, and were celebrated as great religious solemnities, and the friends, parents, and neighbors of the party about to take the vows were invited to attend; while the Templars, on the other hand, shrouded their proceedings in mystery and secrecy, and therefore they *suspected* the worst. The priests thought them guilty, because they were always against the church! Others condemned them because (as they say) the Templars closed their doors against the poor and the humble, and extended hospitality only to the rich and the powerful. The abbot of the monastery of the Holy Cross at Edinburgh declared that they appropriated to themselves the property of their neighbors, right or wrong. The abbot of Dumferlyn knew nothing of his own knowledge against them, but had *heard* much, and *suspected* more. The serving men and the tillers of the lands of the order stated that the chapters were held sometimes by night and sometimes by day, with extraordinary secrecy; and some of the witnesses had heard old men say that the Templars would never have lost the Holy Land if they had been good Christians!

On the 9th of January, A. D. 1310, the examination of witnesses was resumed at London, in the parish church of St. Dunstan's West, near the Temple. The rector of the church of St. Mary de la Strode declared that he had strong *suspicions* of the guilt of the Templars; he had, however, often been at the Temple church, and had observed that the priests performed divine service there just the same as elsewhere. William de Cumbrook, of St. Clement's church, near the Temple, the vicar of St. Martin's-in-the-Fields, and many other priests and clergymen of different churches in London, all declared that they had nothing to allege against the order.

On the 27th of January, Brother John de Stoke, a serving brother of the order of the Temple, of seventeen years' standing, being examined by the inquisitors in the chapel of the Blessed Mary of Berkyngecherche at London, states, amongst other things, that secular persons were allowed to be present at the burial of Templars; that the brethren of the order all received the sacraments of the church at their last hour, and were attended to the grave by a chaplain of the Temple. Being interrogated concerning the burial of the Knight Templar Brother Walter le Bacheler, Grand Preceptor of Ireland, who had been confined in the penitential cell in the Temple, for disobedience to his superiors, and was reported to have been there starved to death, he deposes that the said knight was buried like any other Christian, except that he was not buried in the burying-ground, but in the court of the house of the Temple at London; that he confessed to Brother Richard de Grafton, a priest of the order, then in the island of Cyprus, and partook, as he believed, of the sacrament. He states that he himself and Brother Radulph de Barton carried him to his grave at the dawn of day, and that the deceased knight was in prison, as he believes, for the space of eight weeks; that he was not buried in the habit of his order, and was interred without the cemetery of the brethren, because he was considered to be excommunicated, in pursuance, as he believed, of a rule or statute among the Templars, to the effect that every one who privily made away with the property of the order, and did not acknowledge his fault, was deemed excommunicated.

On the 30th of March, the papal inquisitors opened their commission at Lincoln, and numerous Templars were examined in the chapter-house of the cathedral, amongst whom were some of the veteran warriors of Palestine, who had moistened with their blood the distant plains of the far East. Brother William de Winchester, a member of twenty-six years' standing, stated that he had been received into the order at the castle *de la Roca Guille*, in the province of Armenia, bordering on Syria, by the valiant Grand Master William de Beaujeu. He states that the same mode of reception existed there as in England, and everywhere throughout the order. Brother Robert de Hamilton declares that the girdles said to be worn by the brethren were called girdles of Nazareth, because they had been pressed against the column of the Virgin at that place, and were worn in remembrance of the blessed Mary.

At York, the examination commenced on the 28th of April, and lasted until the 4th of May, during which period twenty-three Templars, prisoners in York Castle, were examined in the chapter-house of the cathedral, and followed the example of their brethren in maintaining their innocence. Brother Thomas de Stanford, a member of thirty years' standing, had been received in the East by the Grand Master William de Beaujeu, and Brother Radulph de Rostona, a priest of the order, of twenty-three years' standing, had been received at the preceptory of Lentini in Sicily, by Brother William de Canello, the Grand Preceptor of Sicily. Brother Stephen de Radenhall refused to reveal the mode of reception, because it formed part of the secrets of the chapter, and if he discovered them he would lose his chamber, be stripped of his mantle, or be committed to prison.[*]

The proceedings against the order in France had, in the mean time, assumed a most sanguinary character. On the 28th of March, (A. D. 1310) five hundred and forty-six Templars, who persisted in maintaining the innocence of their order, were assembled in the garden of the bishop's palace at Paris, to hear the articles of accusation read over to them, and a committee of their number was authorized to draw up a written defense. They asked to have an interview with the Grand Master and the heads of the order, but this was refused. The total number of Templars, immured in the prisons of Paris, was nine hundred. In the course of the examination before the papal commissioners, Brother Laurent de Beaume produced a letter which had been sent to him and his fellow-prisoners at Sens, warning them against a retractation of their confessions in the following terms: *"Sachez que notre pere le pape a mande que tuit cil qui aurent fayt les suizitos confessions devant ses anvouez, qui en cele confessions ne voudroient perseverès, que il sorent mis a damnazion et destruit au feu."* This threat was carried into execution, and Brother Laurent de Beaume was one of the first victims. The defense drawn up by the brethren and presented to the commissioners by Brother Peter de Bologna, begins by stating the origin and objects of their institution, the vows to which they subjected themselves, and the mode in which persons were received into the fraternity. They give a frightful account of the tortures that had been inflicted upon them, and declare that those who had escaped with life from the hands of the tormentors, were either ruined in health or injured in intellect, and that as pardon and forgiveness had been freely offered to those knights who would confess, it was not wonderful that false confessions had been made. They observed that a vast number of knights had died in prison, and they exhorted the commissioners to interrogate the guards, jailers, and executioners, and those who saw them in their last

---

[*] Concil. Mag. Brit. tom. ii. p. 350-383. Acta *Rymeri*, tom. iii. p. 179, 180.

moments, concerning the declarations and confessions they had made at the peril of their souls when dying. They maintained that it was a most extraordinary thing that so many knights of distinguished birth and noble blood, members of the most illustrious families in Europe, should have remained from an early age up to the day of their death, members of the order, and should never, in days of sickness, or at the hour of death, have revealed any of the horrid iniquities and abominations charged against it.[*] All the Templars, indeed, who had made confessions were rapidly following one another's example in retracting them, and maintaining their innocence, and the king hastened to arrest the unfavourable march of events.

The archbishop of Sens, whose ecclesiastical authority extended over the diocese of Paris, having died, the king obtained the vacant see for Philip de Martigny, a creature of his own, who was installed therein in the month of April. In a letter to Clement urging this appointment, Philip reminds the holy pontiff that the new archbishop would have to preside over a provincial council wherein would be transacted many things which immediately concerned the glory of God, the stability of the faith, and of the holy church. Immediately after the enthronement of this new archbishop, the provincial council of Sens was convoked at Paris, and on the 10th of May, all the Templars who had revoked their confessions, and had come forward to maintain the innocence of their order, were dragged before it, and sentence of death was passed upon them by the archbishop in the following terms:—"You have avowed," said he, "that the brethren who are received into the order of the Temple are compelled to renounce Christ and spit upon the cross, and that you yourselves have participated in that crime; you have thus acknowledged that you have fallen into the sin of *heresy.* By your confession and repentance you had merited absolution, and had once more become reconciled to the church. As you have revoked your confession, the church no longer regards you as reconciled, but as having fallen back to your first errors. You are, therefore, *relapsed heretics,* and as such, we condemn you to the fire!" As soon as the commissioners had received intelligence of this extraordinary decree, they despatched messengers to the archbishop and his suffragans, praying them to delay the execution of their sentence, as very many persons affirmed that the Templars who died in prison had proclaimed with their last breath the innocence of their order. But these representations were of no avail. The archbishop, who was paying the price of his elevation to a hard creditor, proceeded to make short work of the business.

The very next morning, (Tuesday, May 12,) fifty-four Templars were handed over to the secular arm, and were led out to execution by the king's officers. They were conducted, at daybreak, into the open country, in the environs of the Porte St. Antoine des Champs at Paris, and were there fastened to stakes driven into the ground, and surrounded by faggots and

---

[*] *Raynouard*, p. 52, 57, 75, ed. 1813. *Dupuy*, p. 138, 139, 174, ed. 1700.

charcoal. In this situation, they saw the torches lighted, and the executioners approaching to accomplish their task, and they were once more offered pardon and favor if they would confess the *guilt* of their order; they persisted in the maintenance of its *innocence*, and were burnt to death in a most cruel manner before slow fires! All historians speak with admiration of the heroism and intrepidity with which they met their fate. Many hundred other Templars were dragged from the dungeons of Paris before the archbishop of Sens and his council. Those whom neither the agony of torture nor the fear of death could overcome, but who remained stedfast amid all their trials in the maintenance of their innocence, were condemned to perpetual imprisonment as *unreconciled heretics*; whilst those who, having made the required confessions of guilt, continued to persevere in them, received absolution, were declared reconciled to the church, and were set at liberty.[*]

On the 18th of August, four other Templars were condemned as relapsed heretics by the council of Sens, and were likewise burnt by the Porte St. Antoine; and it is stated that a hundred and thirteen Templars were, from first to last, burnt at the stake in Paris. Many others were burned in Lorraine; in Normandy; at Carcassone; and nine, or, according to some writers, twenty-nine, were burnt by the archbishop of Rheims at Senlis! King Philip's officers, indeed, not content with their inhuman cruelty towards the living, *invaded the sanctity of the tomb*; they dragged a dead Templar, who had been treasurer of the Temple at Paris, from his grave, and burnt the mouldering corpse as a heretic.

In the midst of all these sanguinary atrocities, the examinations continued before the ecclesiastical tribunals. Many aged and illustrious warriors, who merited a better fate, appeared before their judges pale and trembling. At first they revoked their confessions, declared their innocence, and were remanded to prison; and then, panic-stricken, they demanded to be led back before the papal commissioners, when they abandoned their retractations, persisted in their previous avowals of *guilt*, humbly expressed their sorrow and repentance, and were then pardoned, absolved, and reconciled to the church! The torture still continued to be applied, and out of thirty-three Templars confined in the chateau d'Alaix, four died in prison, and the remaining twenty confessed, amongst other things, the following absurdities:—that in the provincial chapter of the order held at Montpelier, the Templars set up a head and worshipped it; that the devil often appeared there in the shape of a cat, and conversed with the assembled brethren, and promised them a good harvest, with the possession of riches, and all kinds of temporal property. Some asserted that the head worshipped by the fraternity possessed a long beard; others that it was a woman's head; and one of the prisoners declared that as often as this wonderful head was adored, a great number of devils made their appearance in the shape of beautiful women...!!

---

[*] Chron. Cornel. *Zanfliet* apud *Martene*, tom. v. col. 159. *Bocat.* de cas. vir. illustr. lib. ix. cap. 21. *Joan. Can. Sti. Vict.* Contin. de *Nangis*, ad ann. 1310. *Rayn.*

The Knights Templars

We must now unfold the dark page in the history of the order in England. All the Templars in custody in this country had been examined separately, and had, notwithstanding, deposed in substance to the same effect, and given the same account of their reception into the order, and of the oaths that they took. Any reasonable and impartial mind would consequently have been satisfied of the truth of their statements; but it was not the object of the inquisitors to obtain evidence of the *innocence*, but proof of the *guilt* of the order. At first, king Edward the Second, to his honor, forbade the infliction of torture upon the illustrious members of the Temple in his dominions—men who had fought and bled for Christendom, and of whose piety and morals he had a short time before given such ample testimony to the principal sovereigns of Europe. But the virtuous resolution of the weak king was speedily overcome by the all-powerful influence of the Roman pontiff, who wrote to him in the month of June, upbraiding him for preventing the inquisitors from submitting the Templars to the discipline of the rack. Influenced by the admonitions of the pope, and the solicitations of the clergy, king Edward sent orders to the constable of the Tower, to deliver up the Templars to certain gaolers appointed by the inquisitors, in order that the inquisitors might do with the bodies of the Templars whatever should seem fitting, in accordance with ecclesiastical law. The ecclesiastical council then assembled, and ordered that the Templars should be again confined in separate cells; that fresh interrogatories should be prepared, to see if by such means the *truth* could be extracted, and if by straitenings and confinement they would *confess nothing further*, then the torture was to be applied; but it was provided that the examination by torture should be conducted without the PERPETUAL MUTILATION OR DISABLING OF ANY LIMB, AND WITHOUT A VIOLENT EFFUSION OF BLOOD! and the inquisitors and the bishops of London and Chichester were to notify the result to the archbishop of Canterbury, that he might again convene the assembly for the purpose of passing sentence, either of absolution or of condemnation.

Fresh instructions were then sent by the king to the constable of the Tower, and the sheriffs of London, informing them that the king, on account of his respect for the holy apostolical see, had conceded to the inquisitors the power of examining the Templars by TORTURE; and strictly enjoining them to deliver up the Templars to the inquisitors, and receive them back when required so to do. The king then acquainted the mayor, aldermen, and commonalty of his faithful city of London, that out of reverence to the pope he had authorized the inquisitors, sent over by his holiness, to question the Templars by TORTURE; and he commands them, in case it should be notified to them by the inquisitors that the prisons provided by the sheriffs were insufficient for their purposes, to procure without fail fit and convenient houses in the city, or near thereto, for carrying into effect the contemplated measures. Shortly afterwards, he again wrote to the mayor, aldermen, and commonalty of London, acquainting them that the sheriffs had made a return to his writ, to the effect that the four gates (prisons) of the city were not under their charge, and that they could not therefore obtain them for the purposes required; and he commands the mayor, aldermen, and commonalty, to place those four gates at the disposal of the sheriffs. Shortly afterwards orders were given for all the Templars in custody in London to be loaded with chains and fetters! the myrmidons of the inquisitors were to be allowed to make periodical visits to see that the imprisonment was properly carried into effect, and were to be allowed to TORTURE the bodies of the Templars in any way that they might think fit.*

On the 30th of March, A. D. 1311, the examination was resumed before the inquisitors, and the bishops of London and Chichester, at the several churches of St. Martin's Ludgate, and St. Botolph's Bishopsgate. The Templars had now been in prison in England for the space of three years and some months. During the whole of the previous winter they had been confined in chains in the dungeons of the city of London, compelled to receive their scanty supply of food from the officers of the inquisition, and to suffer from cold, from hunger, and from torture. They had been made to endure all the horrors of solitary confinement, and had none to solace or to cheer them during the long hours of their melancholy captivity. They had been already condemned collectively by the pope, as members of an heretical and idolatrous society, and as long as they continued to persist in the truth of their first confessions, and in the avowal of their innocence, they were treated as obstinate, unreconciled heretics, living in a state of excommunication, and doomed, when dead, to everlasting punishment in hell. They had heard of the miserable fate of their brethren in France, and they knew that those who had confessed crimes of which they had never been guilty, had been immediately declared reconciled to the church, had been absolved and set at liberty, and they knew that freedom, pardon, and peace could be immediately purchased by a confession of guilt; notwithstanding all which, every Templar, at this last examination, persisted in the maintenance of his innocence, and in the denial of all knowledge of, or participation in, the crimes and heresies imputed to the order. They were therefore again sent back to their dungeons, and loaded with chains; and the inquisitors, disappointed of the desired confessions, addressed themselves to the enemies of the order for the necessary proofs of guilt.

During the month of April, seventy-two witnesses were examined in the chapter-house of the Holy Trinity. They were nearly all monks, Carmelites, Augustinians, Dominicans, and Minorites; their evidence is all hearsay, and the nature of it will be seen from the following choice specimens:—Henry Thanet, an Irishman, had *heard* that a certain Preceptor of the Pilgrim's Castle was in the habit of making all the brethren he received into the order deny Christ. He had *heard* also that a certain Templar had in his custody a brazen head with two faces, which would

---

* Acta *Rymeri*, tom. iii. p. 194, 195, 224, 225, 227, 230-235. Concil. Mag. Brit. tom. ii. p. 305-314; tom. iii. p. 228, 229.

answer all questions put to it!—Master John de Nassington had *heard* that the Templars celebrated a solemn festival once a year, at which they worshipped a *calf!*—John de Eure, knight, sheriff of the county of York, deposed that he had once invited Brother William de la Fenne, Preceptor of Wesdall, to dine with him, and that after dinner the Preceptor drew a book out of his bosom, and delivered it to the knight's lady to read, who found a piece of paper fastened into the book, on which were written abominable heretical doctrines, to the effect that Christ was not the Son of God, nor born of a virgin, but conceived of the seed of Joseph, the husband of Mary, after the manner of other men, and that Christ was not a true but a false prophet, and was not crucified for the redemption of mankind, but for his own sins; and many other things contrary to the Christian faith. On the production of this important evidence, Brother William de la Fenne was called in and interrogated; he admitted that he had dined with the sheriff of York, and had lent his lady a book to read, but he swore that he was ignorant of the piece of paper fastened into the book, and of its contents. It appears that the sheriff of York had kept this discovery to himself for the space of six years!

William de la Forde, a priest, rector of the parish of Crofton in the diocese of York, had *heard* William de Reynbur, priest of the order of St. Augustine, who was then dead, say, that the Templar, Brother Patrick of Rippon, son of William of Gloucester, had confessed to him, that at his entrance into the order, he was led, clothed only in his shirt and trousers, through a long passage to a secret chamber, and was there made to deny his God and his Saviour; that he was then shown a representation of the crucifixion, and was told that since he had previously honored that emblem he must now dis honor it and spit upon it, and that he did so. "Item dictum fuit ei quod, depositis brachis, dorsum verteret ad crucifixum," and this he did bitterly weeping. After this they brought an image, as it were, of a calf, placed upon an altar, and they told him he must kiss that image, and worship it, and he did so; and after all this they covered up his eyes and led him about, kissing and being kissed by all the brethren, but he could not recollect in what part. The worthy priest was asked when he had *first heard* all these things, and he replied *after* the arrest of the brethren by the king's orders!

Robert of Oteringham, senior of the order of Minorites, stated that on one occasion he was partaking of the hospitality of the Templars at the preceptory of Ribstane in Yorkshire, and that when grace had been said after supper, the chaplain of the order reprimanded the brethren, saying, "The devil will burn you;" and hearing a bustle, he got up, and, as far as he recollects, saw one of the brothers of the Temple, "brachis depositis, tenentem faciem versus occidentem et posteriora versus altare!" He then states, that about twenty years before that time, he was the guest of the Templars, at the preceptory of Wetherby in Yorkshire, and when evening came he heard that the preceptor was not coming to supper, as he was arranging some relics that he had brought with him from the Holy Land,

and afterwards at midnight he heard a confused noise in the chapel, and getting up he looked through the keyhole, and saw a great light therein, either from a fire or from candles, and on the morrow he asked one of the brethren of the Temple the name of the saint in whose honor they had celebrated so grand a festival during the night, and that brother, aghast and turning pale, thinking he had seen what had been done amongst them, said to him, "Go thy way, and if you love me, or have any regard for your own life, never speak of this matter!" Brother John de Wederel, another Minorite, stated that he had lately *heard* in the country, that a Templar, named Robert de Baysat, was once seen running about a meadow uttering, "Alas! alas! that ever I was born, seeing that I have denied God and sold myself to the devil!" Brother N. de Chinon, another Minorite, had *heard* that a certain Templar had a son who peeped through a chink in the wall of the chapter-room and saw a person who was about to be professed, slain because he would not deny Christ, and afterwards the boy was asked by his father to become a Templar, but refused, and he immediately shared the same fate. Twenty other witnesses, who were examined in each other's presence, related similar absurdities.

At this stage of the proceedings, the papal inquisitor, Sicard de Vaur, exhibited two rack-extorted confessions of Templars which had been obtained in France. The first was from Robert de St. Just, who had been received into the order by Brother Himbert, Grand Preceptor of England, but had been arrested in France, and there tortured. In this confession Robert de St. Just states that, on his admission to the vows of the Temple, he denied Christ, and spat *beside* the cross. The second confession had been extorted from Geoffrey de Gonville, Knight of the Order of the Temple, Preceptor of Aquitaine and Poitou. In this confession, (which had been revoked, but of which revocation no notice was taken by the inquisitors,) Geoffrey de Gonville states that he was received into the order in England in the house of the Temple at London, by Brother Robert de Torvile, Knight, the Master of all England, about twenty-eight years before that time; that the Master showed him on a missal the image of Jesus Christ on the cross, and commanded him to deny him who was crucified; that, terribly alarmed, he exclaimed, "Alas! my lord, why should I do this? I will on no account do it." But the Master said to him, "Do it boldly; I swear to thee that the act shall never harm either thy soul or thy conscience;" and then proceeded to inform him that the custom had been introduced into the order by a certain bad Grand Master, who was imprisoned by a certain sultan, and could escape from prison only on condition that he would establish that form of reception in his order, and compel all who were received to deny Christ Jesus! but the deponent remained inflexible; he refused to deny his Saviour, and asked where were his uncle and the other good people who had brought him there, and was told that they were all gone; and at last a compromise took place between him and the Master, who made him take his oath that he would tell all his brethren that he had gone through the customary form, and never reveal that it had been dispensed with! He states also that the ceremony was instituted in memory of St. Peter, who three times denied Christ! This knight had been tortured in the Temple at Paris, by the brothers of St. Dominic, in the presence of the grand inquisitor, and he made his confession when suffering on the rack; he afterwards revoked it, and was then tortured into a withdrawal of his revocation, notwithstanding which the inquisitor made the unhappy wretch, in common with others, put his signature to the following interrogatory, "Interrogatus, utrum *vi* vel *metu carceris* aut *tormentorum* immiscuit in suâ depositione aliquam falsitatem, dicit *quod non!*"

Ferinsius le Mareschal, a secular knight, being examined, declared that his grandfather entered into the order of the Temple, active, healthy, and blithesome as the birds and the dogs, but on the third day from his taking the vows he was dead, and, as he *now suspects*, was killed because he refused to participate in the iniquities practiced by the brethren. An Augustine monk declared that he had heard a Templar say that a man after death had no more soul than a dog. Brother John de Gertia, a Minorite, had *heard* from a certain woman called Cacocaca! who had it from Exvalettus, Preceptor of London, that one of the servants of the Templars entered the Temple hall where the chapter was held, and secreted himself, and after the door had been shut and locked by the last Templar who entered, and the key had been brought by him to the superior, the assembled Templars jumped up and went into another room, and opened a closet, and drew therefrom a certain black figure with shining eyes, and a cross, and they placed the cross before the Master, and the "culum idoli vel figuræ" they placed upon the cross, and carried it to the Master, who kissed the said image, (in ano,) and all the others did the same after him; and when they had finished kissing, they all spat three times upon the cross, except one, who refused, saying, "I was a bad man in the world, and placed myself in this order for the salvation of my soul; what could I do worse? I will not do it;" and then the brethren said to him, "Take heed, and do as you see the order do;" but he answered that he would not do so, and then they placed him in a well which stood in the midst of their house, and covered the well up, and left him to perish. Being asked as to the time when the woman heard this, the deponent stated that she told it to him about fourteen years back at London, where she kept a shop for her husband, Robert Cotacota!

John Walby de Bust, another Minorite, had *heard* John de Dingeston say that *he had heard* that there was in a secret place of the house of the Templars at London a gilded head, and that when one of the masters was on his death-bed, he summoned to his presence several preceptors, and told them that if they wished for power, and dominion, and honor, they must worship that head. Gaspar de Nafferton, chaplain of the parish of Ryde, deposed that he was in the employ of the Templars when William de Pokelington was received into the order; that he well recollected that the said William made his appearance at the Temple on Sunday evening, with the equipage and habit of a member of the order, accompanied by Brother William de la More, the Master of the Temple, Brother William de

Grafton, Preceptor of Ribbestane and Fontebriggs, and other brethren: that the same night, during the first watch, they assembled in the church, and caused the deponent to be awakened to say mass; that, after the celebration of the mass, they made the deponent with his clerk go out into the hall beyond the cloister, and then sent for the person who was to be received; and on his entry into the church, one of the brethren immediately closed all the doors opening into the cloister, so that no one within the chambers could get out, and thus they remained till daylight; but what was done in the church the deponent knew not; the next day, however, he saw the said William clothed in the habit of a Templar, looking very sorrowful. The deponent also declared that he had threatened to peep through a secret door to see what was going on, but was warned that it was inevitable death so to do. He states that the next morning he went into the church, and found the books and crosses all removed from the places in which he had previously left them.

The evidence given before this papal tribunal affords melancholy proof of the immorality, the credulity, and the profligacy of the age. Abandoned women were brought before the inquisitors, and were induced unblushingly to relate, in the presence of the archbishop of Canterbury and the English bishops, the most disgusting and ridiculous enormities; and evidence was taken down by notaries, and quietly listened to by the most learned and distinguished characters of the age, which in these days would be scouted with scorn and contempt from almost every court in Christendom.* On the 22nd of April all the Templars in custody in the Tower and in the prisons of the city were assembled before the inquisitors and the bishops of London and Chichester, in the church of the Holy Trinity, to hear the depositions of the witnesses publicly read. The Templars required copies of these depositions, which were granted them, and they were allowed eight days from that period to bring forward any defenses or privileges they wished to make use of. Subsequently, before the expiration of the eight days, the officer of the bishop of London was sent to the Tower with scriveners and witnesses, to know if they would then set up any matters of defense, to whom the Templars replied that they were unlettered men, ignorant of the law, and that all means of defense were denied them, since they were not permitted to employ those who could afford them fit counsel and advice. They observed, however, that they were desirous of publicly proclaiming the faith, and the religion of themselves and of the order to which they belonged, of showing the privileges conceded to them by the chief pontiffs, and their own

---

* Agnes Lovecote dixit quod ... fratres aperuerunt quandam voltam et perduxerunt de illo loco monstrum quoddam ad formam seu imaginem diaboli, habens loco oculorum lapides rutilantes et illuminantes capitulum, cujus culum osculabantur omnes, primo Magister, et postea alii, et postea ponebant unam crucen nigram ad culum dicti monstri, et spuebant omnes in crucem...! Deponit se audivisse à quâdam *domina* Agnete, quæ dicebat se audivisse à sorore cujusdam Templarii, quod cum ipsa soror denudasset fratrem suum post mortem, credens invenire signa salutis, invenit in braccis dicti Templarii fratis sui crucem pendentem contra anum...! Concil. Mag. Brit. tom. ii. p. 350-364.

depositions taken before the inquisitors, all which they said they wished to make use of in their defense.

On the eighth day, being Thursday the 29th of April, they appeared before the papal inquisitors and the bishops of London and Chichester, in the church of All Saints of Berkyngecherche, and presented to them the following declaration, which they had drawn up amongst themselves, as the only defense they had to offer against the injustice, the tyranny, and the persecution of their powerful oppressors; adding, that if they had in any way done wrong, they were ready to submit themselves to the orders of the church. This declaration is written in the Norman French of that day, and is as follows:—

"*Conue chese seit a nostre honurable père, le ercevesque de Canterbiere, primat de toute Engletere, e a touz prelaz de seinte Elise, e a touz Cristiens, qe touz les frères du Temple que sumes ici assemblez et chescune singulere persone par sen sumes cristien nostre seignur Jesu Crist, e creoms en Dieu Père omnipotent, qui fist ciel e terre, e en Jesu soen fiz, qui fust conceu du Seint Esperit, nez de la Virgine Marie, soeffrit peine e passioun, morut sur la croiz pour touz peccheours, descendist e enferns, e le tierz jour releva de mort en vie, e mounta en ciel, siet au destre soen Père, e vendra au jour de juise, juger les vifs, e les morz, qui fu saunz commencement, e serra saunz fyn; e creoms comme seynte eglise crets, e nous enseigne. E que nostre religion est foundée sus obedience, chasteté, vivre sans propre, aider a conquere la seint terre de Jerusalem, a force e a poer, qui Dieu nous ad preste. E nyoms e firmement en countredioms touz e chescune singulere persone par sei, toutes maneres de heresies e malvaistes, que sount encountre la foi de Seinte Eglise. E prioms pour Dieu e pour charité a vous, que estes en lieu nostre seinte père l'apostoile, que nous puissoms aver lez dretures de seinte église, comme ceus que sount les filz de sainte église, que bien avoms garde, e tenu la foi, e la lei de seinte église, e nostre religion, la quele est bone, honeste e juste, solom les ordenaunces, e les priviléges de la court de Rome avons grauntez, confermez, e canonizez par commun concile, les qels priviléges ensemblement ou lestablisement, e la règle sount en la dite court enregistrez. E mettoms en dur e en mal eu touz Cristiens sauue noz anoisourz, par la ou nous avoms este conversaunt, comment nous avoms nostre vie demene. E se nous avoms rien mesprys de aucun parole en nos examinacions par ignorance de seu, si comme nous sumez genz laics prest sûmes, a ester a lesgard de seint eglise, comme cely que mourust pour nouz en la beneite de croiz. E nous creoms fermement touz les sacremenz de seinte église. E nous vous prioms pour Dieu e pour salvacioun de vous almes, que vous nous jugez si comme vous volez respoundre pour vous et pour nous devaunt Dieu: e que nostre examinement puet estre leu e oii devaunt nous e devaunt le people, salom le respouns e le langage que fust dit devaunt vous, e escrit en papier.*"

"Be it known to our honorable father, the archbishop of Canterbury, primate of all England, and to all the prelates of holy church, and to all

Christians, that all we brethren of the Temple here assembled, and every of one of us are Christians, and believe in our Saviour Jesus Christ, in God the Father omnipotent, &c., &c.... And we believe all that the holy church believes and teaches us. We declare that our religion is founded on vows of obedience, chastity, and poverty, and of aiding in the conquest of the Holy Land of Jerusalem, with all the power and might that God affordeth us. And we firmly deny and contradict, one and all of us, all manner of heresy and evil doings, contrary to the faith of holy church. And for the love of God, and for charity, we beseech you, who represent our holy father the pope, that we may be treated like true children of the church, for we have well guarded and preserved the faith, and the law of the church, and of our own religion, that which is good, honest, and just, according to the ordinances and the privileges of the court of Rome, granted, confirmed, and canonized by common council; the which privileges, together with the rule of our order, are enregistered in the said court. And we would bring forward all Christians, (save our enemies and slanderers,) with whom we are conversant, and among whom we have resided, to say how and in what manner we have spent our lives. And if, in our examinations, we have said or done anything wrong through ignorance of a word, since we are unlettered men, we are ready to suffer for holy church like him who died for us on the blessed cross. And we believe all the sacraments of the church. And we beseech you, for the love of God, and as you hope to be saved, that you judge us as you will have to answer for yourselves and for us before God; and we pray that our examination may be read and heard before ourselves and all the people, in the very language and words in which it was given before you, and written down on paper."

The above declaration was presented by Brother William de la More, the Master of the Temple; the Knights Templars Philip de Mewes, Preceptor of Garwy; William de Burton, Preceptor of Cumbe; Radulph de Maison, Preceptor of Ewell; Michael de Baskevile, Preceptor of London; Thomas de Wothrope, Preceptor of Bistelesham; William de Warwick, Priest; and Thomas de Burton, Chaplain of the Order; together with twenty serving brothers. The same day the inquisitors and the two bishops proceeded to the different prisons of the city to demand if the prisoners confined therein wished to bring forward anything in defense of the order, who severally answered that they would adopt and abide by the declaration made by their brethren in the Tower. In the prison of Aldgate there were confined Brother William de Sautre, Knight, Preceptor of Samford; Brother William de la Ford, Preceptor of Daney; Brother John de Coningeston, Preceptor of Getinges; Roger de Norreis, Preceptor of Cressing; Radolph de Barton, priest, Prior of the New Temple; and several serving brethren of the order. In the prison of Crepelgate were detained William de Egendon, Knight, Preceptor of Schepeley; John de Moun, Knight, Preceptor of Dokesworth; and four serving brethren. In the prison of Ludgate were five serving brethren; and in Newgate was confined Brother Himbert Blanke, Knight, Grand Preceptor of Auvergne.

The Knights Templars

The above declaration of faith and innocence was far from agreeable to the papal inquisitors, who required a confession of *guilt*, and the torture was once more directed to be applied. The king sent fresh orders to the mayor and the sheriffs of the city of London, commanding them to place the Templars in separate dungeons; to load them with chains and fetters; to permit the myrmidons of the inquisitors to pay periodical visits to see that the wishes and intentions of the inquisitors, with regard to the severity of the confinement, were properly carried into effect; and lastly, to inflict TORTURE upon the bodies of the Templars, and generally to do whatever should be thought fitting and expedient in the premises, according to the ecclesiastical law. In conformity with these orders, we learn from the record of the proceedings, that the Templars were placed in solitary confinement in loathsome dungeons; that they were put on a short allowance of bread and water, and periodically visited by the agents of the inquisition; that they were moved from prison to prison, and from dungeon to dungeon; were now treated with rigour, and anon with indulgence; and were then visited by learned prelates, and acute doctors in theology, who, by exhortation, persuasion, and by menace, attempted in every possible mode to wring from them the required avowals! We learn that all the engines of terror wielded by the church were put in force, and that torture was unsparingly applied *"usque ad judicium sanguinis!"* The places in which these atrocious scenes were enacted were the Tower, the prisons of Aldgate, Ludgate, Newgate, Bishopgate, and Crepelgate, the house formerly belonging to John de Banguel, and the tenements once the property of the brethren of penitence.* It appears that some French monks were sent over to administer the torture to the unhappy captives, and that they were questioned and examined in the presence of notaries whilst suffering under the torments of the rack. The relentless perseverance and the incessant exertions of the foreign inquisitors were at last rewarded by a splendid triumph over the powers of endurance of two poor serving brethren, and one chaplain of the order, who were at last induced to make the long desired avowals.

On the 23rd of June, Brother Stephen de Staplebrugge, described as an apostate and fugitive of the order of the Temple, captured by the king's officers in the city of Salisbury, deposed in the house of the head gaoler of Newgate, in the presence of the bishops of London and Chichester, the chancellor of the archbishop of Canterbury, Hugh de Walkeneby, doctor of theology, and other clerical witnesses, that there were two modes of profession in the order of the Temple, the one good and lawful, and the other contrary to the Christian faith; that he himself was received into the order by Brother Brian le Jay, Grand Preceptor of England, at Dynneslee, and was led into the chapel, the door of which was closed as soon as he had entered; that a crucifix was placed before the Master, and that a brother of the Temple, with a drawn sword, stood on either side of him; that the

---

* Acta *Rymeri*, tom. iii. p. 290. MS. Bodl. F. 5, 2. Concil. p. 364, 365. Acta *Rymeri*, tom. iii. p. 228, 231, 232.

Master said to him, "Do you see this image of the crucifixion?" to which he replied, "I see it, my lord;" that the Master then said to him, "You must deny that Christ Jesus was God and man, and that Mary was his mother; and you must spit upon this cross;" which the deponent, through immediate fear of death, did with his mouth, but not with his heart, and he spat *beside* the cross, and not on it; and then falling down upon his knees, with eyes uplifted, with his hands clasped, with bitter tears and sighs, and devout ejaculations, he besought the mercy and the favor of holy church, declaring that he cared not for the death of the body, or for any amount of penance, but only for the salvation of his soul!

On Saturday, the 25th of June, Brother Thomas Tocci de Thoroldeby, serving brother of the order of the Temple, described as an apostate who had escaped from Lincoln after his examination at that place by the papal inquisitors, but had afterwards surrendered himself to the king's officers, was brought before the bishops of London and Chichester, the archdeacon of Salisbury, and others of the clergy in St. Martin's Church, in Vinetriâ; and being again examined, he repeated the statement made in his first deposition, but added some particulars with regard to penances imposed and absolutions pronounced in the chapter, showing the difference between sins and defaults, the priest having to deal with the one, and the Master with the other. He declared that the little cords were worn from honorable motives, and relates a story of his being engaged in a battle against the Saracens, in which he lost his cord, and was punished by the Grand Master for a default in coming home without it. He gives the same account of the secrecy of the chapters as all the other brethren, states that the members of the order were forbidden to confess to the friars mendicants, and were enjoined to confess to their own chaplains; that they did nothing contrary to the Christian faith, and as to their endeavoring to promote the advancement of the order by any means, right or wrong, that exactly the contrary was the case, as there was a statute in the order to the effect, that if any one should be found to have acquired anything unjustly, he should be deprived of his habit, and be expelled the order. Being asked what induced him to become an apostate, and to fly from his order, he replied that it was through fear of death, because the abbot of Lagny, (the papal inquisitor,) when he examined him at Lincoln, asked him if he would not confess anything further, and he answered that he knew of nothing further to confess, unless he was to say things that were not true; and that *the abbot, laying his hand upon his breast, swore by the word of God that he would make him confess before he had done with him!* and that being terribly frightened, he afterwards bribed the gaoler of the castle of Lincoln, giving him forty florins to let him make his escape.

The abbot of Lagny, indeed, was as good as his word, for on the 29th of June, four days after this imprudent avowal, Brother Thomas Tocci de Thoroldeby was brought back to St. Martin's Church, and there, in the presence of the same parties, he made a third confession, in which he declares that, coerced by two Templars with drawn swords in their hands, he denied Christ with his mouth, but not with his heart; and spat *beside* the cross, but not on it; that he was required to spit upon the image of the Virgin Mary, but contrived, instead of doing so, to give her a kiss on the foot. He declares that he had heard Brian le Jay, the Master of the Temple at London, say a hundred times over, that Jesus Christ was not the true God, but a man: and that the smallest hair out of the beard of one Saracen, was of more worth than the whole body of any Christian. He declares that he was once standing in the presence of Brother Brian, when some poor people besought charity of him for the love of God and our lady the blessed Virgin Mary; and he answered, "*Que dame, alez vous pendre a vostre dame*"—"What lady, go and be hanged to your lady," and violently casting a halfpenny into the mud, he made the poor people hunt for it, although it was in the depth of a severe winter. He also relates that, at the chapters, the priest stood like a beast, and had nothing to do but to repeat the psalm, "God be merciful unto us, and bless us," which was read at the closing of the chapter. (The Templars, by the way, must have been strange idolaters to have closed their chapters, in which they are accused of worshipping a cat, a man's head, and a black idol, with the reading of the beautiful psalm, "God be merciful unto us, and bless us, and show us the light of thy countenance, that thy way may be known upon earth, thy saving health among all nations," &c., Psalm lxvii.) This witness further states, that the priest had no power to impose a heavier penance than a day's fast on bread and water, and could not even do that without the permission of the brethren. He is made also to relate that the Templars always favored the Saracens in the holy wars in Palestine, and oppressed the Christians! and he declares, speaking of himself, that for three years before he had never seen the body of Christ without thinking of the devil, nor could he remove that evil thought from his heart by prayer, or in any other way that he knew of; but that very morning he had heard mass with great devotion, and since then had thought only of Christ, and thinks there is no one in the order of the Temple whose soul will be saved, unless a reformation takes place.

Previous to this period, the ecclesiastical council had again assembled, and these last depositions of Brother Stephen de Stapelbrugge and Thomas Tocci de Thoroldeby having been produced before them, the solemn farce of their confession and abjuration was immediately publicly enacted. It is thus described in the record of the proceedings:—"To the praise and glory of the name of the most high Father, and of the Son, and of the Holy Ghost, to the confusion of heretics, and the strengthening of all faithful Christians, begins the public record of the reconciliation of the penitent heretics, returning to the orthodox faith published in the council, celebrated at London in the year 1311. In the name of God, Amen. In the year of the incarnation of our Lord, 1311, on the twenty-seventh day of the month of June, in the hall of the palace of the bishop of London, before the venerable fathers the Lord Robert by the grace of God archbishop of Canterbury, primate of all England, and his suffragans in provincial council assembled, appeared Brother Stephen de Stapelbrugge, of the order of the chivalry of the Temple; and the denying of Christ and the blessed Virgin Mary his mother, the spitting upon the cross, and the heresies and errors acknowledged and confessed by him in his deposition, being displayed, the same Stephen asserted in full council, before the people of the city of London, introduced for the occasion, that all those things so deposed by him were true, and that to that confession he would wholly adhere; humbly confessing his error on his bended knees, with his hands clasped, with much lamentation and many tears, he again and again besought the mercy and pity of holy mother church, offering to abjure all heresies and errors, and praying them to impose on him a fitting penance, and then the book of the holy gospels being placed in his hands, he abjured the aforesaid heresies in this form ;—'I, Brother Stephen de Stapelbrugge, of the order of the chivalry of the Temple, do solemnly confess,' &c., &c., (he repeats his confession, makes his abjuration, and then proceeds;) 'and if at any time hereafter I shall happen to relapse into the same errors, or deviate from any of the articles of the faith, I will account myself *ipso facto* excommunicated; I will stand condemned as a manifest perjured heretic, and the punishment inflicted on perjured relapsed heretics, shall be forthwith imposed upon me without further trial or judgment!!'"

He was then sworn upon the holy gospels to stand to the sentence of the church in the matter, after which Brother Thomas Tocci de Thoroldeby was brought forward to go through the same ceremony, which being concluded, these two poor serving brothers of the order of the Temple, who were so ignorant that they could not write, were made to place their mark on the record of their abjuration. "And then our lord the archbishop of Canterbury, for the purpose of absolving and reconciling to the unity of the church the aforesaid Thomas and Stephen, conceded his authority and that of the whole council to the bishop of London, in the presence of me the notary, specially summoned for the occasion, in these words: 'We grant to you the authority of God, of the blessed Mary, of the blessed Thomas the Martyr our patron, and of all the saints of God (sanctorum atque *sanctarum* Dei) to us conceded, and also the authority of the present council to us transferred, to the end that thou mayest reconcile to the unity of the church these miserables, separated from her by their repudiation of the faith, and now brought back again to her bosom, reserving to ourselves and the council the right of imposing a fit penance for their transgressions!' And as there were two penitents, the bishop of Chichester was joined to the bishop of London for the purpose of pronouncing the absolution, which two bishops, putting on their mitres and pontificals, and being assisted by twelve priests in sacerdotal vestments, placed themselves in seats at the western entrance of the cathedral church of St. Paul, and the penitents, with bended knees, humbly prostrating themselves in prayer upon the steps before the door of the church, the members of the council and the people of the city standing around; and the psalm, *Have mercy upon me, O God, after thy great goodness*, having been chaunted from the beginning to the end, and the subjoined prayers and sermon having been gone through, they absolved the said penitents, and received them back to the unity of the church in the following form:—'In the name of God, Amen. Since by your confession we find that you, Brother Stephen de Stapelbrugge, have denied Christ Jesus and the blessed Virgin Mary, and have spate *beside* the cross, and now taking better advice wishest to return to the unity of the holy church with a true heart and sincere faith, as you assert, and all heretical depravity having for that purpose been previously abjured by you according to the form of the church, we, by the authority of the council, absolve you from the bond of excommunication wherewith you were held fast, and we reconcile you to the unity of the church, if you shall have returned to her in sincerity of heart, and shall have obeyed her injunctions imposed upon you.'" Brother Thomas Tocci de Thoroldeby was then absolved and reconciled to the church in the usual manner, after which various psalms (Gloria Patri, Kyrie Eleyson, Christe Eleyson, &c. &c.) were sung, and prayers were offered up, and then the ceremony was concluded.

On the 1st of July, an avowal of guilt was wrung by the inquisitors from Brother John de Stoke, chaplain of the order, who, being brought before the bishops of London and Chichester in St. Martin's Church, deposed that he was received in the mode mentioned by him on his first examination; but a year and fifteen days after that reception, being at the preceptory of Garwy in the diocese of Hereford, he was called into the chamber of Brother James de Molay, the Grand Master of the order, who, in the presence of two other Templars of foreign extraction, informed him that he wished to make proof of his obedience, and commanded him to take a seat at the foot of the bed, and the deponent did so. The Grand Master then sent into the church for the crucifix, and two serving brothers, with naked swords in their hands, stationed themselves on either side of the doorway. As soon as the crucifix made its appearance, the Grand Master, pointing to the figure of our Saviour nailed thereon, asked the deponent whose image it was, and he answered, "The image of Jesus Christ, who suffered on the cross for the redemption of mankind;" but the Grand Master exclaimed, "Thou sayest wrong, and art much mistaken, for he was the son of a certain woman, and was crucified because he called himself the Son of God, and I myself have been in the place where he was born and crucified, and thou must now deny him whom this image represents." The deponent exclaimed, "Far be it from me to deny my Saviour;" but the Grand Master told him he must do it, or he would be put into a sack and be carried to a place which he would find by no means agreeable, and there were swords in the room, and brothers ready to use them, &c. &c.; and the deponent asked if such was the custom of the order, and if all the brethren did the same; and being answered in the affirmative, he, through fear of immediate death, denied Christ with his *tongue*, but not with his *heart*. Being asked in whom he was told to put his faith after he had denied Christ

Jesus, he replies, "In that great Omnipotent God who created the heaven and the earth!"

On Monday, July 5th, at the request of the ecclesiastical council, the bishop of Chichester had an interview with Sir William de la More, the Master of the Temple, taking with him certain learned lawyers, theologians, and scriveners. He exhorted and earnestly pressed him to abjure the heresies of which he stood convicted, by his own confessions and those of his brethren, respecting the absolutions pronounced by him in the chapters, and submit himself to the disposition of the church; but the Master declared that he had never been guilty of the heresies mentioned, and that he would not abjure crimes which he had never committed; so he was sent back to his dungeon. The next day, the bishops of London, Winchester, and Chichester, had an interview in Southwark with the Knight Templar Philip de Mewes, Preceptor of Garwy, and some serving brethren of the New Temple at London, and told them that they were manifestly guilty of heresy, as appeared from the pope's bulls, and the depositions taken against the order both in England and France, and also from their own confessions regarding the absolutions pronounced in their chapters, explaining to them that they had grievously erred in believing that the Master of the Temple, who was a mere layman, had power to absolve them from their sins by pronouncing absolution, and they warned them that if they persisted in that error they would be condemned as heretics, and that, as they could not clear themselves therefrom, it behoved them to abjure all the heresies of which they were accused. The Templars replied that they were ready to abjure the error they had fallen into respecting the absolution and all heresies of every kind, before the archbishop of Canterbury and the prelates of the council, whenever they should be required so to do, and they humbly and reverently submitted themselves to the orders of the church, beseeching pardon and grace. A sort of compromise was then made with most of the Templars in custody in London. They were required publicly to repeat a form of confession and abjuration drawn up by the bishops of London and Chichester, and were then solemnly absolved and reconciled to the church.

On the 9th of July, Brother Michael de Baskevile, Knight, Preceptor of London, and seventeen other Templars, were absolved and reconciled in full council, in the Episcopal Hall of the see of London, in the presence of a vast concourse of the citizens. On the 10th of the same month, the Preceptors of Dokesworth, Getinges, and Samford, the guardian of the Temple church at London, Brother Radulph de Evesham, chaplain, with other priests, knights, and serving brethren of the order, were absolved by the bishops of London, Exeter, Winchester, and Chichester, in the presence of the archbishop of Canterbury, and the whole ecclesiastical council. The next day many more members of the fraternity were publicly reconciled to the church on the steps before the south door of Saint Paul's cathedral, and were afterwards present at the celebration of high mass in the interior of the sacred edifice, when they advanced in a body towards the high altar bathed in tears, and falling down on their knees, they devoutly kissed the sacred emblems of Christianity. The day after, (July 12,) nineteen other Templars were publicly absolved and reconciled to the church in the same place, in the presence of the earls of Leicester, Pembroke, and Warwick, and afterwards assisted in like manner at the celebration of high mass. The priests of the order made their confessions and abjurations in Latin; the knights pronounced them in Norman French, and the serving brethren for the most part repeated them in English. The vast concourse of people collected together could have comprehended but very little of what was uttered, whilst the appearance of the penitent brethren, and the public spectacle of their recantation, answered the views of the papal inquisitors, and doubtless impressed the commonalty with a conviction of the guilt of the order. Many of the Templars were too *sick* (from the effect of torture) to be brought down to Saint Paul's, and were therefore absolved and reconciled to the church by the bishops of London, Winchester, and Chichester, at Saint Mary's chapel near the Tower. Among these last were many old veteran warriors in the last stage of decrepitude and decay. "They were so old and so infirm," says the public notary who recorded the proceedings, "that they were unable to stand;" their confessions were consequently made before two masters in theology; they were then led before the west door of the chapel, and were publicly reconciled to the church by the bishop of Chichester; after which they were brought into the sacred building, and were placed on their knees before the high altar, which they devoutly kissed, whilst the tears trickled down their furrowed cheeks. All these penitent Templars were now released from prison, and directed to do penance in different monasteries. Precisely the same form of proceeding was followed at York; the reconciliation and absolution being there carried into effect before the south door of the cathedral.*

Similar measures had, in the mean time, been prosecuted against the Templars in all parts of Christendom. On the 18th of March, the pope wrote to the kings of Castile, Leon, Aragon, and Portugal, complaining of the omission to torture the Templars in their dominions. "The bishops and delegates," says the holy pontiff, "have imprudently neglected these means of obtaining the truth; we therefore expressly order them to employ TORTURE against the knights, that the truth may be more readily and completely obtained!" The order for TORTURING the Templars was transmitted to the patriarch of Constantinople, the bishop of Negropont, and the duke of Achaia; and it crossed the seas to the king of Cyprus, and the bishops of Famagousta and Nicosia! The councils of Tarragona and Aragon, after applying the torture, pronounced the order free from heresy. In Portugal and in Germany the Templars were declared innocent: and in no place situate beyond the sphere of the influence of the king of France and his creature the pope was a single Templar condemned to death.†

---

* Concil. Mag. Brit. tom. ii. p. 383-391, 394-401.
† Concilia Hispaniæ, tom. v. p. 223. *Raynouard*, p. 199-204.

On the 16th of October the general council of the church which had been convened by the pope to pronounce the abolition of the order, assembled at Vienne, near Lyons in France. It was opened by the holy pontiff in person, who caused the different confessions and avowals of the Templars to be read over before the assembled nobles and prelates. Although the order was now broken up, and the best and bravest of its members had either perished in the flames or were languishing in dungeons, yet nine fugitive Templars had the courage to present themselves before the council, and demand to be heard in defense of their order, declaring that they were the representatives of from 1,500 to 2,000 Templars, who were wandering about as fugitives and outlaws in the neighborhood of Lyons. Monsieur Raynouard has fortunately brought to light a letter from the pope to king Philip, which states this fact, and also informs us how the holy pontiff acted when he heard that these defenders of the order had presented themselves. Clement caused them to be thrown into prison, where they languished and died. He affected to believe that his life was in danger from the number of the Templars at large, and he immediately took measures to provide for the security of his person.

The assembled fathers, to their honor, expressed their disapprobation of this flagrant act of injustice, and the entire council, with the exception of an Italian prelate, nephew of the pope, and the three French bishops of Rheims, Sens, and Rouen, all creatures of Philip, who had severally condemned large bodies of Templars to be burnt at the stake in their respective dioceses, were unanimously of opinion, that before the suppression of so celebrated and illustrious an order, which had rendered such great and signal services to the Christian faith, the members belonging to it ought to be heard in their own defense.[*] Such a proceeding, however did not suit the views of the pope and king Philip, and the assembly was abruptly dismissed by the holy pontiff, who declared that since they were unwilling to adopt the necessary measures, he himself, out of the plenitude of the papal authority, would supply every defect. Accordingly, at the commencement of the following year, the pope summoned a private consistory; and several cardinals and French bishops having been gained over, the holy pontiff abolished the order by an apostolical ordinance, perpetually prohibiting every one from thenceforth entering into it, or accepting or wearing the habit thereof, or representing themselves to be Templars, on pain of excommunication.[†]

On the 3rd of April, the second session of the council was opened by the pope at Vienne. King Philip and his three sons were present, accompanied by a large body of troops, and the papal decree abolishing the order was published before the assembly. The members of the council appear to have been called together merely to hear the decree read. History

[*] Secund. vit. Clem. 5, p. 43. *Rainald*, ad ann. 1311, n. 55. *Walsingham*, p. 99. Antiq. Britann. p. 210.
[†] *Maratorii* collect. tom. iii. p. 448; tom. x. col. 377. *Mariana*, tom. iii. p. 157. *Raynouard*, p. 191, 192.

does not inform us of any discussion with reference to it, nor of any suffrages having been taken. A few months after the close of these proceedings, Brother William de la More, the Master of the Temple in England, died of a broken heart in his solitary dungeon in the Tower, persisting with his last breath in the maintenance of the innocence of his order. King Edward, in pity for his misfortunes, directed the constable of the Tower to hand over his goods and chattels, valued at the sum of 4*l.* 19*s.* 11*d.*, to his executors, to be employed in the liquidation of his debts, and he commanded Geoffrey de la Lee, guardian of the lands of the Templars, to pay the arrears of his prison pay (2*s.* per diem) to the executor, Roger Hunsingon.

Among the Cotton MS. is a list of the Masters of the Temple, otherwise the Grand Priors or Grand Preceptors of England, compiled under the direction of the prior of the Hospital of Saint John at Clerkenwell, to the intent that the brethren of that fraternity might remember the ancient Masters of the Temple in their prayers.[*] A few names have been omitted which are here supplied. Magister R. de Pointon. Rocelinus de Fossa. Richard de Hastings, (A. D. 1160). Richard Mallebeench. Geoffrey, son of Stephen, (A. D. 1180). Thomas Berard, (A. D. 1200). Amaric de St. Maur, (A. D. 1203). Alan Marcel, (A. D. 1224). Amberaldus, (A. D. 1229). Robert Mountforde, (A. D. 1234). Robert Sanford, (A. D. 1241). Amadeus de Morestello, (A. D. 1254). Himbert Peraut, (A. D. 1270). Robert Turvile, (A. D. 1290). Guido de Foresta, (A. D. 1292). James de Molay, (A. D. 1293). Brian le Jay, (A. D. 1295). William de la More the Martyr.[†]

The only other Templar in England whose fate merits particular attention is Brother Himbert Blanke, the Grand Preceptor of Auvergne. He appears to have been a knight of high honor and of stern unbending pride. From first to last he had boldly protested against the violent proceedings of the inquisitors, and had fearlessly maintained, amid all his trials, his own innocence and that of his order. This illustrious Templar had fought under four successive Grand Masters in defense of the Christian faith in Palestine, and, after the fall of Acre, had led in person several daring expeditions against the infidels. For these meritorious services he was rewarded in the following manner:—After having been tortured and half-starved in the English prisons for the space of five years, he was condemned, as he would make no confession of guilt, to be shut up in a loathsome dungeon, to be loaded with double chains, and to be occasionally visited by the agents of the Inquisition, to see if he would confess *nothing further.*[‡] In this miserable situation he remained until death at last put an end to his sufferings.

---

[*] *Cotton* MS. Nero E. vi. 23 i. Ib. p. 60, fol. 466. Acta *Rymeri,* tom. iii. p. 380.
[†] *Lansdown* MS. 207, E. vol. v. fol. 162, 163, 201, 284, 317, 467. Acta *Rymeri,* tom. i. p. 134, 342, 344, 345, part 3, p. 104. *Matt. Par.* p. 253-255, 258, 270, 314, 615, et in ad. p. 480. Concil. Mag. Brit. tom. ii. p. 340; tom. xi. p. 335, 339, 341, 343, 344. *Prynne,* collect. 3, 143.
[‡] Concil. Mag. Brit. tom. ii. p. 393.

James de Molay, the Grand Master of the Temple, Guy, the Grand Preceptor, a nobleman of illustrious birth, brother to the prince of Dauphiny, Hugh de Peralt, the Visitor-general of the order, and the Grand Preceptor of Aquitaine, had now languished in the prisons of France for the space of five years and a half. The secrets of their dark dungeons were never brought to light, but on the 18th of March, A. D. 1313, a public scaffold was erected before the cathedral church of Notre Dame, at Paris, and the citizens were summoned to hear the order of the Temple convicted by the mouths of its chief officers, of the sins and iniquities charged against it. The four knights, loaded with chains and surrounded by guards, were then brought upon the scaffold by the provost, and the bishop of Alba read their confessions aloud in the presence of the assembled populace. The papal legate then, turning towards the Grand Master and his companions, called upon them to renew, in the hearing of the people, the avowals which they had previously made of the guilt of their order. Hugh de Peralt, the Visitor-general, and the Preceptor of the Temple of Aquitaine, signified their assent to whatever was demanded of them, but the Grand Master, raising his arms bound with chains towards heaven, and advancing to the edge of the scaffold, declared in a loud voice, that to say that which was untrue was a crime, both in the sight of God and man. "I do," said he, "confess my guilt, which consists in having, to my shame and dis honor, suffered myself, through the pain of torture and the fear of death, to give utterance to falsehoods, imputing scandalous sins and iniquities to an illustrious order, which hath nobly served the cause of Christianity. I disdain to seek a wretched and disgraceful existence by engrafting another lie upon the original falsehood." He was here interrupted by the provost and his officers, and Guy, the Grand Preceptor, having commenced with strong asseverations of his innocence, they were both hurried back to prison.

King Philip was no sooner informed of the result, than, upon the first impulse of his indignation, without consulting either pope, or bishop, or ecclesiastical council, he commanded the instant execution of both these gallant noblemen. The same day at dusk they were led out of their dungeons, and were burned to death in a slow and lingering manner upon small fires of charcoal which were kindled on the little island in the Seine, between the king's garden and the convent of Saint Augustine, close to the spot where now stands the equestrian statue of Henri IV.[*] Thus perished the last Grand Master of the Temple.

The fate of the persecutors of the order is not unworthy of notice.

A year and one month after the above horrible execution, the pope was attacked by a dysentery, and speedily hurried to his grave. The dead body was transported to Carpentras, where the court of Rome then resided; it was placed at night in a church which caught fire, and the mortal remains of the holy pontiff were almost entirely consumed. His relations quarrelled

---

[*] *Villani*, lib. viii. cap. 92. *Dupuy*, ed. 1700, p. 71, 128, 139. *Raynouard*, p. 60, 209, 210.

over the immense treasures he left behind him, and a vast sum of money, which had been deposited for safety in a church at Lucca, was stolen by a daring band of German and Italian freebooters. Before the close of the same year, king Philip died of a lingering disease which had baffled all the art of his medical attendants, and the condemned criminal, upon the strength of whose information the Templars were originally arrested, was hanged for fresh crimes. "History attests," says Monsieur Raynouard, "that all those who were foremost in the persecution of the Templars, came to an untimely and miserable death. The last days of Philip were embittered by misfortune; his nobles and clergy leagued against him to resist his exactions; the wives of his three sons were accused of adultery, and two of them were publicly convicted of that crime. The misfortunes of Edward the Second, king of England, and his horrible death in Berkeley Castle, are too well known to be further alluded to."

"The chief cause of the ruin of the Templars," justly remarks Fuller, "was their extraordinary wealth. As Naboth's vineyard was the chiefest ground of his blasphemy, and as in England Sir John Cornwall Lord Fanhope said merrily, not he, but his stately house at Ampthill, in Bedfordshire, was guilty of high treason, so certainly their wealth was the principal cause of their overthrow.... We may believe that king Philip would never have taken away their lives if he might have taken their lands without putting them to death, but the mischief was, he could not get the honey unless he burnt the bees." King Philip, the pope, and the European sovereigns, appear to have disposed of all the personalty of the Templars, the ornaments, jewels, and treasures of their churches and chapels, and during the period of five years, over which the proceedings against the order extended, they remained in the actual receipt of the vast rents and revenues of the fraternity. King Philip put forward a claim upon their lands in France to the extent of two hundred thousand pounds for the expenses of the prosecution, and Louis, his son, claimed a further sum of sixty thousand pounds: "J'ignore," says Voltaire, "ce qui revint au pape, mais je vois evidemment que les frais des cardinaux, des inquisiteurs délégués pour faire ce procès épouvantable monterent à des sommes immenses." The holy pontiff, according to his own account, received only a *small portion* of the personalty of the order, but others make him a large participator in the good things of the fraternity.*

On the imprisonment of the Templars in England, the Temple at London, and all the preceptories dependent upon it, with the manors, farms, houses, lands, and revenues of the order, were placed under the survey of the Court of Exchequer, and extents were directed to be taken of the same, after which they were confided to the care of certain trustworthy persons, styled "Guardians of the lands of the Templars," who were to account for the rents and profits to the king's exchequer. These guardians were directed to pay various pensions to the old servants and retainers of

---

* *Dupuy*, p. 179, 184. *Raynouard*, 197-199. *De Vertis*, liv. iii.

the Templars dwelling in the different preceptories, also the expenses of the prosecution against the order; and they were at different times required to victual the king's castles and strongholds. In the month of February, A. D. 1312, the king gave the Temple manors of Etton and Cave to David, earl of Athol, directing the guardians of the lands and tenements of the Templars in the county of York to hand over to the said earl all the corn in those manors, the oxen, calves, ploughs, and all the goods and chattels of the Templars existing therein, together with the ornaments and utensils of the chapel of the Temple. But on the 16th of May the pope addressed bulls to the king, and to all the earls and barons of the kingdom, setting forth the proceedings of the council of Vienne, and the publication of a papal decree, vesting the property late belonging to the Templars in the brethren of the Hospital of St. John, and he commands them forthwith to place the members of that order in possession thereof. Bulls were also addressed to the archbishops of Canterbury and York and their suffragans, commanding them to enforce by ecclesiastical censures the execution of the papal commands. King Edward and his nobles very properly resisted this decree, and on the 21st of August the king wrote to the Prior of the Hospital of St. John at Clerkenwell, telling him that the pretensions of the pope to dispose of property within the realm of England, without the consent of parliament, were derogatory to the dignity of the crown and the royal authority. The following year the king granted the Temple at London, with the church and all the buildings therein, to Aymer de Valence, earl of Pembroke; and on the 5th of May of the same year, he caused several merchants, from whom he had borrowed money, to be placed in possession of many of the manors of the Templars.*

Yielding, however, at last to the exhortations and menaces of the pope, the king, on the 21st of Nov., A. D. 1313, granted the property to the Hospitallers, and sent orders to the guardians of the lands of the Templars, and to various powerful barons who were in possession of the estates, commanding them to deliver them up to certain parties deputed by the Grand Master and chapter of the Hospital of St. John to receive them. At this period many of the heirs of the donors, whose title had been recognised by the law, were in possession of the lands, and the judges held that the king had no power of his own sole authority to transfer them to the order of the Hospital. The thunders of the Vatican were consequently vigorously made use of, and all the detainers of the property were doomed by the Roman pontiff to everlasting damnation. Pope John, in one of his bulls, dated A. D. 1322, bitterly complains of the disregard by all the king's subjects of the papal commands. He laments that they had hardened their hearts and despised the sentence of excommunication fulminated against them, and declares that his heart was riven with grief to find that even the ecclesiastics, who ought to have been as a wall of defense to the Hospitallers, had themselves been heinously guilty in the premises.†

---

* Acta *Rymeri*, tom. iii. p. 130, 134, 139, 279-297, 321-327, 337, 409, 410. *Dodsworth*, MS. vol. xxxv. p. 65, 67.

The Knights Templars

At last (A. D. 1324) the pope, the bishops, and the Hospitallers, by their united exertions, succeeded in obtaining an act of parliament, vesting all the property late belonging to the Templars in the brethren of the Hospital of St. John, in order that the intentions of the donors might be carried into effect by the appropriation of it to the defense of the Holy Land and the succor of the Christian cause in the East. This statute gave rise to the greatest discontent. The heirs of the donors petitioned parliament for its repeal, alleging that it had been made against law, and against reason, and contrary to the opinion of the judges; and many of the great barons who held the property by a title recognised by the common law, successfully resisted the claims of the order of the Hospital, maintaining that the parliament had no right to interfere with the tenure of private property, and to dispose of their possessions without their consent. This struggle between the heirs of the donors on the one hand, and the Hospitallers on the other, continued for a lengthened period; and in the reign of Edward the Third it was found necessary to pass another act of parliament, confirming the previous statute in their favor, and writs were sent to the sheriffs (A. D. 1334) commanding them to enforce the execution of the acts of the legislature, and to take possession, in the king's name, of all the property unjustly detained from the brethren of the Hospital of St. John.[*]

Whilst the vast possessions, late belonging to the Templars, thus continued to be the subject of contention, the surviving brethren of that dissolved order continued to be treated with the utmost inhumanity and neglect. The ecclesiastical council had assigned to each of them a pension of fourpence a day for subsistence, but this small pittance was not paid, and they were consequently in great danger of dying of hunger. The king, pitying their miserable situation, wrote to the prior of the hospital of St. John at Clerkenwell, earnestly requesting him to take their hard lot into his serious consideration, and not suffer them to come to beggary in the streets. The archbishop of Canterbury also exerted himself in their behalf, and sent letters to the possessors of the property, reproving them for the non-payment of the allotted stipends. "This inhumanity," says he, "awakens our compassion, and penetrates us with the most lively grief. We pray and conjure you in kindness to furnish them, for the love of God and for charity, with the means of subsistence." The archbishop of York caused many of them to be supported in the different monasteries of his diocese.[†]

We have already seen that the Temple at London, the chief house of the English province of the order, had been granted (A. D. 1313) by king Edward the Second to Aymer de Valence, earl of Pembroke. As Thomas earl of Lancaster, the king's cousin and first prince of the blood, however,

[†] Acta *Rymeri*, tom. iii. p. 451, 454, 455, 457, 459-463, 956-959. *Dugd.* Monast. Angl. vol. vi. part 2, p. 809, 849, 850. Rolls of Parliament, vol. ii. p. 41. Concil. Mag. Brit. tom. ii. p. 499.
[*] Statutes at Large, vol. 9. Appendix, p. 23. Rolls of Parliament, vol. ii. p. 41, No. 52. Monast. Angl. p. 880.
[†] Acta *Rymeri*, tom. iii. p. 472. Concil. Mag. Brit. tom. ii. *Walsingham*, p. 99.

claimed the Temple by escheat, as the immediate lord of the fee, the earl of Pembroke, on the 3rd of October, A. D. 1315, at the request of the king, and in consideration of the grant to him by his sovereign of other land, gave up the property to the earl of Lancaster. This earl of Lancaster was president of the council, and the most powerful and opulent subject of the kingdom, and we are told that the students and professors of the common law made interest with him for a lodging in the Temple, and first gained a footing therein as his *lessees*. They took possession of the old Hall and the gloomy cells of the military monks, and converted them into the great and most ancient Common Law University in England. From that period to the present time the retreats of the religious warriors have been devoted to "the studious and eloquent pleaders of causes," a new kind of Templars, who, as Fuller quaintly observes, now "defend one Christian from another, as the old ones did Christians from Pagans."

Subsequently to this event the fee simple or inheritance of the place passed successively through various hands. On the memorable attainder and ignominious execution before his own castle of the earl of Lancaster it reverted to the crown, and was again granted to Aymer de Valence, earl of Pembroke, who was shortly afterwards murdered at Paris. He died without issue, and the Temple accordingly once more vested in the crown.* It was then granted to the royal favorite, Hugh le Despenser the younger, and on his attainder and execution by the Lancastrian faction, it came into the hands of the young king Edward the Third, who had just then ascended the throne, and was committed by him to the keeping of the Mayor of London, his escheator in the city. The mayor closed the gate leading to the waterside, which stood at the bottom of the present Middle Temple Lane, whereby the lawyers were much incommoded in their progress backwards and forwards from the Temple to Westminster. Complaints were made to the king on the subject, who, on the 2nd day of November, in the third year of his reign, (A. D. 1330,) wrote as follows to the mayor:—"The king to the mayor of London, his escheator in the same city. Since we have been given to understand that there ought to be a free passage through the court of the New Temple at London to the river Thames, for our justices, clerks, and others, who may wish to pass by water to Westminster to transact their business, and that you keep the gate of the Temple shut by day, and so prevent those same justices, clerks of ours, and other persons, from passing through the midst of the said court to the waterside, whereby as well our own affairs as those of our people in general are oftentimes greatly delayed, we command you, that you keep the gates of the said Temple open by day, so that our justices and clerks, and other persons who wish to go by water to Westminster may be able so to do by the way to which they have hitherto been accustomed." The following year (A. D. 1331) the king wrote to the mayor, his escheator in the city of London, informing him that

---

* Pat. 8, E. 2. m. 17. Ancient MS. account of the Temple, formerly the property of lord Somers, and afterwards of Nicholls, the celebrated antiquary. Acta *Rymeri*, tom. iii. p. 936, 940. *Lel.* coll. vol. i. p. 668. Rot. Escaet. 1, E. 3. *Dugd.* baron. vol. i. p. 777, 778.

he had been given to understand that the pier in the said court of the Temple, leading to the river, was so broken and decayed, that his clerks and law officers, and others, could no longer get across it, and were consequently prevented from passing by water to Westminster. "We therefore," he proceeds, "being desirous of providing such a remedy as we ought for this evil, command you to do whatever repairs are necessary to the said pier, and to defray the cost thereof out of the proceeds of the lands and rents appertaining to the said Temple now in your custody; and when we shall have been informed of the things done in the matter, the expense shall be allowed you in your account of the same proceeds."*

Two years afterwards (6 E. III., A. D. 1333) the king committed the custody of the Temple to "his beloved clerk," William de Langford, "and farmed out the rents and proceeds thereof to him for the term of ten years, at a rent of 24*l.* per annum, the said William undertaking to keep all the houses and tenements in good order and repair, and so deliver them up at the end of the term." In the mean time, however, the pope and the bishops had been vigorously exerting themselves to obtain a transfer of the property to the order of the Knights Hospitallers of Saint John. The Hospitallers petitioned the king, setting forth that the church, the cloisters, and other places within the Temple, were consecrated and dedicated to the service of God, that they had been unjustly occupied and detained from them by Hugh le Despenser the younger, and, through his attainder, had lately come into the king's hands, and they besought the king to deliver up to them possession thereof. King Edward accordingly commanded the mayor of London, his escheator in that city, to take inquisition concerning the premises.

From this inquisition, and the return thereof, it appears that many of the founders of the Temple Church, and many of the brethren of the order of Knights Templars, then lay buried in the church and cemetery of the Temple; that the bishop of Ely had his lodging in the Temple, known by the name of the bishop of Ely's chamber; that there was a chapel dedicated to St. Thomas-à-Becket, which extended from the door of the Temple Hall as far as the ancient gate of the Temple; also a cloister which began at the bishop of Ely's chamber, and ran in an easterly direction; and that there was a wall which ran in a northerly direction as far as the said king's highway; that in the front part of the cemetery towards the north, bordering on the king's highway, were thirteen houses formerly erected, with the assent and permission of the Master and brethren of the Temple, by Roger Blom, a messenger of the Temple, for the purpose of holding the lights and ornaments of the church; that the land whereon these houses were built, the cemetery, the church, and all the space enclosed between St. Thomas's chapel, the church, the cloisters, and the wall running in a northerly direction, and all the buildings erected thereon, together with the hall, cloisters, and St. Thomas' chapel, were sanctified places dedicated to God;

---

* Acta *Rymeri*, tom. iv. p. 406, 464.

that Hugh le Despenser occupied and detained them unjustly, and that through his attainder and forfeiture, and not otherwise, they came into the king's hands.[*]

After the return of this inquisition, the said sanctified places were assigned to the prior and brethren of the Hospital of Saint John; and the king, on the 11th of January, in the tenth year of his reign, A. D. 1337, directed his writ to the barons of the Exchequer, commanding them to take inquisition of the value of the said sanctified places, so given up to the Hospitallers, and of the residue of the Temple, and certify the same under their seals to the king, in order that a reasonable abatement might be made in William de Langford's rent. From the inquiry made in pursuance of this writ before John de Shoreditch, a baron of the Exchequer, it further appears that on the said residue of the Temple upon the land then remaining in the custody of William de Langford, and withinside the great gate of the Temple, were another HALL and four chambers connected therewith, a kitchen, a garden, a stable, and a chamber beyond the great gate; also eight shops, seven of which stood in Fleet Street, and the eighth in the suburb of London, without the bar of the New Temple; that the annual value of these shops varied from ten to thirteen, fifteen, and sixteen shillings; that the fruit out of the garden of the Temple sold for sixty shillings per annum in the gross, that seven out of the thirteen houses erected by Roger Blom were each of the annual value of eleven shillings; and that the eighth, situated beyond the gate of entrance to the church, was worth four marks per annum. It appears, moreover, that the total annual revenue of the Temple then amounted to 73*l*. 6*s*. 11*d*., equal to about 1,000*l*. of our present money, and that William de Langford was abated 12*l*. 4*s*. 2*d*. of the said rent.[†]

Three years after the taking of this inquisition, and in the thirteenth year of his reign, A. D. 1340, king Edward the Third, in consideration of the sum of one hundred pounds, which the prior of the Knights Hospitallers promised to pay him towards the expense of his expedition into France, granted to the said prior all the residue of the Temple then remaining in the king's hands, to hold, together with the cemetery, cloisters, and the other sanctified places, to the said prior and his brethren, and their successors, of the king and his heirs, for charitable purposes, for ever. From this grant it appears that the porter of the Temple received sixty shillings and tenpence per annum, and twopence a day wages, which were to be paid him by the Hospitallers. At this period Philip Thane was prior of

---

[*] Rot. Escaet. 10, E. 3, 66. Claus. 4, E. 3, p. 1, m. 10.

[†] Sunt etiam ibidem claustrum, capella Sancti Thomæ, et quædam platea terræ eidem capellæ annexata, cum *una aula* et camera supra edificata, quæ sunt loca sancta, et Deo dedicata, et dictæ ecclesiæ annexata, et eidem Priori per idem breve liberata.... Item dicunt, quod præter ista, sunt ibidem in custodia Wilielmi de Langford, infra Magnam Portam dicti Novi Templi, *extra metas et disjunctiones prædictas* una *aula* et quatuor cameræ, una coquina, unum gardinum, unum stabulum, et una camera ultra Magnam Portam prædictam, &c. In memorandis Scacc. inter recorda de Termino Sancti Hilarii. 11 E. 3, in officio Remembratoris Thesaurarii.

the Hospital; and he exerted himself to impart to the celebration of divine service in the Temple Church, the dignity and the splendor it possessed in the time of the Templars. He, with the unanimous consent and approbation of the whole chapter of the Hospital, granted to Hugh de Lichefield, priest, and to his successors, guardians of the Temple Church, towards the improvement of the lights and the celebration of divine service therein, all the land called Ficketzfeld, and the garden called Cotterell Garden; and two years afterwards he made a further grant, to the said Hugh and his successors, of a thousand fagots a year to be cut out of the wood of Lilleston, and carried to the New Temple to keep up the fire in the said church.[*]

King Edward III., in the thirty-fifth year of his reign, A. D. 1362, notwithstanding the grant of the Temple to the Hospitallers, exercised the right of appointing to the porter's office, and by his letter patent he promoted Roger Small to that post for the term of his life, in return for the good service rendered him by the said Roger Small.[†]

It appears that the lawyers in the Temple had at this period their purveyor of provisions as at present, and were then keeping commons or dining together in the hall. The poet Chaucer, who was born at the close of the reign of Edward II., A. D. 1327, and was in high favor at court in the reign of Edward III., thus speaks of the Manciple, or the purveyor of provisions of the lawyers in the Temple:—

"A gentil Manciple was there of the Temple, Of whom achatours mighten take ensample, For to ben wise in bying of vitaille. For whether that he paid or toke by taille, Algate he waited so in his achate, That he was aye before in good estate. Now is not that of God a full fayre grace, That swiche a lewed mannes wit shal pace, The wisdome of an hepe of lerned men?" "Of maisters had he mo than thries ten, That were of lawe expert and curious; Of which there was a dosein in that hous Worthy to ben stewardes of rent and lond Of any lord that is in Englelond, To maken him live by his propre good, In honor detteles, but if he were wood, Or live as scarsly, as him list desire; And able for to helpen all a shire, In any cas that mighte fallen or happe; And yet this manciple sette hir aller cappe."[‡]

At the period of the dissolution of the order of the Templars many of the retainers of the ancient knights were residing in the Temple, supported by pensions from the crown. These were of the class of free servants of office, they held their posts for life, and not having been members of the order, they were not included in the general proscription of the fraternity. On the seizure by the sheriffs and royal officers of the property of their ancient masters, they had been reduced to great distress, and had petitioned the king to be allowed their customary stipends. Edward II. had accordingly granted to Robert Styfford clerk, chaplain of the Temple

---

[*] *Dugd.* Monast. vol. vii. p. 810, 811. Ib. tom. vi. part 2, p. 832.
[†] Pat. 35 E. 3, p. 2, m 33.
[‡] Prologue to the Canterbury Tales. The wages of the Manciples of the Temple, tomp. Henry VIII. were xxxvis. per annum. Bib. *Cotton.* Vitellius, c. 9, f. 320, a.

Church, two deniers a day for his maintenance in the house of the Temple at London, and five shillings a year for necessaries, provided he did service in the Temple Church; and when unable to do so, he was to receive only his food and lodging. Geoffrey Talaver, Geoffrey de Cave, clerk, and John de Shelton, were also, each of them, to receive for their good services, annual pensions for the term of their lives. Some of these retainers, in addition to their various stipends, were to have a gown of the class of free-serving brethren of the order of the Temple each year; one old garment out of the stock of old garments belonging to the brethren; one mark a year for their shoes, &c.; their sons also received so much *per diem*, on condition that they did the daily work of the house.* These domestics and retainers of the ancient brotherhood of the Knights Templars, appear to have transferred their services to the learned society of lawyers established in the Temple, and to have continued and kept alive amongst them many of the ancient customs and observances of the old Knights. The chaplain of the Temple Church took his meals in the hall with the lawyers as he had been wont to do with the Knights Templars; and the rule of their order requiring "two and two to eat together," and "all the fragments to be given in brotherly charity to the domestics," continued to be observed, and prevails to this day; whilst the attendants at table continued to be, and are still called *paniers*, as in the days of the Knights Templars.†

In the sixth year of the reign of Edward III., (A. D. 1333,) a few years after the lawyers had established themselves in the convent of the Temple, the judges of the Court of Common Pleas were made KNIGHTS,‡ being the earliest instance on record of the grant of the honor of knighthood for services purely civil, and the professors of the common law, who had the exclusive privilege of practising in that court, assumed the title or degree of FRERES SERJENS or FRATRES SERVIENTES, so that an order of knights and serving-brethren was most curiously revived in the Temple, and introduced into the profession of the law. It is true that the word *serviens*, *serjen*, or serjeant, was applied to the professors of the law long before the reign of Edward III., but not to denote a *privileged brotherhood*. It was applied to lawyers in common with all persons who did any description of work for another, from the *serviens domini regis ad legem*, who prosecuted the pleas of the crown in the county court, to the *serviens* or *serjen* who walked with his cane before the concubine of the patriarch Heraclius in the streets of Jerusalem. The priest who worked for the Lord was called *serjen de Dieu*, and the lover who served the lady of his affections *serjen d'amour*. It was in the order of the Temple that the word

---

* Acta *Rymeri*, tom. iii. p. 292, 294, 331, 332.
† Thomas of Wothrope, at the trial of the Templars in England, was unable to give an account of the reception of some brethren into the order, quia erat *panetarius* et vacabat circa suum officium. Concil. Mag. Brit. tom. ii. p. 355. Ita appellabant officialem domesticum, qui mensæ panem, mappas et manutergia subministrabat. *Ducange*, Gloss. verb. Panetarius. Concil. Mag. Brit. tom. ii. p. 371-373. MS. Inner Temple Library, div. 9, shelf 5, vol. xvii. fol. 393.
‡ *Dugd*. Orig. Jurid. cap. xxxix. p. 102.

freres serjens or *fratres* servientes first signified an honorary title or degree, and denoted a powerful privileged class of brethren. The *fratres servientes armigeri* or *freres serjens des armes*, of the chivalry of the Temple, were of the rank of gentlemen. They united in their own persons the monastic and the military character, they were allotted one horse each, they wore the cross of the order of the Temple on their breasts, they participated in all the privileges of the brotherhood, and were eligible to the dignity of Preceptor. Large sums of money were frequently given by seculars who had not been advanced to the honor of knighthood, to be admitted amongst this highly esteemed order of men. These *freres serjens* of the Temple wore linen *coifs*, and red caps close over them.* At the ceremony of their admission into the fraternity, the Master of the Temple placed the coif upon their heads, and threw over their shoulders the white mantle of the Temple; he then caused them to sit down on the ground, and gave them a solemn admonition concerning the duties and responsibilities of their profession. The knights and Serjeants of the common law, on the other hand, have ever constituted a privileged *fraternity*, and always address one another by the endearing term *brother*. The religious character of the ancient ceremony of admission into this legal brotherhood, which took place in the Temple Church, and its striking similarity to the ancient mode of reception into the fraternity of the Temple, are curious and remarkable. "Capitalis Justitiarius," says an ancient MS. account of the creation of serjeants-at-law, "monstrabat eis plura bona exempla de eorum prædecessoribus, et tunc. posuit les *coyfes* super eorum capitibus, et induebat eos singulariter de capital de skarletto, et sic creati fuerunt *servientes ad legem*." In his admonitory exhortation, the chief-justice displays to them the moral and religious duties of their profession. "Ambulate in vocatione in quâ vocati estis.... Disce cultum Dei, *reverentiam superioris, misericordiam pauperi*." He tells them the coif is sicut vestis *candida* et immaculata, the emblem of purity and virtue, and he commences a portion of his discourse in the scriptural language used by the popes in the famous bull conceding to the Templars their vast spiritual and temporal privileges, "*Omne datum optimum et omne donum perfectum desursum est descendens a patre luminum,*" &c. &c.† It has been supposed that the coif was first introduced by the clerical practitioners of the common law to hide the *tonsure* of those priests who practiced in the Court of Common Pleas, notwithstanding the ecclesiastical prohibition. This was not the case. The early portraits of our judges exhibit them with a coif of very much larger dimensions than the coifs now worn by the serjeants-at-

---

* *Will. Tyr.* lib. i. p. 50, lib. xii. p. 814. *Dugd.* Hist. Warwickshire, p. 704. Et tune Magister Templi dedit sibim antellum, et imposuit pileum capiti suo, et tune fecit eum sedere ad terram, injungens sibi, &c. Acta *contra Templarios*. Concil. Mag. Brit. tom. ii. p. 300. See also p. 335.
† Ex cod. MS. apud sub-thesaurarium Hosp. Medii Templi, f. 4, a. *Dugd.* Orig. Jurid. cap. 43, 46.

law, very much larger than would be necessary to hide the *mere clerical tonsure*. A covering for that purpose indeed would be absurd.

From the inquisition into the state of the Temple, taken 10 E. III., A. D. 1337, it appears, as we have already seen, that in the time of the Knights Templars there were TWO HALLS in the Temple, the one being the hall of the knights, and the other the hall of the *freres serjens*, or serving-brethren of the order. One of these halls, the present Inner Temple Hall, had been assigned, the year previous to the taking of that inquisition, to the prior and brethren of the Hospital of Saint John, together with the church, cloisters, &c., as before mentioned, whilst the other hall remained in the hands of the crown, and was not granted to the Hospitallers until 13 E. III., A. D. 1340. It was probably soon after this period that the Hospitallers conceded the use of *both halls* to the professors of the law, and these last, from dining apart and being attached to different halls, at last separated into two societies. When the lawyers originally came into the Temple as lessees of the earl of Lancaster, they found engraved upon the ancient buildings the armorial bearings of the order of the Temple, which were, on a shield argent, a plain cross gules, and (*brochant sur le tout*) the holy lamb bearing the banner of the order, surmounted by a red cross. These arms remained the emblem of the Temple until the fifth year of the reign of queen Elizabeth, when unfortunately the society of the Inner Temple, yielding to the advice and persuasion of Master Gerard Leigh, a member of the College of Heralds, abandoned the ancient and honorable device of the Knights Templars, and assumed in its place a galloping winged horse called a Pegasus, or, as it has been explained to us, "a horse striking the earth with its hoof, or *Pegasus luna on a field argent!*" Master Gerard Leigh, we are told, "emblazoned them with precious stones and planets, and by these strange arms he intended to signify that the knowledge acquired at the learned seminary of the Inner Temple would raise the professors of the law to the highest honors, adding, by way of motto, *volat ad æthera virtus*, and he intended to allude to what are esteemed the more liberal sciences, by giving them Pegasus forming the fountain of Hippocrene, by striking his hoof against the rock, as a proper emblem of lawyers becoming poets, as Chaucer and Gower, who were both of the Temple!"

The Society of the Middle Temple, with better taste, still preserves, in that part of the Temple over which its sway extends, the widely-renowned and time- honored badge of the ancient order of the Temple.

On the dissolution of the order of the Hospital of Saint John, (32 Hen. 8,) the Temple once more reverted to the crown, and the lawyers again became the immediate lessees of the sovereign. In the reign of James I., however, some Scotchman attempted to obtain from his majesty a grant of the fee simple or inheritance of the Temple, which being brought to the knowledge of the two law societies, they forthwith made "humble suit" to the king, and obtained a grant of the property to themselves. By letters patent, bearing date at Westminster the 13th of August, in the sixth year of his reign, A. D. 1609, king James granted the Temple to the Benchers of the two societies, their heirs and assigns for ever, for the lodging, reception, and education of the professors and students of the laws of England, the said Benchers yielding and paying to the said king, his heirs and successors, ten pounds yearly for the mansion called the Inner Temple, and ten pounds yearly for the Middle Temple.*

There are but few remains of the ancient Knights Templars now existing in the Temple beyond the Church. The present Inner Temple Hall was the ancient Hall of the Knights, but it has at different periods been so altered and repaired as to have lost almost every trace and vestige of antiquity. In the year 1816 it was nearly rebuilt, and the following extract from "The Report and Observations of the Treasurer on the late Repairs of the Inner Temple Hall," may prove interesting, as showing the state of the edifice previous to that period. "From the proportions, the state of decay, the materials of the eastern and southern walls, the buttresses of the southern front, the pointed form of the roof and arches, and the rude sculpture on the two doors of public entrance, the hall is evidently of very great antiquity.... The northern wall appears to have been rebuilt, except at its two extremities, in modern times, but on the old foundations.... The roof was found to be in a very decayed and precarious state. It appeared to have undergone reparation at three separate periods of time, at each of which timber had been unnecessarily added, so as finally to accumulate a weight which had protruded the northern and southern walls. It became, therefore, indispensable to remove all the timber of the roof, and to replace it in a lighter form. On removing the old wainscoting of the western wall, a perpendicular crack of considerable height and width was discovered, which threatened at any moment the fall of that extremity of the building with its superincumbent roof.... The turret of the clock and the southern front of the hall are only cased with stone; this was done in the year 1741, and very ill executed. The structure of the turret, composed of chalk, ragstone, and rubble, (the same material as the walls of the church,) seems to be very ancient.... The wooden cupola of the bell was so decayed as to let in the rain, and was obliged to be renewed in a form to agree with the other parts of the southern front."

"Notwithstanding the Gothic character of the building, in the year 1680, during the treasurership of Sir Thomas Robinson, prothonotary of C. B., a Grecian screen of the Doric order was erected, surmounted by lions' heads, cones, and other incongruous devices. In the year 1741, during the treasurership of John Blencowe, esq., low windows of Roman architecture were formed in the southern front. The dates of such innovations appear from inscriptions with the respective treasurers' names."

This ancient hall formed the far-famed refectory of the Knights Templars, and was the scene of their proud and sumptuous hospitality. Within its venerable walls they at different periods entertained king John,

---

* *Hargrave*, MS. No. 19, 81, f. 5, fol. 46.

king Henry the Third, the haughty legates of the Roman pontiffs, and the ambassadors of foreign powers. The old custom, alluded to by Matthew Paris, of hanging around the walls the shields and armorial devices of the ancient knights, is still preserved, and each succeeding treasurer of the Temple still continues to hoist his coat of arms on the wall, as in the high and palmy days of the warlike monks of old. Here, in the time of the Knights Templars, the discipline was administered to disobedient brethren, who were scourged upon their bare backs with leathern thongs. Here also was kept, according to the depositions of the witnesses who brought such dark and terrible accusations against the Templars before the ecclesiastical tribunal assembled in London, the famous black idol with shining eyes, and the gilded head, which the Templars worshipped! and from hence was taken the refractory knight, who having refused to spit upon the cross, was plunged into the well which stood in the middle of the Temple court! The general chapters of the Templars were frequently held in the Temple Hall, and the vicar of the church of St. Clements at Sandwich, swore before the Papal inquisitors assembled at London, that he had heard that a boy had been murdered by the Templars in the Temple, because he had crept by stealth into the Hall to witness the proceedings of the assembled brethren.

At the west end of the hall are considerable remains of the ancient convent of the Knights. A groined Gothic arch of the same style of architecture as the oldest part of the Temple Church forms the roof of the present buttery, and in the apartment beyond is a groined vaulted ceiling of great beauty. The ribs of the arches in both rooms are elegantly moulded, but are sadly disfigured with a thick coating of plaster and barbarous whitewash. In the cellars underneath these rooms are some old walls of immense thickness, the remains of an ancient window, a curious fireplace, and some elegant pointed Gothic arches corresponding with the ceilings above; but they are now, alas! shrouded in darkness, choked with modern brick partitions and staircases, and soiled with the damp and dust of many centuries. These interesting remains form an upper and an under story, the floor of the upper story being on a level with the floor of the hall, and the floor of the under story on a level with the terrace on the south side thereof. They were formerly connected with the church by means of a covered way or cloister, which ran at right angles with them over the site of the present cloister-chambers, and communicated with the upper and under story of the chapel of St. Anne, which formerly stood on the south side of the church. By means of this corridor and chapel the brethren of the Temple had private access to the church for the performance of their strict religious duties, and of their secret ceremonies of admitting novices to the vows of the order. In 9 Jac. I., A. D. 1612, some brick buildings three stories high were erected over this ancient cloister by Francis Tate, esq., and being burnt down a few years afterwards, the interesting covered way which connected the church with the ancient convent was involved in the general destruction, as appears from the following inscription upon the present buildings:—Vetustissima Templariorum porticu igne consumpta, anno

1678, Nova hæc, sumptibus Medii Templi extructa, anno 1681, Gulielmo Whitelocke armigero, thesaurario. "The very ancient portico of the Templars being consumed by fire in the year 1678, these new buildings were erected at the expense of the Middle Temple in the year 1681, during the treasurership of William Whitelocke, esq."

The cloisters of the Templars formed the medium of communication between the halls, of the church, and the cells of the serving brethren of the order. During the formation of the present new entrance into the Temple, by the church, at the bottom of the Inner Temple lane, a considerable portion of the brickwork of the old houses was pulled down, and an ancient wall of great thickness was disclosed. It was composed of chalk, ragstone, and rubble, exactly resembling the walls of the church. It ran in a direction east and west, and appeared to have formed the extreme northern boundary of the old convent. The exact site of the remaining buildings of the ancient Temple cannot now be determined with certainty.

Among the many interesting objects to be seen in the ancient church of the Knights Templars which still exists in a wonderful state of preservation, is the Penitential Cell, a dreary place of solitary confinement formed within the thick wall of the building, only four feet six inches long and two feet six inches wide, so narrow and small that a grown person cannot lie down within it.* In this narrow prison the disobedient brethren of the ancient Templars were temporarily confined in chains and fetters, "in order that their souls might be saved from the eternal prison of hell." The hinges and catch of a door firmly attached to the doorway of this dreary chamber still remain, and at the bottom of the staircase is a stone recess or cupboard, where bread and water were placed for the prisoner. In this cell Brother Walter le Bachelor, Knight, Grand Preceptor of Ireland, is said to have been starved to death.

THE END.

---

* For an account of the Temple Church and its antiquities, see *Addison's* "Temple Church."

Printed in Great Britain
by Amazon